INDIA and JAPAN

Past, Present and Future

INDIA and JAPAN

Past, Present and Future

Rajaram Panda

KW Publishers Pvt Ltd
New Delhi

ISBN 978-81-967900-4-2 Hardback

Published in India by Kalpana Shukla

KW Publishers Pvt Ltd
4676/21, First Floor, Ansari Road
Daryaganj, New Delhi 110002
Phone: +91 11 43528107
Marketing: kw@kwpub.in
Editorial: production@kwpub.in
Website: www.kwpub.in

Printed and Bound in India

Contents

Acknowledgements

The project of this book was supported by the Prime Ministers Museum and Library (PMML), with a two-year Fellowship from 2021-2023. The author wishes to express gratitude to the PMML and Library staff for their assistance throughout the fellowship period. The discussions with the other fellows were very beneficial, and they, too, deserve praise.

1

Introduction

The regional security landscape in the Indo-Pacific is in a state of flux. Several state and non-state actors continue to threaten peace and stability in the region. Certain countries have attempted to implement unilateral policies with little respect for global rules, which are unacceptable for law-abiding nations. In particular, China's unilateralism on regional issues such as South China Sea, which it claims almost entirely, has irked other claimants. When the Philippines went to the International Court for arbitration and obtained a verdict in its favour in July 2016, China rejected it outright, knowing well that the Court lacked the enforcing power of its judgment. Besides its sustained military militarization, its muscle-flexing behaviour creates a sense of unease in the rest of Asia. While it has territorial disputes with Japan over the Senkaku islands, China has a festering boundary dispute with India that shows no signs of early resolution.

Several bilateral, trilateral and regional dispute settlement mechanisms have proven to be ineffective or have had no tangible impact. North Korea's nuclear and missile development programmes have injected a new sense of volatility in the security environment in the region. Former American President Donald Trump's outreach initiative that resulted in three summits in Singapore, Panmunjom and Hanoi raised temporary hope for a breakthrough. The efforts of the liberal South Korean President Moon Jae-in to engage with the North Korean President Kim Jong-un and his summit diplomacy also yielded no result. As a result, the North Korean issue remains a matter of concern. As the spectre of a conflict looks real over North Korea's weaponization, the potential adversarial countries are positioning themselves either to strengthen their existing bilateral security relationships with the US, or seek new partners, or even beef up their own preparedness to cope with the evolving grim situation. There have also been talks in certain quarters, both in Japan and South Korea, if the time is appropriate now to revisit their nuclear options to counter the North Korean threat.

Against this background, this book intends to analyse in-depth this dimension of the security situation in which the roles of India and Japan shall be the key focus. Following a preliminary examination of the nature of relationships between India and Japan during the post-War years, and how they evolved during the Congress and later the UPA rules, the study shall conduct a micro-analysis to examine how India-Japan bilateral ties have strengthened under the tenures of Prime Minister Narendra Modi in India and Shinzo Abe in Japan, and subsequently during successive governments. In the process, it will also be examined what factors contributed to Abe emerging as the longest-serving prime minister of Japan after a phase of political instability when the ruling Liberal Democratic Party lost its political space until Abe resurrected it in 2012.[1] Since then, and after the emergence of Modi in India's political firmament, the kind of bonhomie that both leaders developed has been the most remarkable development in the India-Japan relationships. Though the focus will be on how the two leaders found common interests and viewpoints to address the common regional and global challenges, the most recent of which is coping with the outbreak of the Coronavirus, which become a global menace. With a platform built for making the bilateral ties robust by sustained efforts from both sides, Abe resigned due to health concerns and was succeeded by Yoshihide Suga. Suga committed to carrying on Abe's legacy while deepening and expanding the partnership in all dimensions. Unfortunately, Suga proved to be a failure and had to unceremoniously withdraw from the presidential race of the LDP. The tenure during the current Fumio Kishida administration looks promising, as he has come up with many new initiatives.

Historical Connect

A discussion on the past and how relations between the two countries have evolved over the years will help to posit the contemporary situation in context of making an objective assessment of the issues identified for serious analysis.

The relationship between the two countries is not recent; it dates back centuries. This relationship is not something artificial but of two real friends without any hiccups throughout their long journey. During the long history, ties remain rooted in spiritual affinity and strong cultural and civilizational bonds. Like India's relations with the Southeast Asian regions and the link of Buddhism, relations with Japan and the rest of Northeast Asia have remained strong over centuries too. Delivering her speech at the Japan Foundation Award receiving ceremony in Tokyo on October 29, 2010, Professor Savitri Vishwanathan remarked, "Although Japan was aware of the existence of India with the introduction of Buddhism through China even as early as the 8th century, India was blissfully unaware of even the existence of a country called Japan. There were no travellers from Japan, as in the case of China. Indian priests, who reached Japan from China and were respected, did not return to India to talk about Japan. Study of Sanskrit by the Japanese helped them to evolve a simpler phonetic script, the Buddhist scriptures stimulated their curiosity about India (tenjiku) the divine land, where Buddha was born. However, they did not succeed in visiting India. It is interesting to note that the Japanese perceptions of India were first formed through the prism of China and later, through that of the West. The ignorance of the Japanese about the actual conditions in India, including the geographical position was dispelled to a certain extent by the accounts obtained from the Portuguese and the Dutch in the 16th century. However, Japan's seclusion policy in 1639 did not permit the Japanese to travel outside Japan and knowledge about India had to be limited to the accounts received from the Dutch. These accounts informed the Japanese that India came under foreign rule first by the Muslims and later by the British and there was lack of resistance on the part of Indians to preserve their country's honour and cultural heritage. This was a source of great disappointment to the Japanese intellectuals and resulted in a negative appraisal of India."[2]

The oldest documented direct encounter between India and Japan occurred at Nara's Todaiji Temple, where an Indian monk, Bodhisena, performed the consecration or eye-opening of the towering statue of Lord Buddha in 752 AD. A brief explanation of the significance of this event is relevant to connect the evolution of bilateral ties through contemporary times with the continuation of spiritual bonds.

Japan's history can be broadly divided into three major periods during which the country was internationalized. Indian history has also passed through various periods such as Maurya, Gupta and others, to depict the ancient period, followed by the Delhi Sultanate, the Mediaeval period and finally the British period. The post-independence India is known as the Modern period. The internationalization process has been a huge learning process for enriching the cultures in both the countries.

Similarly, after passing through many such periods, Japan also entered the modern era beginning with the Meiji Restoration in 1868, which continues till today and contributes to the internationalization process. When Portuguese traders arrived in Japan in 1543, Japan saw the brutal suppression of Christianity by the Tokugawa Shogunate. During its 264- year rule, the government issued the seclusion edict, ushering in over 250 years of relative isolation. The Tokugawa period, also called Edo Period (1603-1867), the final period of traditional Japan, a time of internal peace, political stability and economic growth under the shogunate (military dictatorship) founded by Tokugawa Ieyasu. The shogunate achieved hegemony over the entire country by balancing the power of potentially hostile domains with strategically placed allies and collateral houses. During this long period, Japan was under the rule of the Tokugawa shogunate and the country's 300 daimyo. The shogun had his capital in Edo, the modern Tokyo, which derived its name as Edo period and the dynasty began with Ieyasu's victory over Hideyoshi's forces at the Battle of Sekigahara, and the consolidation of political power around the Tokugawa clan and its daimyo allies in Japan's east, on the Kanto plain.[3] This marked the beginning of nearly three full centuries of shogunal rule by the Tokugawa family, established on March 24, 1603, and nearly equivalent period of peace and stability in which competing daimyo were kept in check through a system of alternate attendance and tribute known as sankinkotai.

The shogunate under Tokugawa Iemitsu chose to implement policy through a number of edicts from 1633-39 known as Sakoku (closed country), heralding an isolationist foreign policy of the Japanese shogunate, under which relations and trade between Japan and other countries were severely limited.[4] Nearly all foreigners were barred from entering Japan and the common Japanese people were kept from leaving the country for a period of over 220 years. Such a policy ended after 1853, when the American Blackships commanded by Matthew Perry forced the opening of Japan to American (and by extension, Western) trade through a series of unequal treaties. The period ended with the Meiji Restoration on May 3, 1868, after the fall of Edo.[5]

Despite the political upheaval of recent years, the India link may be traced back to the early sixth century, when Japan borrowed extensively from Tang China and the kingdoms on the Korean Peninsula. Japan embraced political institutions and culture from the Asian mainland, with Buddhism undoubtedly the most important import. This connection remains relevant till today in the India-Japan context.

Buddhism and Role of Bodhisena

Amid these cultural and spiritual links, cultural assets from India reached Japan when Chinese and Korean monks brought copies of important sutras and frescoes from the walls of Indian temples and monasteries. Murals in the Horyuji temple in Nara, the cradle of Japanese Buddhism, feature improvised Japanese with an Indian accent. This implies that Japan absorbed Indian influences a long time ago. With the Tang empire in disarray, monks and traders, together with some official Japanese ambassadors, decided to risk ocean passage and undertook the perilous journey to India in the late ninth century, conveying Buddha's teachings. Soon enough, Buddhist imprint took root as more and more Japanese came under the spell of Buddhist philosophy and were also encouraged by official patronage.

During the early stages of Buddhism taking root, the ruling class used Buddhism as a vehicle for supporting the state. That spirit led Emperor Shomu to order the creation of a giant statue (daibutsu) of the Locana (Vaircana) Buddha—the primordial Buddha of the universe—at the Todaiji temple in Nara in 741. Despite the fact that this huge project wreaked havoc on state finances, it was inspired by China's Tang dynasty, which had already built a giant Locana Buddha at Luoyang. The project cost Japan greatly, as the statue used much of Japan's bronze and was made entirely of imported gold.[6]

It may be worth reinforcing, what is probably already known to many readers, that the eye-opening ceremony (kaigen or kaigan) was held in 752. This was a truly international affair, and was attended by Empress Koken, retired Emperor Shomu, Empress Dowager Komyo, 10,000 guests, including monks from China and the Korean kingdoms of Paekche, Kudara and Silla, and 4,000 dancers to celebrate the completion of the Buddha. In the context of the relevance of this study, these historical links are relevant even today.

Why was the eye-opening ceremony or consecration important, and what did it signify then and now? In Buddhism, the "painting in" of the eyes of a statue signifies its "awakening", thereby endowing the statue with spiritual properties, so that the image is believed to resemble a living Buddha. What is remarkable and noteworthy in the context of historical connect is that the event was officiated by an Indian priest and monk Bodhisena, who was the first Indian to reach Japan's shores. This fact is established by documentary evidence. The brush Bodhisena used, as well as some of the Tempyo-era costumes, masks and other utensils used during the ceremony, are preserved in the Shosoin treasure house near Todaiji, signifying the importance and respect Japan attaches to the century-old event.

The journey of Bodhisena, the Indian monk, to Japan during a time when travel was difficult is a well-known story and deserves to be mentioned again here. According to author and sociologist John Carroll, his study on Bodhisena which is based on fragmentary and sometimes contradictory documentary evidences, suggest that Bodhisena was born into a Brahmin family in the city of Madurai around 704, when Buddhism was into its long decline in the land of its birth.[7] According to the story, while traversing the

South China Sea, Bodhisena was shipwrecked but was saved by an Indian by birth who was trading pearls in the kingdom of Champa, Vietnam.[8] This saviour himself became a monk and travelled with Bodhisena to China and eventually to Japan. Bodhisena wanted to meet Manjusri, the boshisattva of visionary insight who lived in Mount Wutai and for whom he had great admiration. However, when told that Manjusri had moved to Japan, he too moved to Japan on the invitation by a Japanese official delegation that was in China with them in 736.

While in Japan, Bodhisena met a Japanese monk Gyoki, who took him to Heian-kyo at Nara and introduced him to the Emperor. Later, a Buddhist retreat called Ryosenji was built on Mount Tomi for the Indian monk. When Bodhisena died, aged 57 or 25 years after coming to Japan, he was cremated and buried there. Ryosenji is located about eight kilometres from central Nara, near Tomio station, and is a major site for Buddhists. Some Japanese seems to have visited India around that time but the claim cannot be verified by evidence. For instance, one Japanese monk Kongo Sanmai (Sanskrit name Vajrasmadhi) is believed to have reached India via Tang China and studied at the great Buddhist intellectual centre at Nalanda. After years of neglect when Buddhism declined, this great centre of learning was reduced to ruins until recently, when it was revived with the support of India and some Asian nations, where Buddhist influence contributed a great deal to the region's spiritual connect. Though it may be difficult to restore Nalanda's ancient glory, the effort to revive its memory is commendable.

Bodhisena's coming to Japan and officiating at the Todaiji dedication had a huge historical impact, but the cultural impact was greater. Instrumental music and court dancing that originated in India are preserved and practiced till today. With the monk's influence, Sanskrit also gained popularity. Daibutsu symbolized Buddhist unity transcending borders.

In contemporary times, prominent Indians associated with Japan were Swami Vivekananda, Nobel laureate Rabindranath Tagore, entrepreneur JRD Tata, freedom fighter Netaji Subhash Chandra Bose and Justice Radha Binod Pal. Another Indian freedom fighter, Rash Behari Bose, played an equally crucial role in fostering relations between India and Japan. Each of these luminaries had a significant impact on the friendship between the two countries. Though a brief account of each of these individuals may bring value to our inquiry, another level of relations flourished with the blessing of the British, who ruled India at that time.

Role of the Tatas

At the level of commercial links at the time, the roles of Jamshetji Nuserwanji Tata (1839-1904 AD) and later entrepreneur Jehangir Ratanji Dadabhoy Tata, popularly known as J.R.D. Tata (1904-1993) in fostering India-Japan relations are extremely important. Even before Japan entered the war, it was surfing many countries around the world, and more particularly within Asia, for precious raw materials for its first stage of economic development. Japan identified India an important import source of cotton and cotton yarns to meet the increasing demand of its textile industry. This brought the Japanese to India. At that time, India was a British colony, and Japan was careful not to displease the British as it realized that it needed the support of Britain to facilitate the imports from India. With the endorsement of the British, the Japanese could trade with the cotton growers, and even establish ginning factories in the fields thus giving an opportunity for interaction between Indians and Japanese. With the help of the imports of cotton and cotton yarns from India, Japan's textile industry flourished, enabling Japan to export silk yarn and silk textiles as early as the 19th century, which were considered as sophisticated and cheap.

Not to be overlooked is the importance of those companies in promoting Indo-Japan shipping venture to enable Indian businessmen to transport goods at lowest freight rates using their own ships for transporting cotton, cotton yarn, etc. The role of the Tata Co. is no less significant. Towards this end, Jamshetji Tata went to Japan to meet Shibusawa Eiichi for talks. This joint venture for shipping would have led to greater interaction between Japanese and Indians. Before this could take off successfully, Tatas had to bow out because of the price wars by the British and European Companies. However, the Japanese shipping company Nippon Yusen Kaisha (NYK) was allowed to transport goods between India and Japan, but with restrictions about the number of voyages and also the ports the ships could use. According to reports, NYK ships sought Indian crew members. The Indian crew had a positive opinion of the Japanese, both in terms of pay and treatment. Probably, the Indians saw these foreigners as different from their British masters and developed an affinity for them. While the Indian shipping partnership was stifled, Indian businesses trading with Japan received a boost. Indian trading houses were opened in Kobe and Yokohama and the number of Indians visiting Japan for trading purposes increased. While raw cotton accounted for 50 per cent of Japanese imports, other commodities like pig iron, teak, jute, gunny bags, natural rubber, oils and fats, leather, etc., were also traded with Japan. The exports from Japan consisted of cotton and silk textiles, matchsticks and other miscellaneous products. Interactions between Indians and Japanese increased.

Tata's visit also yielded other results: establishment of silk farms in Mysore for production of silk under the guidance and supervision of two Japanese experts, so that development of sericulture could be done on scientific lines.

Swami Vivekanand's Japan visit

At the intellectual level, Swami Vivekananda's visit to Japan on his way to the World Congress of Religions in 1893 provided the Indian people with a new perspective on Japan and the Japanese. His first-hand observations about Japan through his letters, lectures, etc., had only one message for the young students of India, "Look East", go to Japan and learn from them about the development strategy of the Meiji Government and how they implemented their plans. He also conveyed to the Indians his impressions of other traits of the Japanese, such as their discipline and cleanliness. Vivekananda admired Japan's emphasis on compulsory universal education. Vivekananda's call to the youth led to many Indian students going to Japan for higher education to learn about scientific and technological advancements. Indian students under the aegis of the Oriental Youngmen's association also hoped that Japan would serve as a hub for Asian students to exchange ideas, provide mutual encouragement and, on finishing their studies, be pioneers in bringing about development and enlightenment for

Asia. Thus, knowledge gained in Japan seemed to offer opportunities and hope for the bright future of Asia.

Vivekananda's stirring speech at the Art Institute of Chicago on September 11, 1893, in which he lamented about sectarianism, bigotry, and their horrible descendants that have filled the beautiful Earth with violence and sent whole nations into despair, left an indelible mark across generations.[9] Who funded the trip of the monk to Chicago? Not many are aware that Maharaja Ajit Singh Bahadur, the erstwhile ruler of Khetri, sponsored the trip for his guru and friend. On his return, the spiritual leader visited Khetri as a mark of respect and gratitude. Vivekananda was born as Narendra Dutta, aka Swami Bibidishanand, on January 12, 1983. It was an accidental meet between the Swami and the Maharaja in 1888 at Mount Abu, where they tried decoding various strands of spirituality, yoga and universalism.

During one such conversation, Singh told Swami Vivekananda to wear a turban as a shield to protect himself from the dust storms of Rajasthan. The Maharaja also provided a saffron robe, which later became Swami Vivekananda's traditional attire. Interestingly, Singh had bestowed the name 'Vivekananda' to him as mentioned in the book 'Living Vedanta' by Chaturvedi Badrinath.[10]

Visits of Vivesvaraya and Syed Ross Masud

When M. Visvesvaraya (1860-1962) from the southern state of Mysore visited Japan in 1898, he was struck by the country's emphasis on universal education, as well as the priority placed on vocational and compulsory education. Visvesvaraya saw Japan as a working model for India, believing that education and planned economic development were critical to India's quick rise. The government should actively participate in the service of commerce and industry. Visvesvaraya, as the Dewan of Mysore, could get his ideas implemented in the field of education and industry, as Mysore was a princely state with no British government interference. Visvesvaraya's book Reconstructing India, published in 1920, referred to Japan's modernization.[11] Another princely state, Hyderabad, sent Syed Ross Masud to Japan to study Japan's educational system and his report was published in 1923.[12] Thus, the educated elite were being informed about the conditions in Japan and how India could follow Japan in its development. In short, a very favourable impression of Japan was projected among Indians.

Tagore and Okakura

Second, the intellectual partnership between Nobel laureate Gurudev Rabindranath Tagore (1861-1941)[13] and Japanese art historian and curator Tenshin Okakura (1862-1913) was path-breaking in the context of Asian renaissance and a new awakening in asserting Asian identity. Tagore was the first non-European Nobel Laureate Bengali poet to visit Japan in 1916. Tagore wrote *Japanjatri* (A Traveller to Japan) in 1919, which is a major work of travel literature and a key document in the study of India-Japan relations.

Indeed, Bengal has a special place in the long history of cultural relations with Japan.[14] This dates back to 1902, the year which marks a historical meeting between two great intellectuals, Tenshin Okakura and Rabindranath Tagore in Calcutta. Okakura was deeply impressed by the revivalist movement on culture and art. During his short stay in Calcutta, he came into contact with the nationalist leaders of Bengal. Subsequently he played a significant part in the formation of the 'Anushilan Shamity', which waged a violent anti-imperialist movement in Bengal.

On returning to Japan, Okakura sent two distinguished artists, Yokoyama Taikan and Shimomura Kanzan, to Calcutta, where they met Tagore and exchanged opinions and artistic views. In 1905, Jinnosuke Sano, a former student of Keio University, came to Santiniketan. He was a judo instructor. During his three years of stay at Santiniketan, he also taught Japanese, apart from teaching Jujutsu. Tagore's five visits to Japan—1916, 1917, 1924, and 1929 (twice)—brought him into contact with a remarkable group of intellectuals and artists of Bengal and Japan. In fact, the subsequent narration of events shall demonstrate that Bengal had a special affinity with Japan for over a century.[15]

After meeting Tagore for the first time in Calcutta in 1902, Okakura returned to Japan, where he became an overnight celebrity at the outbreak of the Pacific War. The following year he published a book called *The Ideals of the East—Asia is one,* which was subsequently celebrated posthumously as the most powerful expression of Japanese wartime aspirations, and Okakura was considered a visionary of Japanese political ascendancy in Asia. But during his lifetime, Okakura was known as a bureaucrat, art philosopher, and museum curator devoted to the protection of Asian art. His most important achievement was the restoration of Japanese pictorial art (nihonga). Employing the individualism and art philosophy of the West, he encouraged artists in late-nineteenth-century Japan to create a new artistic tradition and cultural identity reflecting modern Japan's dynamic social and cultural change. This thesis aims to transcend the gap between the principally intellectual and aesthetic investigations of Okakura's lifetime achievements and the primarily political examinations of his appropriation in wartime Japan. Though these two distinguished friends met only few times, their friendship endured, and the consequences of this friendship included the artistic and intellectual movements of the early 20th century.

Rustom Barucha's magisterial work on this friendship is a must-read for anyone interested to know the history of India-Japan relations.[16] The book weaves an intricate tapestry of ideas relating to pan-Asianism, nationalism, cosmopolitanism and friendship, and positions the early modernist tensions of the period within-and against-the spectre of a unified Asia that concealed considerable political differences. Okakura's *The Ideals of the East*[17] and *The Awakening of the East* posited well with Tagore's radical critique of Nationalism, providing deep insights into how the Orient travelled with and beyond Asia.

Reviewing the book for *The Japan Times*, David Burleigh remarks that the idea of "Asia" was then a recent notion, positing a common inheritance and purpose among the countries of the East to counter the dominance of the West.[18] The eventual result was stress on the liberation movement from imperial control and then independence. There could be differing interpretations when Barucha writes about Okakura's 1903 volume *The Ideals of the East*. He suggests that "Asia was less a political entity than a metaphysical and spiritual realm". Okakura's other book, *The Awakening of the East*, published after his death evokes similar differing opinions and perspectives. Words such "national exclusiveness" and "cultural schizophrenia" appear bewildering, but some Japanese writers have used them after reading Okakura's books.

Even though the Tagore-Okakura friendship has been widely discussed and written about, both had differing perspectives on a variety of matters. For both, the term "nationalism" has different implications. While Tagore's focus was primarily on India, Okakura looked more to the West and helped build the Boston Museum as curator by acquiring artefacts mainly from Japan and China but hardly anything from India, which troubled Tagore, and Tagore started viewing and re-examining what exactly Okakura meant when he said in the opening sentence of his book "Asia is one". When Tagore visited Japan in 1916 on a lecture tour, he was critical of Japan's preoccupations with material progress and did not mention Okakura in his lectures. Following the posthumous publication of The Awakening of the East in 1938, Tagore's relationship with a younger Japanese acquaintance, Yone Noguchi (1875-1947), deteriorated due to Japan's conduct in the Chinese war.[19] Noguchi was educated in the United States, married an American after multiple affairs, had a child, and eventually returned to Japan, where he followed the prevailing political trends. In short, he supported Japan's right-wing policies. He had a furious letter exchange in 1938, which ended their friendship due to political and philosophical differences. During the World War II, he supported the Japanese cause, advocating a non-holds-barred assault on the Western countries he had once admired. Noguchi visited India in 1935-36 to garner support for Japanese objectives in East Asia, but had little success.

There were other differences between Tagore's and Okakura's life styles. While Tagore dressed in flowing robes and expressed his views eloquently, particularly in his native Bengali, using English as an appendage and as a mere additional tool, Okakura presented himself as a Japanese in traditional costumes but communicated mainly in English and scarcely wrote in his own language. Interestingly, Tagore is the only person to have become the author of two national anthems (those of India and Bangladesh). While Okakura enhanced a marvellous museum collection in a country other than his own, Tagore established a university to continue his legacy in Bengal.

The differences between the two friends became too glaring when Japan, after defeating great powers such as Russia and China, which temporarily resonated with Asian awakening against the imperial West and seeking its own Asian identity, chose a militaristic adventurist policy to colonize Asia, which Tagore disapproved but was endorsed by Okakura. In particular, Tagore was critical of Japan's Greater Asia Co-Prosperity Sphere definition.[20]

From admiration of Japan, Tagore turned into a critic of Japan, particularly after Japan chose to adopt an aggressive foreign policy. Though the Sino-Japanese war of 1894-95, the Russo-Japanese war of 1904-5 and then Japan ousting China from Korea caught the attention of Indian intellectuals and the people in general, Tagore was troubled by Japan's aggressive behaviour. Also, the Indian businessmen engaged in cotton and textile trade became very apprehensive of Japan ousting them from the Chinese markets. Thus, there were both expectations and also a sense of worry over Japan.

Yet, admiration of Indian intellectuals as well as freedom fighters of India reached sky-high when Japan defeated China and Russia, interpreted in many quarters as a dwarf defeating two giants in a short span of time, raising the spectre of an Asian renaissance and a new awakening. Indian nationalist leaders like Bal Gangadhar Tilak stated that Japan's victory had broken the myth of the superiority and invincibility of the Europeans over Asians. Inspired by Japan's successes, he felt that Indian freedom fighters can follow Japan's example and feel confident that they, too, could do the same with a sense of national pride. Japan thus boosted the confidence of the Asian nations in their struggle against western nations. There was high expectation in the leadership of Japan to fight the west.

In November 2003, a new museum commemorating the connection between Japan and Tagore with a grant from Mitsubishi Corp India was established at Rabindra Bharati University in Kolkata where rare memorabilia chronicling the poet's many visits to Japan and its deep influence on him were housed. The influence on Tagore was more literary and spiritual, reflecting Tagore's personal bent. But, the artefact did express discretely Tagore's dismay at what he saw as signs of militant nationalism, especially during his visit in 1916. It reminded him of the unthinking, belligerent chauvinism that he felt had led to the outbreak of war in Europe and did not represent the best of Japan.

The political situation in the post-Taisho era and the subsequent Showa era stands in dramatic contrast to the post-War years, particularly if seen in light of the post-War Constitution. This is what Tagore had envisioned the best for Japan even before Japan entered into the conflicts and started the colonisation process under the umbrella of the Greater East Asia Co-Prosperity Sphere, which ultimately became Japan's undoing, ending in disaster and Japan's defeat. Had Tagore been alive today, he probably would have not approved the recent trends in viewing nationalism in a similar light, though one cannot imagine what remedy Tagore could have offered as the geopolitical situation in the present times is slowly shifting to one that precipitated the two World Wars. Tagore had travelled to as many as 35 countries, offering his non-sectarian views, and had become a virtual citizen of the world as he understood both the East and the West from a similar prism.

His visit to Japan in 1916 was different from earlier visits as he started viewing his perspective of Japan more critically. On the one hand, Tagore admired Japan's economic, industrial and scientific advances as well as Japan's cultural and literary traditions, especially the verse form of haiku, which he appreciated for its emotional restraint. On the other hand, he was troubled by the seeds of divergence in those values and the strident patriotism, which was manifesting in Japan.[21] In 1938, Tagore expressed his "utter sorrow" over these events and predicted in a letter to Noguchi, who had become an advocate for Japan's expansionist goals in Asia. He wrote: "I know that one day the disillusionment of your people will be complete, and through laborious centuries they will have to clear the debris of their civilization wrought to ruin by their own warlords run amok. They will realize that the aggressive war on China is insignificant as compared to the destruction of the inner spirit of chivalry of Japan, which is proceeding with a ferocious severity." As subsequent developments showed when Japan drifted to a comprehensive path of militant nationalism, Tagore's prophetic words came true.

When the war-renouncing Constitution was enshrined by the Occupation forces (the issue is debatable if it was imposed or had Japan's consent to adopt as many views exist), Tagore was dead. Had he been alive, he would probably have read the Constitution from the perspective of an attempt to restore the original spirit of Japan. Tagore could have probably conceded that Japan require decades, if not centuries, to undo the damage to its own image. It remains unclear and also difficult to imagine what perspective Tagore would have offered as Japan's neighbours that faced violence at the hands of Japan's military continue to read a nationalistic, scheming and aggressive agenda, whose culture he had praised from a larger Asian perspective and saw as the embodiment of harmony, forbearance and benevolence.

Hariprabha-Takeda Matrimony

We learn more about life in Japan not just from intellectuals, but also from the account of Hariprabha, a commoner who married a Japanese, Uemon Takeda, owner of a soap factory in Dhaka in 1907. Hariprabha visited Japan along with her husband in 1912 to meet his family living in Niwa (Aichi prefecture). She was impressed by the courteous and friendly policemen in Koban (police beat box). They were not an object of fear like the British police force, back in India. Another account by an industrialist and statesman, Sir Lalubhai Samaldas, who had an opportunity to visit Japan's various institutions also stresses on the Japanese people's sense of cleanliness. He also had a very favourable impression of Japanese politeness and manners, their thoroughness in what they do, their work ethic and sense of commitment. Therefore, if we sum up the perception of Indians about Japan from the late 19th century to the turn of the 20th century, it was that Indians should learn from Japan's achievements in the fields of education, science, technology, etc. Admiration for Japan's social and cultural traditions led to a call to adapt their cleanliness and their behaviour in social life. One might be tempted to connect Prime Minister Narendra Modi's initiative to promote Swacha Bharat and Atmanirbhar programs that resonates with Japanese practices and lifestyles dating back to centuries.

The saga of Hariprabha-Uemon Takeda's marriage in an age when international marriages were frowned upon is an interesting footnote in the evolution of India-Japan relations at the people-to-people level. As is customary in most marriages when the woman moves to her husband's home after marriage, Hariprabha had to travel to Japan to meet her in-laws. Hariprabha Mullick (1890-1972), a Brahmo Bengali woman, wrote a travelogue titled *Bango Mohilar Japan Jatra* (A Bengali lady's visit to Japan) and published in 1915, wherein one finds mention of Uemon Takeda (b. 1875). The travelogue offers a Bengali woman's perspective of a Japanese household in the early 1900s with reflections on contemporary Japanese society and culture. This was the earliest published travelogue on Japan by a Bengali woman.[22] Hariprabha and Uemon were interviewed in Japan after their arrival there. From the interview published in the daily on December 16, 1912, it transpires that Uemon was 37 years old and his wife was 22 when they arrived in Japan.

Let me elaborate on the Hariprabha-Takeda matrimony to connect the intercultural connect between India and Japan of the past with the present, wherein people-to-people contact is often stressed in diplomatic parlour for fostering mutual understanding. Seen from this perspective, the governmental initiatives such as the Indian Council for Cultural Relations in India and Japan Foundation in Japan are playing a pioneering role in bridging India-Japan relationship. This backdrop is immensely helpful in deepening economic and defence/security relations, albeit in an invisible way. Joseph Nye's soft power concept stems from this narrative.

The diary of Hariprabha Basu Mallik (1890-1972) called *Bongomohilar Japan Jatra or A Bengali Woman's Journey to Japan,* was published by her sister Kumari Santiprabha Mallik in November 1915 in Dacca. The diary portrays Japanese family and social life during the Taisho and early Meiji eras. Uemon Takeda was not in touch with his parents back home for almost a decade, which made them think that Uemon had died in British India. When Hariprabha travelled to her sasurbari in 1912 after her marriage to Uemon in 1907, Uemon's parents were delighted to welcome their son and foreign daughter-in-law. Viewed differently, Hariprabha's travel to Japan was both a "reckless adventure", and an incitement of Brahmo Samaj's "women's emancipation" culture. Hariprabha and her family were Brahmo Samajist. The Brahmo Samaj was a reformist movement within Hinduism and advocated equality of caste, creed and religion. The movement was responsible to a large extent in creating modern India. When Hariprabha's diary was published it created great "excitement among the women of Calcutta" who saw her experience as an opening of new horizons.

In 1915, the Indian revolutionary, Rash Behari Bose, fled to Japan. It was only four years after Hariprabha's visit that Rabindranath Tagore visited Japan for the first time in 1916. Hariprabha was a strange new face in her husband's village community. Many people came to see her foreignness. Hariprabha was treated with great care and love by the Takeda family. The village society was especially nice to her, eager to meet her and listen to her stories. The magic of the mysterious foreigner added to her attraction. Hariprabha stayed in Japan for four months with her husband experiencing family life at close quarters. Her simple-mindedness and purity of intention created a perceptive prose in her diary. By the time she started her journey back to India on April 12, 1913, she had captured the essence of Japanese middle-class life. She returned to Dacca on May 8, 1913, after 25 days of travel. In these four months she basked in the "love and attention of everyone", jotting down her experiences. She would return to Japan two more times.

Brahmo Samaj Heritage Hariprabha never intended to write for publication, but as a Brahmo Samajist felt it was her duty to write about her life. Also the egalitarian ethos that Brahmo Samaj promoted made it easy for her to describe a foreign society with alacrity. Indeed, Brahmo Samaj encouraged such cross-cultural encounters as early as the twentieth century. When Hariprabha proposed to her youngest sister Santiprabha the idea of marrying Toshan, the younger brother of Uemon, she rejected it. But Hariprabha imbibed the ideas of Brahmo Samaj quite sincerely. She followed their example even when it caused her great misery. While Uemon died early due to acute depression and ill-health, Hariprabha died in 1972 in Calcutta.

Hariprabha was a keen observer of Japanese life and society. Mukesh Williams writes, "Many Indian bureaucrats and businessmen have written about Japanese family life, economic dealings and food shortage during the war years. But Hariprabha's diary carries picture-book observations of Japanese homes, gardens, hospitality, food, city architecture, village life, child rearing, girl's education, cooking, daily living, women's hairstyles, kimonos, newspaper reading habits, bathing, washing hair, makeup and curiosity about foreigners. The early entries are short and carry snippets of daily events. But towards the end the discussion becomes more complex and lengthy, covering many aspects of Japanese life such as winter clothing, fire safety, kimono, footwear, rice preparation, respect for work, part time jobs, position of women and marriage rituals. Hariprabha keenly observed the social life of Japan especially the woman's position—health care, domestic work, marriage and child rearing. The Bengali journal Bangadarshan brought out two articles by her. The first one was called Japane Santan Palon o Narisiksha or Child Rearing and Women's Education in Japan and the second Japaner Nari or Women in Japan. Both bring out the themes of women's position in Japan. Later Manjushree Sinha compiled these writings under the title Bongomohilar Japan Jatra o Onannyo Rachana (2009)."[23]

Her Diary

Hariprabha's diary of 66 pages packs a lot of detail about her feelings about her river and sea voyages. She had a literary and religious bent of mind, as she evoked metaphors of the sea and divinity through her descriptions and religious songs. Her journey takes her through Rangoon, Penang, Singapore, Hong Kong, Shanghai to Port Moji in Kitakyushu. She heaves a sigh of relief having arrived in Japan. She keenly observed various Japanese customs such as marriage, drinking sake, dressing in expensive silk and going to the in-laws house in a rickshaw and so on. She also notices that the Japanese mother is the centre of the family. Hariprabha had an eye for detail.

She was extremely fortunate to travel to Japan in the aftermath of the euphoric victory in the Russo-Japanese War of 1904-5. Through her diary entries, we see a slowly modernising Japan that retains the legacy of the past in its manners, transport and architecture. Usually she avoids referring to the political life of Japan as she does not want to disrupt the status quo. However, occasionally a few details about politics do creep in. Hariprabha finds Kyoto as a city of "pilgrimage" shaped by its temples, with wide verandahs for meditation and aesthetic pleasure. Osaka lives up to its reputation as a commercial center with its "factories and business".

Inspired by the Takeda story, the Bangladeshi film director Tanvir Mokammel made a documentary called *The Japanese Wife* in 2012. In 2014 Somdatta Mandal, professor of English at Visva-Bharati University, completed translating the book from Bengali to English. But publishers delayed, and the book changed hands. It was finally published by Jadavpur University Press in 2019.

Their Meeting & Marriage

How did Hariprabha and Uemon meet for the first time? Both met first in Dacca. She was 22 and he was 37. Uemon like many other young men had travelled to British India in "search of a living". He travelled to Bengal and found a job in the Bulbul soap factory in Dacca as a technical overseer. The company was owned by Hariprabha's father Sashibhushan Basu Mallick. As a Japanese immigrant to India, Uemon felt bored not being able to meet people. The desire to socialize forced him to attend Brahmo Samaj meetings. It is at one of these meetings that Uemon met Hariprabha and courted her. Hariprabha's mother Nagendrabala realized Uemon's entrepreneurial character and persuaded her husband to allow their eldest daughter marry Uemon. Nagendrabala's assessment of Uemon's character proved correct as he started his own manufacturing company and helped his in-laws in the philanthropic efforts. He was joined by his brother Toshan, but for nine years, Uemon did not communicate with his parents. In the essay "The Japan that Hariprabha Saw" Kazuhiro Watanabe has the answer. In the year 1912, when Hariprabha came with her husband to Japan, the Emperor Mutsuhito died signalling the end of the long Meiji Era and then dawned the Taisho era.

Was Hariprabha keen to visit Japan and prepared to undertake the tumultuous long sea journey? She was. As a traditional Indian woman, she was yearning to receive the blessings of her in-laws but was not a conformist to the idea of sangsar, which meant a married woman's real home was her in-laws. Being a Brahmo Samajist, she had strong faith in the power of the divine to shape her destiny. Perhaps she wanted to pay obeisance: to the gods of her in-laws who were Jodo-shu Buddhist. Indeed, Hariprabha was far ahead of the times in taking the plunge and marrying a foreigner outside her caste and nationality, posing a great challenge to the conservative decadent society of Bengal, though she was not at the same page with her younger sister who spurned her proposal to marry Uemon's younger brother, Toshon, and was therefore conservative about international marriage. What is noteworthy is that while whereas the Bengali middle class journeyed to Europe and England for pilgrimage, study, or marriage relocation, or with their husbands, travel to Japan was an exception as it was a relatively unknown destination.

Two More Visits to Japan

The Takedas revisited Japan two more times, once in 1924 and then again in 1941. Her trip in 1924 was short but dates are not available. The third trip in 1941 was the longest. Hostilities between the United States and Japan were increasing. As part of the repatriation drive organized by the Japanese government, the couple left Bombay on 2 November in a Japanese ship with 1,200 Japanese nationals and reached Kobe on 21 November. Hariprabha chronicles both the wars and the bombing of Pearl Harbor and cities of Hiroshima and Nagasaki. She saw food shortages during the war and lived a life of penury as her husband fell sick. For some time, on the advice of Rash Behari Bose and with the direct encouragement from Subhas Chandra Bose, she worked as a radio announcer of the secret broadcast service of the Azad Hind Fauj or the Indian National Army. Also some of her Indian friends like Rash Behari Bose, Justice Radha Binod Pal and others helped her with her daily needs and perhaps gave her money to buy her passage back to Bengal. She returned with her sick husband on board the British ship Eastern Saga from Yokohama in 1948. A flood in 1968 spoilt all her possessions. So she came to Calcutta and spent the last two and a half years of her life with her nephew Surojit Dasgupta and his wife Manju. Her husband became deeply depressed by Japan's defeat in World War II.

She went to Japan for the third time with her husband in 1941 and returned in 1948. Uemon was very sick and died soon after their return. He suffered from acute depression as he could not accept the defeat of Japan. During her third stay she wrote about the war and its impact on Japan, ravaged by the War or Juddha Jarjarita Japan. She got connected to both the Boses who were in Japan—Subhas Chandra and Rash Behari. According to Mandal, "her first trip was romantic but the second was patriotic."

An Inspirational Wife

A dutiful wife, war reporter, event chronicler and social reformer, Hariprabha's travel diary and other writings continue to inspire the Bengali middle class in India. About seven and a half years of her Japanese experience feeds into the Asian sense of pride created by Okakura Tenshin and corroborated by Tagore. Tagore's own writings on Japan in Japan Jatri were a "poet's vision of that country", while Hariprabha delves deep into the hearts of the common people. Hariprabha's diary brings alive the process of modernization Japan was going through during the Taisho and Meiji eras and the freedom struggle India was engaged in. Her diary is an important addition to the female travelogue literature of the early 20th century. This is a glorious chapter in the history of India-Japan relation in the historical context that is often overlooked by contemporary Indian scholars of Japanese studies in India. Bhabani Sen Gupta, the late eminent Indian scholar who was frequently misunderstood in the academic community due to his unconventional but fearless views, stated at a conference organised by the author in the 1990s at the Indian International Centre that we must project the past to understand the present and the present to understand the future. This was a significant statement with immediate and long-term implications. He went on to say that today's scholars are too afraid to face scholarly examination. Hariprabha's example, which is often overlooked, must share space along with Rash Behari Bose, Netaji Subash Chandra Bose and Justice Radha Binod Pal.

Other Early Bengal Connect

Hariprabha-Uemon matrimony is not the only standalone example of Bengal's early connection with Japan. There were also other Bengalis who visited Japan those days. Manmathanath Ghosh visited Japan on April 1, 1906, and stayed on for three years. His travel experiences and impressions are found in the three books that he wrote about Japan, all published in 1915. The first book called the *Japan Probash* (Abroad in Japan), published in 1910 is the first Bengali book ever written on Japan. His other two books on Japan issues are *Nobyo Japan* (The New Japan), and *Supto Japan* (The Hidden Japan). He was basically an entrepreneur and his objective was to acquire Japanese technique so that he could apply it in the Indian setting. He again returned to Japan for a second time in 1933 to procure some modern technology to apply in his business. The three books written by Ghosh tell the tales of the then Japanese socio-economic life, and the untold aspects.[24]

Rise in Japan's Ambitions and Geopolitical Churning

When all these aforementioned developments were proceeding at a snail's pace both in the economic as well as cultural domains, India felt a sense of betrayal when Japan entered into the Anglo-Japanese Alliance in 1902. The Indian bitterness further sharpened when the alliance was extended in 1905 as it signified that Japan, in the interests of British imperialism, would act as a bulwark against Russian expansionism in India. India was shocked as Japan's defeat of China and Russia had raised hopes of Indian nationalists to fight against the British imperialists. When the treaty was revised in 1911, Russia ceased to be a potential enemy as Russia and England had reached an accord. In view of this power realignment, a new feeling began to emerge in Japan that the Japan-Britain honeymoon must end. Japan started viewing Britain in a different prism.

Indirectly, souring of Japan-Britain relations worked in India's favour as Indian revolutionaries who had taken refuge in Japan felt safe to pursue their activities openly and not secretively. Japan's focus shifted after it annexed Korea in 1910 and demanded extraterritorial rights in China to be at par with other Western powers, thereby using the same methods as adopted by the West. This was the first demonstration of Japan's ambitions. It aspired to be accepted as a member of the West on a position of equality. As it transpired in the subsequent decades, this ended with perilous consequences. A detailed analysis of this is beyond the scope of this book.

Developments Back in India

In India, spurred by the developments in Japan, anti-British movement started gathering steam. Indian revolutionaries called upon the people to boycott British products and encouraged to use the local produce, particularly those produced in Maharashtra and Bengal. Interestingly and as a sign of goodwill and sentiment for Japanese people, the call to boycott foreign products did not include goods produced in Japan. After the Russo-Japanese War, many Indians went to Japan for studies or sought refuge in Japan to escape the suppression of the British in India. Another interesting aspect in the evolution of the relationship deserves mention. In 1897, Okuma Shigenobu, a statesman in the Meiji period, had established the Indo-Japan study circle to study the problems in India. In 1907, he became the President of the Waseda University and established a Centre for Indian Studies in the University. The Indian students studying there organized a function in honour of Shivaji, the 17th century hero of Maharashtra, whose call for Swaraj (self rule) had inspired the nationalist movement in India. Okuma disappointed the Indian youth in Japan by urging them to pursue their studies and not resorting to violence. The Indian students were not only disappointed but also realized that Japan had constraints put by the Anglo-Japanese Alliance on the Japanese Government. Disappointed, the Indian youth left Japan to pursue their ideals in their home land. Though Okuma was supporting Japan's position to play the role of a policeman in the East for Britain and was acting as per the terms of the Anglo-Japanese Alliance, things turned sour soon, thereby giving a new impetus to Indian revolutionaries who had made Japan as their base.

Changes in the International Situation—Japan Softens Towards Asian Nationalist Movements

Much to Japan's disappointment, the Allied Powers did not provide the desired assistance in order for Japan to be regarded equally with the Western powers. It was not permitted to view China as its own sphere of influence. The West was concerned about Japan's newly gained naval might and wished to limit it, seeing Japan as a potential competitor to its colonial ambitions. Meanwhile, America's worldwide dominance had grown significantly, while Britain's had commensurately diminished. This emboldened America to put pressure on Britain to abrogate the Alliance relationship with Japan. A relatively weak Britain had to succumb to American pressure, and the Anglo-Japanese Alliance was finally abrogated in 1923.

The establishment of a communist power in Russia in 1917, even before the end of the War, also changed the international situation. All the attempts made by Japan to prove to the Western powers through its successful economic development and military prowess that it was different from other Asian nations, could not get for Japan a different treatment in the matter of immigration policy of the Western nations. All these factors led to a change in Japan's attitude towards the nationalist movements in Asia. While at the people's level, support for the movement had been there, the covert support given by the Government to the Indian revolutionaries in Japan was a new factor. Japan resisted the pressures from the British to ferret out the revolutionaries and deport them. This becomes clear when we examine the case of Rash Bihari Bose, who sought refuge in Japan.

Role of Rash Behari Bose

The next historical connect with Japan in contemporary times is the role of freedom fighter Rash Behari Bose, which is often underplayed in India and is not widely known, and therefore needs to be highlighted. As one of the unsung heroes and freedom fighters of India, the story of his role in India's struggle for freedom is a significant episode in the history of Indian independence movement.[25]

As an officer of the British Raj, Rash Bihari Bose had come under the influence of extremists in the Indian national movement, like Aurobindo Ghose, Bal Gangadhar Tilak, and Bipin Chandra Pal. In 1905, when the British colonial power portioned Bengal, Bose quit his job as an officer of the British Raj and became a revolutionary. The colonial power issued a death warrant against him for his alleged involvement in some conspiracies against Lord Hardinge, then British Viceroy of India, and to bring about a general uprising of Indian soldiers starting from the Lahore barracks. Bose fled India for Japan in 1915 where he did the groundwork for the foundation of Netaji

Subhash Chandra Bose's Azad Hind Fauj by writing about the colonized India's struggle for freedom in the contemporary Japanese publications.

The account of Bose's escape from India to reach Japan is an interesting story that needs reiteration. Indeed, Bose's story forms a vital part of India's struggle for independence, and the victory which was finally achieved was in no small measure due to his organizational skill and wonderful spirit of sacrifice. Referring to the role of Bose as the founder of the Indian National Army, the former Prime Minister of Burma (now Myanmar) Thakin Nu observed that "if Netaji came out in the fight as Garibaldi of the movement, Rash Behari Bose's part in the drama was more than of a Mazzini."[26] Not many are aware that Rash Behari Bose was the founder of the Indian National Army (INA), though it is often credited to Netaji Subash Chandra Bose. This historical fallacy needs to be corrected. Even A.M. Nair who opened an Indian restaurant in Ginza and a popular outlet for the Japanese and wrote his memoir, *An Indian Freedom Fighter in Japan*, mentions that he worked as the liaison officer of Rash Behari Bose who led two important Japan-backed organizations, the Indian Independence League and the Indian National Army, and opines that Bash Behari has been unfairly minimized and the contribution of the more famous Subash Chandra Bose greatly inflated.[27] Nair died in 1990 but his restaurant bearing his name leaves another example of cultural connect through Indian food between the two countries, besides Nakamuraya, which will be discussed in details later in this Chapter.

Nair laments that in contemporary India, Subhas's stature appears to have increased. While esteeming Subash's charisma and patriotism, he slams his lack of realism and his dictatorial tendencies. Nair does concede that the INA galvanised the rebel army, resulting in mutiny by the Navy in Bombay. British India saw the writing was on the wall. Nair also acted on several occasions as interpreter for Justice Radha Binod Behari Pal, the only judge who gave his dissenting judgement at the Tokyo War Crimes Trials declaring all "A-Class" (political) defendants innocent. Pal's stinging counter to allegations of Japanese conspiracy to wage war was profound and this can be deciphered from his statement: "Many powerful nations are living this sort of life, and if these acts are criminal, then the entire international community is living a criminal life."

Rash Behari Bose was a revolutionary even from his student days. That time, Bengal was the hotbed of political firmament, which is why the British decided to shift the capital from Calcutta (now Kolkata) to Delhi. After the abortive attempt to eliminate Lord Hardinge, Rash Behari foisted the British attempt to nab him and escaped to Japan under the assumed name of Raja P.N. Tagore, presenting himself to the Commissioner of Police, Calcutta, as one of Gurudev Tagore's secretaries, proceeding to Japan to make arrangements for his visit to Tokyo, from where he continued the revolutionary movement.

After reaching Tokyo in June 1915, Bose soon reached out to the Japanese sympathizers. Japan had already entered into an alliance relationship with Great Britain and signed the Anglo-Japanese Alliance (1902-23), which bound both Japan and Britain to assist one another in safeguarding respective interests in China and Korea. Directed against Russian expansionism in the Far East, it was a cornerstone of British and Japanese policy in Asia until after World War I.[28] Therefore, the Japanese government was forced to direct Rash Behari to leave the shores of Japan. However, Bose got the support from the Japanese people and protection by hiding him in the cellar of an influential hotel Nakamuraya.

On entering Japan, he was introduced to Sun Yat Sen by Bhagwan Singh of the Gadar Party, and got into the network of the so-called "Pan-Asianists", both Chinese and Japanese. He also got the sympathy and support of right wing leaders like Toyama Mitsuru, Ohkawa Shumei, etc. But it is the support of common people, which enabled him to carry out his activities.

When a British ship had fired at a Japanese merchant carrier, Japan was provoked and relationships between Japan and Britain soured. In order to hurt the pride and prestige of Britain, Japan went soft against Bose, encouraging him to come out of his hiding to carry on his revolutionary movement against the British rule in India. Japan also withdrew the deportation order issued against Bose based on the terms of the Anglo-Japanese alliance. During his stay at Nakamuraya, the owner of the restaurant Mr. and Mrs. Zoma bestowed Bose with affection and care, offering their eldest daughter Toshiko in marriage to Rash Behari. Thus, Rash Behari became the son-in-law in the Land of the Rising Sun but never forgot his Motherland.

A marriage photograph of Toshiko and Rash Behari Bose

Interestingly, though the Japanese government had issued an expulsion order against Bose, but these orders were never seriously implemented. When Bose found that the British would not allow him to enter India, he became a Japanese citizen in 1923. The Japanese press had also criticized the government and started a campaign against the deportation orders. The Japanese openly supported the Indians' right to gain freedom by cooperating with Japan. Rash Behari Bose expanded his activities into China and other Southeast Asian countries. He participated in pan-Asian conferences that advocated for Asian unification and the development of an Asian race union to achieve world peace based on justice and equal opportunity. It was also decided at these sessions that Asia would be freed from European dominance under Japanese leadership. Rash Behari Bose also enlightened the Japanese through his writings in Japanese journals like Kaizo, Toho Jiron, and Gekkan Nihon and public lectures about the nationalist movement in India. He sharply criticized the British Rule in India. He also warned Japan that after World War I, Japan should be more watchful of a closer relationship between Britain and America. At the same time, he strongly criticized Japan's China policy. The Indian national leaders were initially quite receptive to the idea of Pan-Asia proposed by Japan, but Japan's aggressive policy towards China was strongly condemned. All sections of Indians, whether of the nationalist movement in India, or those in Japan were clear that they would not tolerate the control of Japan over India, even if India gains freedom from the British with Japan's assistance. However, the leaders of the Congress were keen to strengthen cultural, economic and political relations with Japan. For this purpose, an Indian National Committee was formed with A.N. Sahay, who was in Japan as its President. The purpose of the Committee was to create better understanding and friendship between Indians and Japanese.

Here, two issues deserve special mention: founding of the Azad Hind Fauz and the popularization of Indian curry, which is a craze in Japan till today. A great opportunity unfolded in 1942 when World War II had already broken out, Singapore fell into the hands of Japan. Japan took many Indians, Australians and British as prisoners of war. At that time, another Indian revolutionary, Subhas Chandra Bose, was in Germany seeking help. Rash Behari was toying with the idea of forming a Liberation Army and invade India from outside with the help of Japan. Encouraged by Japan's support, Rash Behari floated the idea of building the Azad Hind Fauz for the purpose. Subash Chandra Bose undertook a most arduous journey in a submarine from Germany on February 8, 1943, and reached Singapore. When Rash Behari invited Subash Chandra Bose to lead this force, Subash was happy to accept the offer and assumed the Supreme Command of the Free Indian National Army in August 1943. Reposing his faith on the forces he had created and handed over the reins to Subash Chandra Bose, Rash Behari died of heart attack on January 21, 1945, and thus could not see his beloved country become independent. In 1959, when the ashes of Rash Behari were brought to India by his daughter, Tetsu Higuchi, Dr. Rajendra Prasad, then President of India, paid to the noble son of Bharat a glowing tribute in which he said, "Rash Behari Bose was one of those well-known patriots whose love for the Motherland and burning desire to see her free could never be curbed."

Rash Behari Bose is mostly known as a revolutionary in India, but he is remembered in Japan for another thing, which only few know. During his stay in Japan, he introduced an authentic Indian curry that is a key dish on the menu at Tokyo's popular restaurants, even today. When detective agencies hired by the British traced his whereabouts in Tokyo, Rash Behari moved to Shinjuku, a commercial district of Tokyo then and even now where he found a hideout. The hideout was the Nakamuraya bakery, owned by Aizo Soma and Kotsuko Soma. This couple supported India's struggle for independence and therefore sheltered Rash Behari Bose in the basement of the house. Gradually, Rash Behari developed a bond of affection with the Soma family. It was where he shared the recipe of his favourite Indian chicken curry, making the Indian curry popular in the Soma house. The bond between Rash Behari and the Somas thickened when the latter offered their eldest daughter in marriage with Rash Behari.[29] The marriage was solemnised in 1918. The Soma family made a brave decision to marry their daughter to a foreigner during a time when such a system was frowned upon in Japan during those days. Toshiko not only willingly accepted the life of a social outcast, but also shouldered most of the domestic responsibilities letting Bose to pursue his goal of Indian independence with unwavering devotion.

One can interpret this development as a sign of Japan's cultural internationalisation and paved the way for intercultural marriages widely popular in contemporary times. This however does not eliminate or change the mindset of the native Japanese completely, as they continue to view children born of mixed marriages suspiciously and contemptuously, referring to them as 'hafus', which means that those children are half-Japanese and continue to face many legal hurdles to be accepted as full Japanese citizens. Priyanka Yoshikawa, born of a Japanese mother and an Indian father, hogged international limelight when she was crowned Miss Japan in 2015 and many Japanese questioned her selection as she was a 'hafu'. That was an unnecessary controversy which could have been avoided. It is important to understand how, despite being modern, Japan cannot abandon many old beliefs and traditions. Whether it is a happy blend of tradition and modernity remains a matter of debate.

Coming back to Rash Behari issue, it is unclear how much Toshiko contributed to Rash Behari's mission to free India from the British, as not much information is available. Toshiko died prematurely of tuberculosis in

1925, at the age of 28, leaving behind two children. This unexpected turn of events upset Rash Behari Bose. He had to care for the two infants and also required financial assistance. As a result, the bereaved Bose teamed up with his father-in-law to create a tiny restaurant on top of the Nakamuraya bakery, where he prepared and served his beloved chicken curry to the residents, as well as other Indian cuisine. The aroma of Indian spices used in curry preparation attracted many Japanese to the Indian cuisine and became an instant hit. Thus, was born Indo Karii, a blend of Indian curry and Japanese rice. The print media popularised the curry as Rash Behari's "Taste of love and revolution", thereby catapulting Nakamuraya's popularity and contributing to its success in business. Bose developed health problems related to the lungs and was hospitalised in 1944. He breathed his last in January 1945, even before World War II ended, leaving behind Nakamuraya's Indo Karii, which continues to be a household name and popular dish in Japan.[30] The restaurant still exists in Shinjuku ward and was renovated in 2015 with more space so that 100 people can dine at the same time.

When visiting the restaurant, one cannot miss the painting of a young girl staring out at the world with maturity beyond her years. The menu bears an unusual slogan: "The taste of love and revolution". The young girl was the eldest daughter of the Soma couple, who owned and operated Nakamuraya in the early twentieth century. In 1923, the young lady married Rash Behari, an Indian rebel who devised the curry known in Japan as Indo karii. The details have been discussed elsewhere in this book.

The Somas were "a dynamic and radical couple …Their circle included activists, poets, and university professors as well as artists—locals, returnees, and non-Japanese alike". They actively encouraged artists they admired by providing studio space and accommodations in an annexe behind the bakery. It was there that famed painter Tsune Nakamura created the portrait of their 15-year-old daughter Toshiko which hangs in the alcove of the curry restaurant. The infatuated Tsune also completed several more portraits of the girl, including a nude study that critics praised but her Christian school teachers did not.

Another member of their salon was the sculptor Rokuzan, who had studied under Rodin in Paris, thanks to financial support from the Somas.

Like many artists of the era, he died young. His final piece was an erotically charged female figure that bore a striking similarity to the woman he loved, Kokko Soma.

More interesting information has emerged about Rash Behari and Toshiko's marriage. When Bose was under surveillance, the Japanese authorities might have easily traced and deported Rash Behari to stand justice in India under the Anglo-Japanese alliance of the Taisho era (1912-1926). But this did not happen. There could be two reasons: Japanese military was angry when a British ship fired and sank a Japanese vessel, whether knowingly or unwillingly, and so chose to go easy on Rash Behari in protest. Rash Behari, on the other hand, was allowed to carry out his revolutionary operations without interference. The second reason was that the formidable Toyama, who himself was jailed as a young man for anti-government violence, knew how to keep his secret intact. Toshiko was enlisted as an inconspicuous bearer of messages to and from Bose who was kept by the Somas in secrecy. That gave Toyama the idea of Bose-Toshiko matrimonial alliance. Kokko, Toshiko's mother, had rejected the penniless painter Tsune Nakamura (the maker of the portrait hanging in the Nakamuraya restaurant) as a suitable mach for her daughter. But an Indian on the run was even a worse bet. According to Nakajima, Kokko left the decision to her daughter, explaining that it would be no ordinary marriage and might end in disgrace or death. Toshiko more matured than her age answered: "I know that. You and father are worried, but please let me go ahead." Such information is unknown to Indian readers and must be highlighted in view of the historical importance defining India-Japan relations. The Rash Behari-Toshiko marriage took place in secrecy in Mitsuru Toyama's residence, with witnesses including Foreign Minister Shinpei Goto and future Prime Minister Tsuyoshi Inukai, both enthusiastic pan-Asianists. In order to allay suspicion, Toshiko and the Soma couple breached custom by travelling to the ceremony by a streetcar and in ordinary clothes. Toshiko's wedding kimono had been sent directly to Toyama's house by the Takashimaya department store.[31]

According to *Bose of Nakamuraya*, by Professor Takeshi Nakajima, Bose wanted to prove that the curry the Japanese were used to was a colonial invention. Getting his recipe on the Nakamuraya menu was therefore "part of his anti-colonial struggle, by trying to win back India's food culture from British hands."[32]

Though sushi and soba are important parts of traditional Japanese lunch and dinner, curry and rice have become equally important parts of Japanese diet. The Japanese Navy even has a "curry Friday" tradition when all navy canteens offer curry and rice as a Friday staple. Since 2001, the company sells ready-to-eat packaged curries using the original Bose recipe to convenience stores. These accounted for almost half the sales value of the 2.6 billion yen the Nakamura Processed Foods division made in 2016.[33]

There are plenty of stories written in recent times on this Rash Behari saga and his relatively unknown aspects of life and activities have reached the public imagination. This historical connect is extremely relevant in the contemporary times, when both India and Japan are facing new challenges, and this cultural connect provides additional heft.

When World War II broke out and Singapore fell to Japan in 1942, there were around 32,000 Indian prisoners-of-war in Southeast Asia. Major Fujiwara who was in charge of Singapore offered to assist the Indian soldiers if they were willing to fight against the British. Rash Behari left Tokyo and reached Bangkok to pursue his aim to liberate India from British yoke with the help of the Japanese. He founded the Independence League, with the Indian National Army as its military wing. He also invited Indian representatives from other Asian countries to join the struggle. In May 1943, Subash Chandra Bose had reached Japan in a secretive submarine journey from Berlin, where both the Boses met. Being impressed with the younger Bose, Rash Behari transferred the leadership of the League to the younger charismatic Subash Chandra. This organisation played a significant role in weakening the British hold in India. Though Mahatma Gandhi's strategy of non-violence as the primary tool finally led to India's liberation, and disapproved Subash Chandra's approach to achieve the same objective by military means, Subash Chandra's contribution to India's independence is no less important.

Yukihiko Yamada writes that two Boses, and their Japanese connect shall remain fresh in the memory of the Japanese people, both for the freedom movement and introduction of Indian curry and that the Japanese would never forget.[34] Both had strong connect with Japan, friends of Japan, and key forces behind the formation of the Indian National Army (INA), the Azad Hind Fauz, which was floated to free India from the colonial rule of Britain, and both also died in the same year-1945—Rash Behari in Japan and Subash Chandra Bose in Taiwan. Not many are aware that while Rash Behari hailed from West Bengal, Subash Chandra Bose was born in Cuttack, Odisha.

Savitri Vishwanathan observes: "The early victories of Japan in South East Asia even made an Indian leader like Mahatma Gandhi ponder about the possibility of using Japan in achieving self-rule, once the British were forced to leave India, unable to resist the Japanese Army. Although the Indian National Army could not finally successfully enter India and were badly defeated, the INA interlude brought Indians and Japanese closer. As Nehru put it, even in the defeat and subsequent prosecution of the INA officers, INA became "a symbol of India fighting for independence".[35]

There are multiple interpretations on Bose's introduction of the Indo karii. Peter Tasker writes for Japan Forward that the Western obsession with popularising Western cuisine, which he refers to as the Progressive Club Sandwich, was motivated by a desire to demonstrate Western moral superiority over Japanese backwardness. In this mix, Bose's Indo karii offering a different suite of flavour was a moral high for the Japanese and therefore an Indian alternative history of modern Japan.[36]

In recent times, new interpretations have emerged that link the Indo Karii to the Quad idea. According to one viewpoint, the Quad, which plays an important role in Japan's foreign policy, originated with Rash Behari Bose and Nakamuraya during Japan's Taisho era of intellectual vitality.[37] Peter Tasker writes, modern-day Japan needs revolutionaries like Bose, institutions like Nakamuraya, and the willingness to absorb the "complex and unpredictable mix of influences across the globe".[38] Bose and Somas were great admirers of Rabindranath Tagore and welcomed him several times during his five trips to Japan. Bose did not live to see his motherland free from the British colonial rule. He died of an illness in January 1945. His son Masahide, "straight and excellent" (a name chosen by Toyama), died in the Battle of Okinawa. His daughter, Tetsuko, "child of wisdom", passed away in 2016 at the age of 93. She lived most of her life in the RB Building in Harajuku, named after her father and constructed on the site he acquired in the mid-1920s.

Another interesting anecdote emerges from Nair's memoirs is that he befriended many Japanese military contacts and encouraged them to fight against the British, while silently urging his customers to fight against the British. One of his closest military contacts, War Minister Seishiro Itagaki who received the death sentence, while another General Yoshijiro Umezu, died in prison. Nair writes that one of his military contacts made a dark joke that had MacArthur known about his complicity in provoking the Japanese to join Indian freedom fighters to fight against the British, Nair could have been booked as War Criminal Number One but the Supreme Commander MacArthur missed it. Nair remained an Indian citizen all his life, but because of the espionage and undercover work, he was treated by Japan's top military figures as equivalent to a Major-General in rank.

The Progressive Club Sandwich, with its assumption of Western moral superiority and Japanese backwardness, is still a popular comfort food. It has a long history, beginning with the "opening" of Japan by Commodore Perry's gunboats in the 1850s, and its influence can be found today in innumerable op-eds, books, and academic papers.

What gave the Taisho era (1912-1926) its freewheeling dynamism—so different to what came before and after—was this willingness to cross boundaries and the intellectual ferment that it generated. Tagore was welcome by the Soma family during his five trips to Japan. He had become increasingly critical of Japan's imitation of Western modernisation.

Controversy over Subash Chandra's Death

It is already established that Subash Chandra Bose died in a plane crash. However, conspiracy theories appeared emerged hours of his death and persisted for decades and kept alive various martial myths about Bose. Many of his supporters in India and elsewhere refused to believe the fact or the circumstances surrounding his death. According to credible sources, Subash died of third-degree burns on August 18, 1945, after the overloaded bomber in which he was being transported by the Japanese crashed in Taihoku, now Taipei.

Subash was marginalized within Congress in his own country and was a target for British surveillance. He chose to embrace the fascist powers as allies against the British and fled India, first to Hitler's Germany, then, on a German submarine, to the Japanese-occupied Singapore. Where he was going in the bomber, and who else were in the same bomber, became the centre of controversy. Though many written works on his death are available, and many more will be published in the future, offering various and sometimes contradictory versions, one work by an Indian journalist Harin Shah from the Bombay-based *Free Press Journal* who visited Taiwan months after the crash and wrote a small book containing a lot of insights from first-hand information, has not received the desired publicity.[39]

His observations are revealing after speaking with many people, including the nurse who took care of Subash in the South-Gate Military Hospital, the Chief the Taipei City Health and Hygiene Bureau Dr. Kaw King Yen, the keeper of the crematorium who cremated Netaji's body, Chu Tsung, some students and many more. The nurse in the hospital was candid even to the point of showing the bed in which Bose breathed his last.[40]

Though there was no dispute about Netaji's death in the plane crash and serious burns, Dr. Kaw presented a different explanation for the disaster. He believed Netaji intended to go to Soviet Russia, and the Japanese did not want him to flee to Russia. Dr. Kaw believed that the Japanese purposely sank the plane shortly after it took off from the airport with the goal of killing him. Though Shah attempted to investigate more to determine the basis of his opinion, Dr. Kaw was unable to provide any other information. His theory seems to be based more on speculation. But there are more reasons that could testify to Dr. Kaw's suspicions. But the information provided by Shah in his observation that the anxious Japanese military officers advised the Director of the Bureau to cremate Netaji's body and keep this confidential gives room for suspicion. For example, Sister Tsan Pi Sha who was at Netaji's bedside when he breathed his last had no clue when and where Netaji was cremated.

Shah felt that local Japanese authorities were acting under acute tension and confusion to surrender. He observes: "It is possible they were acting on orders from Tokyo."[41] Even Col Habibur Rehman, Netaji's companion, suggested shifting the body either to Singapore or Tokyo, but the Japanese rejected his offer.

As the mystery surrounding Netaji's death grew, the Indian government formed multiple investigating bodies to determine the truth. The Figgess Report (1946), Shah Nawaz Committee (1956), Khosla Commission (1970), Mukherjee Commission (2005), and the Japanese government report (1956) were all declassified in September 2016. The findings of all these committees and commissions created more controversies than concrete results. None of them were able to decode the mystery of Netaji's disappearance. The mystery continued until people in India had to accept that Netaji died in Taiwan. Like the recognition accorded by Japan to Justice Radha Binod Pal, who has a memorial at Yasukuni Shrine, Netaji has also his pride of place in Japan, demonstrating the deep friendship and mutual respect between India and Japan. There is a memorial of Subash Chandra Bose in the compound of the Renkoji Temple, Tokyo, where Bose's ashes are stored in the temple in a golden pagoda. Bose died on August 18, 1945. His ashes arrived in Japan in early September 1945; after a memorial service, they were accepted by the temple on September 18, 1945.

Mystery Continued with the Story of Gumnami Baba

For a long time, everyone, including his family members, refused to believe the news of the death of a legendary personality, one of India's most revered icons. This refusal to embrace the truth sparked a few mysteries when Gumnami Baba, a recluse sadhu from Uttar Pradesh, was spotted bearing an uncanny likeness to Netaji. The notion grew that the Baba was Netaji in disguise.[42] Even after his death in 1985, people continued to believe that he was Netaji in disguise. Though Netaji did not appear, the myth lives on. A book authored by Anju Dhar and Chandrachur Ghose on Netaji further perpetuates the mystery.[43] Srijit Mukherjee's film Gumnaami (2019) based on the book, sparked a backlash from Netaji's family, who viewed the plot as fictional and an insult to him. As a result, the mystery has not been solved. The inability to understand the mystery surrounding Netaji draws more people to his captivating charm. Netaji's disappearance is one of India's most enduring political mysteries.

Role of Justice Radha Binod Pal

Another important factor cementing India-Japan relations relates to the role played by Justice Radha Binod Pal at the International Military Tribunal for the Far East, known as the 'Tokyo Trial', whereas the representative of the British power much to the surprise of the British being the sole judge gave the dissenting judgement exonerating the Japanese of any war crimes.

At the end of the Second World War, the leaders of the defeated Axis powers were tried for crimes against peace, war crimes, and crimes against humanity in two specially established international military tribunals. Unlike at the vaunted Nuremberg trials, the judgment of the less-illustrious Tokyo tribunal was not unanimous. In his dissenting opinion, Justice Radha Binod Pal of India comprehensively disagreed with all aspects of the trial, finding all defendants "not guilty" of the charges levelled against them. Despite being considered quite incendiary at that time, the dissenting opinion has been largely overlooked by International Relations scholarship who analyze the development of legal norms and institutions in global politics. Despite its numerous limitations, the questions posed in Pal's dissent concerning criminality, authority, and justice, while placed in a specific historical context, are far from settled.[44]

Justice Pal (January 27, 1886–January 10, 1967) was one of the three Asian judges appointed to the Tokyo Trials of Japanese war crimes committed during World War II. Among all the judges of the tribunal, Justice Pal was the only one who submitted a judgment which insisted all defendants were not guilty. Justice Pal found strong evidence that members of the Japanese armed forces committed crimes against civilians in several of the regions they occupied, as well as prisoners of war. However, he issued a decision that called into doubt the tribunal's legality and findings. He believed that the tribunal's legality was doubtful and questionable because the underlying basis for passing judgement was the spirit of retribution, and not impartial justice.

He concluded: "I would hold that every one of the accused must be found not guilty of every one of the charges in the indictment and should be acquitted on all those charges." Justice Pal never intended to offer a juridical argument on whether a sentence of not guilty would have been a correct one. However, he argued that the United States had clearly provoked the war with Japan and expected Japan to act. He argued that "Even contemporary historians could think that as for the present war, the Principality of Monaco, the Grand Duchy of Luxembourg, would have taken up arms against the United States on receipt of such a note[45] as the State Department sent the Japanese Government on the eve of Pearl Harbor." He also noted that, "Questions of law are not decided in an intellectual quarantine area in which legal doctrine and the local history of the dispute alone are retained and all else is forcibly excluded. We cannot afford to be ignorant of the world in which disputes arise."

In his lone dissent, Judge Pal refers to the trial as a "sham employment of legal process for the satisfaction of a thirst for revenge." According to Norimitsu Onishi, while he fully acknowledged Japan's war atrocities – including the Nanjing massacre—he said they were covered in the Class B and Class C trials.[46] Judge Pal noted, "I might mention in this connection that even the published accounts of Nanking 'rape' could not be accepted by the world without some suspicion of exaggeration."[47]

Furthermore, Justice Pal believed that the exclusion of Western colonialism and the use of the atomic bomb by the US from the list of crimes, as well as the exclusion of judges from the vanquished nations on the bench, signified the "failure of the Tribunal to provide anything other than the opportunity for the victors to retaliate." Pal wrote that the Tokyo Trials were an exercise in victor's justice and that the Allies were equally culpable in acts such as strategic bombings of civilian targets. Regardless of his personal opinions about Japan, he deemed it appropriate to dissent from the judgement of his "learned brothers" to embody his love for absolute truth and justice.

On November 12, 1948, the former Prime Minister of Japan, Hideki Tojo, and some others were sentenced to death for war crimes by the Tribunal and many sentenced with life imprisonment.[48] "Guilty", pronounced one judge after another, until a voice thundered, "Not Guilty!". The disbelieving gasps came first followed by complete silence. That voice of dissent came from Indian Justice Radha Binod Pal.

The majority opinion finally prevailed and wartime prime minister Hideki Tojo and six other war criminals were executed in Tokyo on December 23, 1948. According to declassified US documents that have since surfaced, the ashes of those executed were scattered over the Pacific Ocean. This clears up a decades-old mystery over the final disposal of the remains. The documents kept at the US National Archives and Records Administration in Washington give information on the final disposition of the remains following the convictions handed down by the International Military Tribunal for the Far East. The finding was made by a full-time lecturer and specialist on Japanese war criminals at Tokyo's Nihon University, Hiroaki Takazawa, discovered two documents in 2018 that provide details on the final handling of the remains following the convictions handed down by the International Military Tribunal for the Far East.

The first document of December 23, 1948, the day of the executions, makes a brief mention of the ash-scattering operation. The second document of January 4, 1949, gives more details. Both of them were written by Maj. Luther Frierson of the Eighth U.S. Army based in Yokohama, who was in charge of the operation. Frierson wrote that he was present at the early morning hangings in Sugamo Prison, and accompanied the seven corpses when they were transferred to Yokohama by truck. The remains were later cremated and placed in separate urns, which were then loaded onto a liaison plane used by the U.S. Eighth Army. Frierson writes: "We proceeded to a point approximately 30 miles (48 kilometers) over the Pacific Ocean east of Yokohama where I personally scattered the cremated remains over a wide area in accordance with letter GHQ, August 13, 1948."[49]

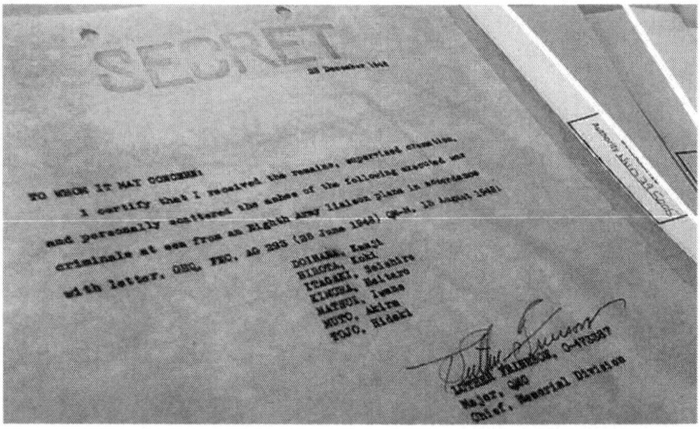

The letter from General Headquarters in Tokyo where Gen. Douglas MacArthur reigned as Supreme Commander of the Allied powers during the U.S. occupation, stated: "The remains of executed war criminals in the custody of the United States Army shall be cremated and the ashes disposed of secretly at sea." Adequate precautions were taken to ensure that news photographers did not get wind of the journey from Sugamo Prison to Yokohama. Though the documents offered no explanation for GHQ's decision to scatter the ashes secretly at sea, William Sebald, the chief of the diplomatic section of GHQ, said in his book, "With MacArthur in Japan: A Personal History of the Occupation", published by Asahi Shimbun Co., "The ashes were planned to be scattered around to prevent the graves of the executed war leaders from being deified in the future."[50]

After Japan's surrender, the Supreme Commander of Allied Forces (SCAP), a position created at the start of the occupation of Japan on August 14, 1945, was headed by General Douglas MacArthur who oversaw Japan's transition into a democratic system. The Emperor's powers were drastically curtailed and made a figure head and symbol of the State. In greater wisdom, the institution of the Emperor, seen as a demi-God by the Japanese people, was not tempered with. All military potentials were destroyed and a Constitution was virtually imposed on Japan with a peace clause enshrined in Article 9.[51] By inserting another clause in Article 96, it virtually closed option for any future attempt to amend any Article. The Occupation period ended in 1952 after Japan signed the San Francisco Peace Treaty on September 8, 1951. Independent India refused to sign this treaty but chose to sign a separate treaty with Japan in 1952, symbolising mutual respect. Then Prime Minister Jawaharlal Nehru felt that signing a separate peace treaty gave Japan a due place of honour and equality among the community of free nations. In the Peace Treaty, India waived all reparation claims against Japan. This also marked a defining moment in the bilateral relations, setting the tone for the future. This gesture by India, as well as Justice Pal's dissenting judgement, are significant milestones in India-Japan ties, in addition to the others highlighted and detailed in this Chapter. These experiences struck an emotional chord with the people of both countries, contributing significantly to their mutual love and respect.

The American occupation of Japan ended in 1952 after Japan signed the San Francisco Peace Treaty and accepted the Tokyo trial's verdict. Japan had no other choice. Its morale was low, and its spirit was sinking. At this important juncture, India stood up and embraced its friend snatched away by the Western colonial powers with a warm hug. Thus started a new chapter, and since then, relationships have deepened and flourished in all fronts, regaining the lost glory of friendship.

The end of the Occupation also lifted a ban on the publication of Justice Pal's 1,235-page dissent. Patriots in Japan taking pride in their past glory and tradition took an opportunity to use this as the basis of their argument that the Tokyo trials were biased. Some academics also opine that the trials were a basis for shifting blame from the Emperor to Tojo as the culprit of the War. Psychologist and cultural critic Ashish Nandy argues that Judge Pal's lone dissenting opinion, that the Japanese soldiers were only following orders and that the acts committed by them were not illegal in an indictable sense, was because of "his long exposure to the traditional laws of India", combined with a sense of "Asian solidarity" within the "larger Afro-Asian context of nationalism." In 1966, Pal visited Japan and said that he had admired Japan from an early age for being the only Asian nation that "stood up against the West". Pal was awarded the Order of the Sacred Treasure's First Class by the Emperor of Japan. Pal is adored by Japanese patriots, and a monument to him exists on the grounds of the Yasukuni Shrine. Pal's monument was erected following his death. There is another monument of Pal at Kyoto Ryozen Gokoku Shrine.

Yasukuni Shrine (Jinja) is a Shinto shrine in Chiyoda, Tokyo, Japan. It was founded by Emperor Meiji and commemorates anyone who had died in service of the Empire of Japan. The Honden shrine commemorates anyone who died on behalf of the empire, including not only soldiers, relief workers, factory workers, and other citizens, but also those not of Japanese ethnicity such as Taiwanese and Koreans who served Japan. The engraved words from Radha Binod Pal say: "When time shall have softened passion and prejudice, when Reason shall have stripped the mask from misrepresentation, then Justice, holding evenly her scales, will require much of past censure and praise to change places."

The popular (also controversial) Yasukuni Shrine in the vicinity of the Indian Embassy in Kudanshita, Tokyo, Japan. Five million people visit Yasukuni Jinja every year to pay their respects to the enshrined souls.

The impact of Justice Pal's judgment is so huge that it has become a talking point in praise and admiration of his courage and conviction to stand up to his integrity in upholding jurisprudence and the neutrality in delivering the judgment without succumbing to any pressure or influence from any side. His dissenting voice is frequently mentioned by Indian diplomats and political leaders in the context of Indo-Japanese friendship and solidarity.

On April 29, 2005, in his remarks at a banquet in New Delhi in honour of the visiting Japanese Prime Minister Junichiro Koizumi, Prime Minister Manmohan Singh said: "It is a noteworthy fact that though we have gone through various phases in our relationship, in times of difficulty, we have stood by each other. … The dissenting judgement of Judge Radha Binod Pal is well-known to the Japanese people and will always symbolise the affection and regard our people have for your country." Further, while delivering a speech in the Japanese Diet on December 14, 2006, Prime Minister Singh stated: "The principled judgment of Judge Radha Binod Pal after the War is remembered even today in Japan." On August 23, 2007, Japanese Prime Minister Shinzō Abe met Pal's son, Prasanta, in Kolkata and appreciated Dr Pal's role during the course of trials. Dr Radha Binod Pal was awarded Padma Vibhushan in 1959. Prasanta along with his wife, Minati, were invited to Kyoto, in Japan, as guests of honour to inaugurate a statue of Justice Pal in the hall. Prasanta donated to the Memorial the pen used by his father to sign the dissenting judgment in 1948.[52] He died in 2009 at the age of 83.

Justice Pal was one of the 11 members of the tribunal set up by the Allied powers and by General Douglas MacArthur as the representative of British India. Justice Pal standing in the back row, first on the left.

Nearly six decades after his death, Justice Pal remains a big personality in the Japanese consciousness. A grateful Japan has not forgotten this famous Indian judge. Delivering the famous speech in the Indian Parliament in August in 2007, Prime Minister Abe had remarked: "Justice Pal is highly respected even today by many Japanese for the noble spirit of courage he exhibited during the International Military Tribunal for the Far East."[53] After his short tenure of one year in 2006-7 as Prime Minister, Abe went on to become the longest-serving Prime Minister of Japan from 2012 to 2020, when he resigned on health grounds. During this long tenure, Abe, with his nationalist credentials and backed by like-minded academics and nationalist politicians, pushed forward a revisionist view of Japan's wartime history. Judge Pal sprang back into the spotlight, resurrecting the Japanese spirit where he remains a touchstone of the culture wars surrounding the Tokyo trials.[54] It remains unclear why the British and American authorities selected Justice Pal, who held strong views on the colonial powers and sympathised with the anti-colonial struggle in India. As an Asian nationalist, he saw things very differently from the other judges. Justice Pal was bold enough to describe the atomic bombings of Hiroshima and Nagasaki by the United States as the worst atrocities of the war, comparable with Nazi crimes.

There can never be unanimous acclaim for Justice Pal in Japan or India. Some people in Japan disagree with Pal's perspective on the Nankin massacre and believe he was overly harsh. There is also a minority belief that, while Japan inspired admiration as an Asian nation contending with Western powers, there was equal concern over its colonisation of Asia. Those who hold such view say that Justice Pal, being an Indian and Bengali himself, must have been aware of the activities of Indian anti-colonialists such as fellow revolutionaries such as Rash Behari Bose Pal and Subash Chandra Bose, which could have indirectly influenced his views.

The Tokyo trial ended but left many legal issues and interpretations unanswered and debatable, which continue to affect Japan in modern times. The templates of trial involving the composition of the judges, criteria of their inclusion, fixing either individual or collective/institutional/representative responsibility and many more continue to impact Japan's present legal system.

Who decided to attack Pearl Harbour that triggered the War?

There is considerable controversy regarding who made the decision to attack Pearl Harbour, which sparked the war. According to the entry of the journal written by Saburo Hyakutake (1872-1963) on October 13, 1941, the Emperor Hirohito was ready to go to war against the US. The note below supports this view.

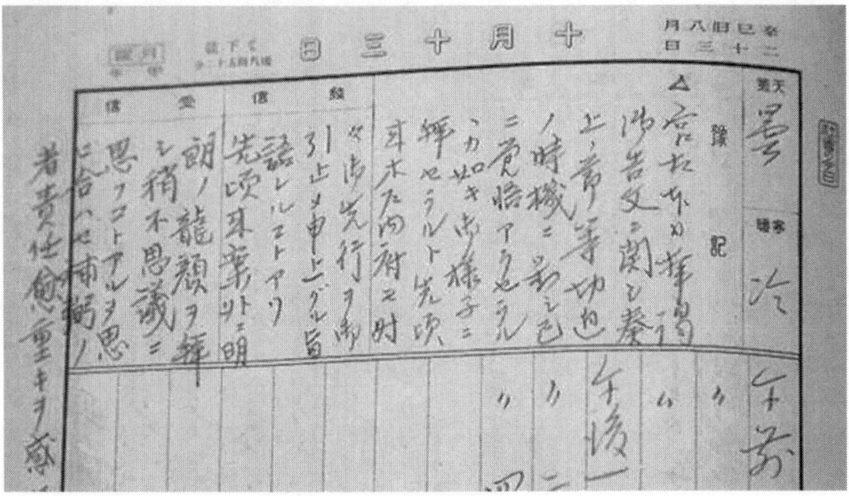

If this note is credible that Emperor Hirohito was preparing for war against the US about two months before Japan attacked Pearl Harbour, it automatically raises the question of wartime responsibilities.[55] Hyakutake, who served as the grand chamberlain for the emperor for eight years until 1944, penned a diary wherein he mentioned that the emperor was making progress in terms of battle preparations. This revelation surfaced when Hyakutake's relatives deposited a total of 25 diaries and pocket notebooks as well as memos, written by him to the library of the University of Tokyo's graduate schools for law and politics in 2019 and became available to the public in September 2021, marking the 80th year of Japan's attack on Pearl Harbour on December 7, 1941.[56]

The allied powers did not accuse Emperor Showa before the Tokyo War Crimes Tribunal. It was stated that the Emperor was wary of war and preferred peace, but grudgingly accepted to the war urged by the administration and military. Though this was the long-held position, certain contemporary studies of modern Japanese history based on records dispute that narrative, supporting the notion that the emperor was pleased with Japan's involvement in the conflict with the West. Hyakutake's diary is a significant record penned by one of the close aides. His descriptions of the emperor's attitude towards the war may lead to further research on the suspected complicity in going to war.

General MacArthur, in his wisdom, did not consider Showa Tenno (Emperor Hirohito) to take responsibility for the war by requiring his abdication from the throne. Since the military went to the war in the name of the Tenno, exonerating him of war responsibility is an issue that Japan continues to confront in its wartime history. The Tenno remained on the throne for 44 years after the end of the war, serving as a constant reminder to many East Asian countries of the wartime period. While MacArthur's judgment to keep the Emperor on the throne remains debatable, it is possible that the post-war bitterness of other East Asian countries could have been substantially altered. If that had happened, his son and successor, now Emperor Emeritus Akihito, would have served on the throne for 73 years by the time he stepped down in 2019.[57] Thus, debates over the conspiracy and representative/individual accountability for events and errors over which they had no visible control or prevention continues to trouble the academic and legal communities. It is unclear if the Tokyo trial established or strengthened Japan's idea of individual responsibility. If the Emperor was not held accountable, the question of who was accountable remains unanswered. To put it another way, while everyone was responsible for the conflict, no single person could be held accountable. Justice Pal's dissenting decision must be viewed in light of the broader legal perspective.

Establishment of Diplomatic Relations

After World War II, in 1949, Indian Prime Minister Jawaharlal Nehru donated two Indian baby elephants (one named Indira) to the Ueno Zoo in Tokyo as all the animals had perished in the aerial bombing, which showed India's eagerness to bring some cheer to the Japanese children in war-devastated Japan. Japan was also invited to take part in the Asian games in 1951, even before gaining independence. To enable Japan to rebuild its ruined economy, India signed a barter agreement with Japan for supplying raw cotton on January 20, 1948. This brought a ray of light into the lives of the Japanese people, who still had yet to recover from their defeat in the war.

India took keen interest in the San Francisco Peace Conference but did not sign the Treaty. India had various objections to the Anglo-American draft. In India's policy towards the peace settlement, there was an underlying desire that there should be no vindictive action and the settlement should be capable of wiping out hatred from the minds of the people concerned. India felt that the treaty failed to grant Japan a position of honour and equality among nations. India objected to the continued stationing of foreign troops in Japan even after the end of the occupation. In India's view the exclusion of the People's Republic of China from the negotiations could not be justified. India also strongly protested against provisions relating to the disposition of territories taken away from Japan. Therefore, India did not sign the San Francisco Treaty. A big section of Japanese people welcomed the Indian attitude since they, too, supported the idea of a 'separate treaty'. India justified its stand by concluding a separate peace treaty with Japan on June 9, 1952[58] after Japan got back her sovereignty. It was a Treaty of friendship and goodwill. The Treaty had provisions for the restoration of the Japanese assets in India and renunciations of reparation claims.

Japan and India also established diplomatic relations on April 28, 1952.[59] This treaty was one of the first peace treaties Japan signed after World War II. Since then, the two countries have enjoyed cordial relations. In the post-World War II period, India's iron ore helped a great deal in Japan's recovery from the devastation. Following Japanese Prime Minister Nobusuke Kishi's visit to India in 1957, Japan started providing yen loans to India in 1958, as the first yen loan aid extended by Japan.

In the first decade, after diplomatic ties were established, several high-level exchanges took place, beginning with Kishi's visit to India in May 1957, Prime Minister Jawaharlal Nehru's visit to Japan the same year in October 1957, followed by President Rajendra Prasad's visit to Japan in 1958. Japan started providing yen loans to India in 1958. Their Highnesses, the then-Japanese Crown Prince Akihito and Crown Princess Michiko paid a visit to India in 1960, which boosted relations to new heights. Japan's reliability as a friend was tested in 1991 when it was one of the few countries that helped India out of the balance of payment crisis. After Prime Minister Hayato Ikeda's visit to India in 1961, the next visit by a Japanese Prime Minister came after 23 years in 1984, when Yasuhiro Nakasone chose to visit India, even though Indian Prime Minister Indira Gandhi travelled to Japan twice in 1969 and 1982. Following Nakasone's visit, Prime Minister Rajiv Gandhi followed his mother's footsteps and visited Japan twice in 1985 and 1987. Despite historically favourable relations, India's Prime Minister P.V. Narasimha Rao implemented economic liberalisation in 1991, hastening this baby step in bilateral relations.

The low-key nature of the bilateral ties was not directly related to any conflict of interests or on any issue, but had geopolitical considerations. To summarise, after the birth of communism and the division of the world into two camps on ideological grounds, each led by the USSR and the US, while Japan was tied with the US by security alliance relationship and identified with the capitalist bloc, many other countries joined the USSR camp which was identified as the socialist group. India did not join either of the camps instead proposed the concept of non-alignment, which arose from its colonial heritage. It pursued a policy of establishing a welfare state with a socialist economic model. This ideological schism widened the gulf between India and Japan. Moreover, India's share of iron ore in the Japanese imports declined quickly as India was unable to meet Japan's rising demand as a result of its rapid economic growth in the 1960s and 1970s. After countries such as Australia had exploited enormous amount of resources and sought markets, Japan shifted its supply sources, sourcing the bulk of its resource imports from Australia.[60] The details are discussed in a separate Chapter.

Further, when India became involved in the Bangladesh Liberation War centring on the atrocities of the Pakistan army and the resultant millions of refugees entering into India, while the US provided security support to Pakistan, India signed a Peace and Friendship Treaty with the USSR, thereby providing fodder to critics who argued that it was the demise of its non-alignment policy. This is an issue on which much academic discourse has taken place, with some endorsing and others rejecting. There could never be a consensus on such a contentious matter. Despite these terrible experiences, Indian political leaders remained committed to India's neutrality and socialist ideology. India has always claimed to have maintained the policy of "strategic autonomy" in its international affairs. The ground for improving India-Japan relations was not found congenial enough, and therefore growth remained stagnant.

Souring of Ties Post-1998

May 1998 was another milestone in India-Japan relations, not in a positive but negative sense, when relations between the two countries entered into the worst phase of their relationship during the post-War years when India, defying a worldwide ban, conducted three nuclear tests, evoking sharp outcry.[61] Japan responded by suspending its Official Development Assistance (ODA) to India, and Japanese business houses withheld plans to invest in India. Both countries lost a golden opportunity to start a new partnership, which lasted until August 2000, when Prime Minister Yoshiro Mori decided to visit India in August 2000. The years 1998-2000 were the worst period in their bilateral relationship since World War II. In India, Prime Minister Hashimoto Ryutaro's reactions were perceived as too harsh. Japan was not content with its own stance; it mounted a campaign against India at several international fora and co-sponsored a resolution in the UN Security Council exhorting both India and Pakistan to stop the nuclear race and join the international regime for non-proliferation. Japan made its ODA conditional to India's compliance to the nuclear Non-Proliferation Treaty (NPT) and Comprehensive Test Ban Treaty (CTBT).[62]

In taking such a strong position, Japan failed to appreciate the circumstance under which India had to conduct the nuclear test. Even while Japan remains under the US security umbrella, it is nevertheless sensitive to nuclear issues because of its past experience. India understands Japan's position. But what disappointed India was Japan's failure to appreciate India's security dilemma as the security environment in South Asia had deteriorated. It is possible that Hashimoto was under intense domestic pressure that led his government to overreact at that time. His popularity had plummeted as a result of his failure to revive the country's economy after a protracted period of recession. Financial scandals rocked the banking system, putting pressure on the Hashimoto government. The ensuing election to the Upper House in July 1998 was also a factor in the position that Japan took on India's nuclear test. Besides adhering to Japan's 1992 ODA Charter, which included 'conditionals' such as not extending ODA to nuclear weapon nations or governments whose actions may favour nuclear proliferation, Hashimoto personally campaigned as a proponent of global nonproliferation. India's nuclear weapons program was perceived as a threat to the stability to the global nuclear order that Japan wanted to champion and persevere.[63] Be that as it may, for unforeseen reasons, Hashimoto had adopted an unfavourable stance towards India, and to the extent of being anti-Indian, demonstrating his narrow-minded worldview and one who could not assess and examine international relations from a larger and long-term perspective.

Elsewhere, India's detonation of nuclear explosion was seen as signalling its determination to abandon decades of ambiguity and declare itself a nuclear state. The Pokharan test, also known as the "Smiling Buddha", was conducted at the same place where India conducted its first nuclear test on May 18, 1974. This paved the way for the Indian scientists to design "nuclear weapons of different yields for different applications and for different delivery systems", meaning that the explosions were meant to test different types of nuclear warheads for India's fast-developing missile program, which has a mix of delivery vehicles to reach targets as close as Pakistan and as distant as China.[64]

The Pokharan tests changed India's image around the world. It was counterintuitive. The world started to acknowledge India as a responsible nuclear power. For the Indian strategists, it was ad infinitum as that from 1974 despite decades of economic and technological sanctions, India had remained true to the highest NPT standards despite being an NPT outlier. While harmonising itself with the global nuclear order, the tests and their aftermath ironically destroyed the prevalent 'nuclear superstructure.'[65] The Nuclear Suppliers Group (NSG) was formed in reaction to the Indian tests to check international nuclear proliferation. The NSG decided in 1992 to require full-scope IAEA safeguards for any new nuclear export deals, which effectively ruled out nuclear exports to India, but it waived this restriction on nuclear trade with India as part of the Indo-US civilian nuclear agreement in 2008. The tests were necessary to end India's international isolation and provided the basis for reconciliation with the global nuclear order, and redefined India's relationship with the US. There was a dramatic turnaround in Japan's policy towards India in 1998, when it was extremely critical and reacted with sharp measures, came to the party by signing a Civil Nuclear Cooperation Agreement on November 11, 2016, when Prime Minister Narendra Modi visited Japan. The 1998 tests proved to be a turning point in India's engagement with the world, which was long overdue. Continued compliance to the new nuclear security order has become the new mantra for assuring Indian security. The agreement for cooperation in the peaceful uses of nuclear energy entered into force on July 20, 2017, with exchange of diplomatic notes between the two sides.[66]

With this, India has become the first non-NPT country with which Japan signed a Civil Nuclear Agreement. Despite the protracted negotiations that started following a joint statement in 2006 between Prime Minister Manmohan Singh and Japanese Prime Minister Shinzo Abe, the agreement could not be realized mainly because India did not fit into Japan's 'Hikaku

San Gensoku' or three non-nuclear principles. These principles adopted in a resolution by Japanese Diet (parliament), state that Japan would neither possess nor manufacture nuclear weapons, nor shall it permit their introduction into Japanese territory. However, the discussions took five years to move to the negotiation stage in 2010. The delay was due to political opposition within Japan from anti-nuclear lobbies and media. Subsequently, India signed such civil nuclear deals with 10 other countries: the United States, Russia, South Korea, Mongolia, France, Namibia, Argentina, Canada, Kazakhstan and Australia.

Significance of Mori's 2000 Visit to India and After: Why Now and Not Earlier?

When Japanese Prime Minister Yoshiro Mori decided to break the prolonged logjam in the bilateral ties by choosing to visit India in August 2000, almost a decade after the economic liberation policy was launched, bilateral ties started to make significant improvement with the establishment of a '*Global Partnership*' between the two sides.[67]

However, Mori's August 2000 visit must be considered in light of US President Bill Clinton's visit to India in March of that year. This was the first by a US President since Jimmy Carter toured in 1978 and marked a shift in "Washington's orientation in the region away from its previous Cold War alliance with Pakistan and towards a new, as yet tentative and economic relationship with India".[68] His five-day stay that also took him to the centre of India's burgeoning software and computer industries, had hidden salience which Japan had failed to notice earlier. In signing a joint "vision" statement with Indian Prime Minister Atal Behari Vajpayee, two of the world's largest democracies announced that "the character of the 21st century world will depend on the success of (our) cooperation for peace, prosperity, democracy and freedom".

Though the visit was planned even before it happened and was delayed because of India's 1998 nuclear tests, Clinton had already made his economic calculations. Clinton had noticed the remarkable advance India had made in computer software and technology industries, and how a large pool graduates, who are paid a fraction of the salaries received by their counterparts in Europe or the US, carry out the labour-intensive work of computer programming. A report by the management consulting firm McKinsey & Company forecasted that by the end of the decade, the Indian software industry could earn $87 billion and employ over 2 million people had awakened the Clinton administration and neglecting India was no longer an option. Regrettably, Japan lacked such vision and awakened from its long slumber in planning Yoshiro Mori's visit to India just 4 months after Clinton's visit. Symonds writes "A global bidding war has broken out for Indian brains."[69]

Simultaneously, the US policy underwent a strategic shift, with a renewed emphasis on India. Following the demise of the Soviet Union, America's new priority was on combating terrorism. Cooperation with India was identified as a requirement for meeting this challenge. Despite this "tilt" towards India, the possession of nuclear arsenals, while a source of anxiety, was not viewed as a "direct threat". This resulted in a clear awareness of India's security requirements in the US policy. Others saw this US stance as a tacit acceptance of a nuclear-armed India.

There was another dimension to this new US strategic orientation. In certain quarters in the US, the Clinton administration's tacit acceptance of India as a nuclear-armed country could be used as a useful tool against China, which continued to support Pakistan. In other words, India was seen as a strategic counterweight to China. China hawks in both India and America started dreaming of a "strategic partnership" between the two great democracies.[70] Was this new friendship the beginning of an anti-China axis, as evidenced by the future foundation of QUAD? Opinions disagree and have no finality because India's ideal of "strategic autonomy" is unlikely to be easily negotiated away.

Impact of Clinton's visit to India on Japan

During all of these changes, Japan was concerned that it might be left out of this new power orientation. As a US security alliance partner, it could not afford to take a different approach at the risk of incurring US wrath. Seeing the bigger picture, Prime Minister Mori decided to reach out to India, not wanting to miss out on the immense potential of India's IT industry. Though there were other variables behind Mori's decision to visit India just four months after Clinton's visit, this significant shift in focus and rethinking on Japan's part heralded a glorious chapter in the India-Japan relations in all dimensions. For the first time, the strategic dimension of the relationship was emphasised.

There is yet another view on this. This view contends that Mori's decisiom to build a global partnership with India was probably driven by the simmering displeasure with US President Bill Clinton's bonhomie with China in the 1990s, and therefore building an opinion inside Japan to look for alternatives and not solely depend on the US alliance was a tempting option. This could be farther from the truth as Clinton's strategic calculation clearly demonstrated a departure from the established China policy for decades. In Mori's calculation, India emerged as an attractive candidate in whom it could invest for broader security and strategic cooperation, again on the lines of what Clinton thought. Mori was undoubtedly confident that India would fit well into the developing security matrix that was emerging in the area, with China on the verge of reclaiming its lost grandeur and India and Japan able to join forces with the new narrative. Mori's outreach to India in 2000 proved to be a masterstroke, as the years passed. The fact that the later Quad idea originated from Japan with Prime Minister Abe Shinzo at the helm in 2007 and required several years to crystallise demonstrates that the roots were sown during Clinton's March 2000 visit to India. There were other issues as well.

Japan was dismayed by the Asian financial crisis of 1997-98, as well as the United States' rejection of its proposal to establish an Asian Monetary Fund with a $10 billion capital to aid affected countries. Around this time, Japan also warmed up to ASEAN to push more economic integration policies by supporting the initiative of expanding ASEAN by including Japan, China and South Korea.

Indeed, it need not be overlooked that the foundation of sculpting a defence partnership between the two countries was laid in January 2000, seven months before Mori's historic visit in August, when India's Defence Minister George Fernandes visited Tokyo to initiate defence dialogue. This was the Indian Defence Minister's first visit to Japan, and he highlighted the necessity of strengthening bilateral defence cooperation. In truth, Fernandes envisioned a bigger India-Japan-China alliance to address the region's security issues, believing that Eastern civilization and culture have much to give the world provided the ugly side of geopolitics and power games are not allowed as obstacles.[71]

Since Prime Minister Junichiro Koizumi visit to India in April 2005, India-Japan annual summit meetings have been held in respective capitals. When Prime Minister Manmohan Singh visited Japan in December 2006, the India-Japan relationship was elevated to a Global and Strategic Partnership. In September 2014, Prime Minister Narendra Modi paid an official visit to Japan and had a summit meeting with Prime Minister Abe. They concurred to upgrade the bilateral relationship to "Special Strategic and Global Partnership." In December 2015, Prime Minister Abe paid an official visit to India and had a summit meeting with Prime Minister Narendra Modi. The two Prime Ministers resolved to transform the Japan-India Special Strategic and Global Partnership into a deep, broad-based and action-oriented partnership, which reflects a broad convergence of their long-term political, economic and strategic goals. They announced "Japan and India Vision 2025 Special Strategic and Global Partnership Working Together for Peace and Prosperity of the Indo-Pacific Region and the World" a joint statement that would serve as a guide post for the "new era in Japan-India relations."[72]

The graph of India-Japan relations continued to rise since then. The year 2013 was a monumental year with Emperor Akihito and Empress Michiko making their first visit to India from November 30 to December 6, 2013,[73] followed by Abe Shinzo's visit in January 2014 as the Chief Guest at the Republic Day celebrations. This was the first time a Japanese Prime Minister had received the distinction since India's independence. Bilateral relations were upgraded to "Special Strategic and Global Partnership", during Prime Minister Modi's formal visit to Japan for the Annual Summit conference in August-September 2016, India's first visit outside of its immediate neighbourhood.

Modi's visit to Japan on October 28-29, 2018, for the 13th Annual Summit provided further impetus to bilateral ties, building upon the momentum created by his earlier visits to Japan in 2014 and 2016, as well as the visits of Abe to India in 2015 and 2017. During the Summit, both Prime Ministers outlined the shared vision for future India-Japan relations. In a special gesture, Abe hosted Modi for a private dinner at his ancestral home in Yamanashi, the first such reception to be extended to a foreign leader. Japan's announcement of joining the International Solar Alliance (ISA), Exchange of Notes concerning the provision of seven Yen loan projects including the Project for the Construction of MAHSR (High Speed Rail), Currency Swap Agreement, India-Japan Digital Partnership and Implementing Arrangement for deeper cooperation between Japan Maritime Self-Defence Force and Indian Navy, and MOC on Healthcare were among the 32 MoUs/Agreements signed during the summit. Soon, 57 Japanese companies declared investments totalling $ 2.5 billion in India, while 15 Indian companies announced investments in Japan.

Modi then visited Japan on June 27-29, 2019, to participate in G20 Summit held in Osaka. On the sidelines, he held a bilateral meeting with Abe and discussed broad range of topics of mutual interest. Thereafter, Modi and Abe met on the sidelines of G7 Summit in Biarritz (August 2019), Eastern Economic Forum in Vladivostok (September 2019), and ASEAN-related summit meetings in Bangkok (November 2019). In August 2020, Abe announced stepping down from the office of Prime Minister on health grounds but not before having a telephone talk with Modi during which both welcomed the signing of Agreement Concerning Reciprocal Provision of Supplies and Services between the Self-Defense Forces of Japan and the Indian Armed Forces (so-called "Acquisition and Cross-Servicing Agreement", or ACSA) on September 9, 2020.

Abe was succeeded by Yoshihide Suga, who continued with the legacy left behind by Abe in fostering bilateral ties. Though both Modi and Suga remained in touch on phone, the surging coronavirus compelled Suga to cancel his scheduled visit to India in late April 2021. Both leaders remained committed to promote bilateral cooperation in the fields of security and economic cooperation, and affirmed their intention to steadily advance the High Speed Rail project and facilitate people-to-people exchanges. Plans were carved out to celebrate the 70th anniversary of the establishment of diplomatic relations between Japan and India in 2022 through events, with expectations that the COVID-19 would have ebbed out by then. The virtual route also remained open if needed.

After Emperor Akihito abdicated the throne, and his son Naruhito succeeded him, thereby inaugurating the Reiwa Era. On October 21-23, 2019, President Ram Nath Kovind attended Emperor Naruhito's enthronement ceremony, as well as other related rituals.

Apart from the Annual Summits, Foreign Ministers' Bilateral Strategic Dialogue, Defense Ministers' Meeting, NSA-level Dialogue, 2+2 Ministerial Meeting, FOC Consultations and other bilateral dialogue mechanisms ensure regular high-level functional engagements. Bilateral Strategic Dialogue led by Foreign Ministers was held on June 29, 2019, on the sidelines of G20 Summit in Osaka, and Defense Ministerial Meeting was held on September 2, 2019, in Tokyo. India-Japan Foreign Ministers' meeting was also held on September 26, 2019 on the sidelines of the 74th Session of the United Nations General Assembly, followed by a meeting in Nagoya on the sidelines of G20 Foreign Minister's meeting held on November 22-23, 2019. Japanese Foreign Minister Motegi Toshimitsu and Defense Minister Kono Taro visited India for the first India-Japan 2+2 Foreign and Defence Ministerial Meeting held in New Delhi on November 30, 2019. Secretary General of National Security Secretariat of Japan Kitamura Shigeru visited India to hold NSA level dialogue in November 2019. On November 7, 2019, MoS for External Affairs Shri V Muraleedharan met Nakatani Shinichi, Parliamentary Vice Minister for External Affairs of Japan on the sidelines of Indian Ocean Rim Association (IORA) in Abu Dhabi. Lok Sabha Speaker Om Birla visited Japan to participate in G-20 Speakers Summit in November 2019. External Affairs Minister S. Jayashankar visited Tokyo on October 6-7, 2020, to attend the FM-level India-Japan-Australia-US Quad meeting, and held the latest round of FM-level Bilateral Strategic Dialogue on the sidelines also held on September 26, 2019, on the sidelines of 74th Session of the United Nations.

There are also other forums for bilateral dialogues on a host of issues. The Act East Forum, established in 2017, aims to provide a platform for India-Japan collaboration under the rubric of India's "Act East Policy" and Japan's "Free and Open Indo-Pacific Vision". The Forum identifies specific projects for economic modernization of India's North-East region. This aspect of India-Japan cooperation shall be dealt at length in a separate Chapter in this book. The 5th meeting of the Act East Forum was held on January 28, 2021, in New Delhi. The inaugural India-Japan Space Dialogue was held in New Delhi on March 8, 2019, for enhancing bilateral cooperation in outer space and information exchange on respective space policies. The 3rd round of Cyber Dialogue was held in February 2019 in Tokyo; 5th round of India-Japan Maritime Affairs Dialogue and 8th round of Bilateral Consultations on Disarmament, Non-Proliferation and Export Control were held in December 2019 in Tokyo; 3rd round of consultations on Civil Nuclear Cooperation was held in February 2020 in Tokyo.

It appears that China's ascent has emerged as the primary impetus for not only bringing India and Japan closer together than ever before but also for complementing the shared ideals and reciprocal complementarities that both countries have experienced over generations. These factors have aided either side in using China in ways that benefit their national interests. The proliferation of regional institutional mechanisms that have emerged in recent years throughout Asia to address various elements of regional challenges has also aided India and Japan in developing their partnerships. This is not to say that every issue and concern confronting the region and individual nations are resolved through such institutions. However, their importance cannot be overstated, as these processes have proven extraordinarily beneficial in limiting specific crises that carry the seeds of potential conflagration. The subsequent Chapters will cover various challenges that have impacted India-Japan ties in the past and present. The conclusion and final chapter will describe a road map for how bilateral ties will and should progress, which the author feels would be helpful guide to the policy makers to consider.

Notes

1. See, "Japan's Longest-Serving Prime Ministers", November 20, 2019, https://www.nippon.com/en/features/h00296/japan%E2%80%99s-longest-serving-prime-ministers.html
2. Savitri Vishwanathan, "India and Japan: Changing Perceptions", https://www.jpf.go.jp/e/about/award/archive/2010/dl/Savitri_Vishwanathan.pdf
3. https://www.japanpitt.pitt.edu/timeline/tokugawa-period-1603-1868

4. "Tokugawa Shogunate Closed Country Policy", http://world-history-education-resources.com/tokugawa-shogunate/country-closed-tokugawa-shogunate.html
5. For a thoughtful, primarily political history, resting on a careful study of both Japanese and western sources till the end of World War II, see Yanaga Chitoshi, *Japan Since Perry* (1949), New York, p. 692.
6. Shōmu-tenno was the 45th Emperor of Japan, (born in 701; died on June 21, 756), according to the traditional order of succession. He devoted huge sums of money to the creation of magnificent Buddhist temples and artefacts during his reign. During his reign, Buddhism virtually became the official state religion. In 729, his consort, a member of the powerful Fujiwara family, was declared the Empress, shattering the precedent that all Empress consorts had to be princesses of the blood, https://www.britannica.com/biography/Shomu-emperor-of-Japan
7. John Carroll, "Bodhisena: The Indian Monk Who Opened Eyes in Nara", *Japan Forward*, September 26, 2020, https://japan-forward.com/bookmark-bodhisena-the-indian-monk-who-opened-eyes-in-nara/
8. Champa is another city in Vietnam where Buddhism left its imprint, converting many Vietnamese people to Buddhism. One can see many Hindu temples in Champa even today. For detailed information on this aspect, see Rajaram Panda, ed., *India-Vietnam Relations Retrospect & Prospect* (2016), ICCR and Northern Book Centre, New Delhi, p. 240.
9. Gopi Karelia, "The Bond that moved Swami Vivekananda to say 'You Are (my) only Friend in This Life", August 23, 2021, https://www.thebetterindia.com/261033/swami-vivekananda-letters-read-online-maharaja-khetri-friendship/
10. See, Chaturvedi Badrinath, *Swami Vivekananda: Living Vedanta*, Penguin Books, 2006, p. 452.
11. Sir M. Visvesvaraya, *Reconstructing India* (1920), P.S. Kings and Sons Ltd., London, p. 352.
12. Masood, Sayyid Ross, *Japan and Its Educational System: Being a Report Compiled for the Government of His Exalted Highness the Nizam* (Hyderabad, Andhra Pradesh, India: Government Central Press, 1923). For Masood, the most important events in the political history of Japan were the Meiji Restoration of 1868 and the constitution of 1889 granted by the emperor. He was particularly impressed by the respect shown for the emperor as the patriarchal head with semi-divine status.
13. Rabindranath Tagore was the first Asian to win a Nobel Peace Prize in Literature for his work *Geetanjali* in 1913. The same year, his friend Okakura Tenshin left the world, a short life but on whose works outlived him.
14. Anushilan Samiti (bodybuilding society) was a Bengali Indian organisation in the first quarter of the 20th century that supported revolutionary violence as the means for ending British rule in India. In the year 1902, it was founded by Satish Chandra with three other accomplices: Pramatha Mitra, Aurobindo Ghose and Sarala Devi. The organisation arose from a conglomeration of local youth groups and gyms (akhara) in Bengal in 1902.

It had two prominent, somewhat independent, arms in East and West Bengal: Dhaka Anushilan Samiti (centred in Dhaka, modern day Bangladesh), and the Jugantar group (centred at Calcutta). From its foundation to its dissolution during the 1930s, the Samiti challenged British rule in India by engaging in militant nationalism, including bombings, assassinations and politically motivated violence.

Nationalist writings and publications by Aurobindo and Barin, including Bande Mataram and Jugantar, had a widespread influence on Bengal youth and helped Anushilan Samiti to gain popularity in Bengal. In 1908, young recruits Khudiram Bose and Prafulla Chaki were sent on a mission to Muzaffarpur to assassinate chief presidency magistrate D. H. Kingsford. They bombed a carriage that they mistook for Kingsford's, killing two Englishwomen. Bose was arrested while attempting to flee and Chaki committed suicide. It was also involved in the Kakori conspiracy, the Chittagong armoury raid and other actions.

The people associated with this samiti were Sri Aurobindo, Deshabandhu Chittaranjan Das, Surendranath Tagore, Jatindranath Banerjee, BaghaJatin, Bhupendra Natha Datta, Barindra Ghosh etc. After Aurobindo's retirement, the western Anushilan Samiti found a more prominent leader in Bagha Jatin, who emerged as the Jugantar. Keshav Baliram Hedgewar, the founder of the Hindu nationalist organization Rashtriya Swayamsevak Sangh (RSS), was an alumnus of the Anushilan Samiti.

15. See, two-part article by Rajaram Panda, "Bengal and Japan-I" and "Bengal and Japan-II", *The Statesman*, July 9 and 10, 2021.
16. See, Rustom Bharucha, *Another Asia. Rabindranath Tagore & Okakura Tenshin*, (2006), Oxford University Press, New Delhi, p. 326.
17. Toshiya Kaneko, "Cultural light, political shadow: Okakura Tenshin (1862–1913) and the Japanese crisis of national identity, 1880-1941", https://repository.upenn.edu/dissertations/AAI3054959/
18. David Burleigh, "A friendship's influence across Asia: Japan's Okakura Tenshin and India's Rabindranath Tagore", *The Japan Times*, October 28, 2007, https://www.japantimes.co.jp/culture/2007/10/28/books/book-reviews/a-friendships-influence-across-asia/
19. For the background of Noguchi's life, see https://everything.explained.today/Yone_Noguchi/
20. There are varying opinions on this Greater Asia Co-Prosperity Sphere Concept. Those who endorse Japan's approach take the position that Japan did not want that the resources of Asia should be taken away by the Western colonial powers for the good of their peoples but must remain for the benefit of Asian people. However, if this was the original and sincere intention, the method that Japan adopted to materialise this objective against the Asian people was wrong. When Okakura endorsed Japan's approach, Tagore opposed it. A resource-deficient Japan probably wanted a policy to secure resources from Asia that it desperately needed, which drove it to choose such an aggressive militaristic policy. As it transpired later, it was a wrong choice.

21. "Rabindranath Tagore and Japan", *The Japan Times*, editorial, September 7, 2003, https://www.japantimes.co.jp/opinion/2003/09/07/editorials/rabindranath-tagore-and-japan/
22. In a two-part article, Madhurima Mukhopadhyay writes about Harirapha's extraordinary experiences in Japan, evaluating the tiny 64-page candid account of a Bengali woman of human relations between the peoples of India and Japan and the historical importance of it. See, "Uemon and Hariprabha Takeda: Travelling into Lives", https://refugeewatchonline.wordpress.com/2017/10/04/uemon-and-hariprabha-takeda-travelling-into-lives/. The review article titled "A Bengali Bride in the Land of the Rising Sun: Review of Somdatta Mandal's The Journey of a Bengali Woman in Japan and Other Essay", (Translation of Hariprabha Takeda's *Banglo Mohilar* Japan Jatra o Ananya Bachana? by Swati Ganguly provides more insights into this exotic romance enough to be the stuff of fiction. See, vol. 11, no. 3, October-December 2019, http://rupkatha.com/v11n3.php
23. Mukesh Williams, "Hariprabha Takeda's Diary – an Indian Woman's Observations of Taisho & Meiji Japan", *Japan Spotlight*, September-October 2021, pp. 50-53. https://www.jef.or.jp/journal/pdf/239th_HRAC.pdf
24. Subrat Kumar Das, "Manmathanath Ghosh's Japan Probas: The initial Bangla-language book on Japan", https://www.academia.edu/12143810/Manmathanath_Ghosh_s_Japan_Probash_The_initial Bangla_language_book_on_Japan
25. "Freedom Fighter Rash Behari Bose's Favourite Indian Curry: A Taste of Romance and Revolution in Japan", https://www.indianeagle.com/travelbeats/
26. "Rash Behari Bose: The founder of Indian National Army", November 29, 2009, https://haindavakeralam.com/rash-behari-bose-founder-of-hk10962
27. A.M. Nair, *An Indian Freedom Fighter in Japan,* Vikas Publishing House, 1986, p. 364.
28. https://www.britannica.com/topic/Anglo-Japanese-Alliance.
29. There are differing views about Rash Behari Bose's marriage with Toshiko. One version says that the Soma couple offered their eldest daughter in marriage with Rash Behari. The other version says that it was Bose who asked Aizo and Kotsuko's permission to marry their eldest daughter. Irrespective of which version was correct, the truism is that Toshiko had fallen in love with Bose who reciprocated her feelings. The Soma family was also fond of Bose. The couple married in a simple ceremony in July 1918. There is yet another version of the story according to which a right-wing politician Mitsuru Toyama, who introduced Rash Behari to the Soma family, requested the Soma family to get their eldest daughter married to Rash Behari Bose.
30. Sanchari Pal, "The Other Bose: How an Indian Freedom Fighter's Curry Became a Sensation in Japan", July 21, 2017, https://www.thebetterindia.com/109063/rash-behari-bose-ina-nakamuraya-curry-japan/
31. Peter Tasker, "What Have Love, Curry, and the Quad Got to Do with Japan's Security?, *Japan Forward,* June 6, 2021, https://japan-forward.com/bookmark-what-have-love-curry-and-the-quad-got-to-do-with-japans-security/

32. Takeshi Nakajima, *Bose of Nakamuraya: An Indian Revolutionary in Japan* (2009), Bibliophile South Asia, New Delhi, p. 324.
33. Pallavi Aiyar, "Bose of Nakamuraya", *The Hindu*, February 6, 2018, https://www.thehindu.com/opinion/op-ed/bose-of-nakamuraya/article22661567.ece
34. Yukihiko Yamada, "The tale of two Boses, their Japanese connect and authentic Indian curry", November 10, 2019, https://www.asiancommunitynews.com/the-tale-of-two-boses-their-japanese-connect-and-authentic-indian-curry/#:~:text=He%20married%20Toshiko%20in%201918%2C%20and%20he%20acquired,the%
35. SavitriVishwanathan, n. 2.
36. Peter Tasker, "Curried Narratives: Indian Alternative History of Modern Japan", *Japan Forward*, July 29, 2021, https://japan-forward.com/curried-narratives-indias-alternative-history-of-modern-japan/
37. Peter Tasker, "Love, Curry, and the Quad: A Curious Story of Japan's Indian Connection", *Japan Forward*, June 5, 2021, https://japan-forward.com/bookmark-love-curry-and-the-quad-a-curious-story-of-japans-indian-connection/
38. Peter Tasker, 'What have Love, Curry, and the Quad Got to Do with Japan's Security?", *Japan Forward*, June 5, 2021, https://japan-forward.com/bookmark-what-have-love-curry-and-the-quad-got-to-do-with-japans-security/
39. Harin Shah, *Verdict from Formosa: Gallant End of Netaji* (Atam Ram & Sons, 1956), p. 158.
40. The Formosan nurse's name was Sister who was by Netaji's side till his death. She also confirmed this by showing the cot that was occupied by Netaji's companion Col. Habibur Rehman. It was Habib who took the ashes of Netaji to Tokyo
41. Harin Shah, n. 39.
42. Priyanka Basu, "Netaji and Gumnami Baba—An Uncanny Resemblance", January 21, 2021, https://monomousumi.com/netaji-and-gumnami-baba-an-uncanny-resemblance-one-mystery/
43. See, Anju Dhar and Chandrachur, *Conundrum: Subhas Bose's Life After Death*, (Vitasta Publishing Pvt Ltd, 2019), p.834. For a review of the book, see M.R. Narayan Swamy, "Did Netaji Live, Die in India Post 1947", *Mainstream*, Vol. LIX No. 39, New Delhi, September 11, 2021, http://mainstreamweekly.net/article11514.html
44. For an assessment of Pal's dissent in order to recover its unique and critical insights into the relationship between imperialism and the development of international law, see Latha Varadarajan, "The trials of imperialism: Radhabinod Pal's dissent at the Tokyo tribunal", *European Journal of International Relations,* December 10, 2014, https://journals.sagepub.com/doi/10.1177/1354066114555775
45. Known as the Hull note, officially the 'Outline of Proposed Basis for Agreement Between the United States and Japan', was the final proposal delivered to Japan by the United States before the attack on Pearl Harbor and the Japanese declaration of war. The note was delivered on November 26, 1941, and is named for Secretary of State Cordell Hull. It was the culmination of a series of events leading to the attack on Pearl Harbor. Notably it repeats previous American demands for Japan

to withdraw from China and French Indo-China. No further American proposals were made before the attack on Pearl Harbor, as the US government had received intelligence that Japan was preparing an invasion of Thailand.

46. Norimitsu Onishi, "Decades After War Trials, Japan Still Honors a Dissenting Judge", *The New York Times,* August 31, 2007, https://www.nytimes.com/2007/08/31/world/asia/31memo.html
47. Nanjing Massacre, conventional Nanking Massacre, also called Rape of Nanjing, (December 1937–January 1938), mass killing and ravaging of Chinese citizens and capitulated soldiers by soldiers of the Japanese Imperial Army after its seizure of Nanjing, China, on December 13, 1937, during the Sino-Japanese War that preceded World War II, October 22, 2020, https://www.britannica.com/event/Nanjing-Massacre. New facts have emerged recently with proper evidences, showing that China's claim of 300,000 being massacred was exaggerated. For details, see the two-part article https://japan-forward.com/bookmark-ignoring-evidence-of-fewer-nanjing-massacre-victims-the-west-chooses-to-believe-china/, and https://japan-forward.com/bookmark-politics-keeps-the-west-holding-on-to-300000-nanjing-massacre-tally/
48. For the details of the accused and the judges, and various aspects of the trial, see, https://ww2db.com/battle_spec.php?battle_id=221
49. Naotaka Fujita, "Tojo's ashes scattered over ocean with those of 6 others", *The Asahi Shimbun*, June 8, 2021, http://www.asahi.com/ajw/articles/14368165
50. William Sebald, "With MacArthur in Japan: A Personal History of the Occupation", (Tokyo: Asahi Shimbun Co, 1965), p. 318.
51. There is a lot of debate about amending this peace clause in response to the changing security environment in the region. This aspect will be discussed in a later Chapter of this study.
52. "The Dissenting Indian", *Deccan Herald,* August 14, 2021, https://www.deccanherald.com/content/88645/dissenting-indian.html
53. See, Abe's address on "Confluence of the two Seas", August 22, 2007, https://www.mofa.go.jp/region/asia-paci/pmv0708/speech-2.html
54. NorimitsuOnishi, n. 24.
55. Ryuichi Kitano, "Diary: Hirohito prepared for U.S. war before Pearl Harbor attack", *The Asahi Shimbun*, December 6, 2021, https://www.asahi.com/ajw/articles/14496398
56. Ibid.
57. For a two-part article by Edo Naito on this contentious issue, see *Japan Forward,* August 7, 2021, https://japan-forward.com/bookmark-tracing-asia-pacifics-woes-to-the-mishandled-tokyo-war-crimes-trial/ and https://japan-forward.com/bookmark-failures-of-tokyo-war-crimes-trial-hound-modern-day-japan/
58. For the detail conditions in the treaty, see https://www.mea.gov.in/bilateraldocuments.htm?dtl/7012/Treaty_of_Peace
59. https://www.mofa.go.jp/region/asia-paci/india/data.html
60. See Rajaram Panda, *Pacific Partnership: Japan-Australia Resource Diplomacy* (1982), Manthan Publications, Rohtak.

61. John F. Burns, "India sets 3 nuclear blasts, defying a worldwide ban; tests brings a sharp outcry", *The New York Times,* May 12, 1998, https://www.nytimes.com/1998/05/12/world/india-sets-3-nuclear-blasts-defying-a-worldwide-ban-tests-bring-a-sharp-outcry.html
62. Rajaram Panda, "Changing Dynamics of India-Japan Relations: Future Trends", in Akihiro Iwashita, ed., *India-Japan Dialogue: Challenge and Potential* (Slavic Research Center, Hokkaido University, Sapporo), July 2011, https://src-h.slav.hokudai.ac.jp/rp/publications/no06/01_Panda.pdf
63. The two paragraphs are taken from the author's earlier publication in the above-cited reference.
64. Burns, n. 61.
65. "How 1998 Pokhran tests changed India's image", *The Economic Times,* May 12, 2018, https://economictimes.indiatimes.com/news/politics-and-nation/how-1998-pokhran-tests-changed-indias-image/a-sudden-decision/slideshow/64135032.cms
66. Sanjna Sudan, "Indo-Japan Civil Nuclear Agreement: A Win-Win?", November 16, 2016, https://www.diplomaticourier.com/posts/indo-japan-civil-nuclear-agreement-win-win
67. https://www.mofa.go.jp/region/asia-paci/india/data.html
68. Peter Symonds, "Clinton visit to the Indian subcontinent sets a new strategic orientation", March 23, 2000, https://www.wsws.org/en/articles/2000/03/ind-m23.html
69. Ibid.
70. "The elephant and the Pekinese", *The Economist,* March 18, 2000, https://www.economist.com/special/2000/03/16/the-elephant-and-the-pekinese
71. Rajaram Panda, "India and Japan" Strengthening Defence Cooperation", December 22, 2009, https://idsa.in/idsacomments/IndiaandJapanStrengtheningDefenceCooperation_rpanda_221209
72. https://www.mofa.go.jp/region/asia-paci/india/data.html
73. See, Rajaram Panda, "Significance of Royal Visit and India-Japan Relations", *C3S Paper No. 2042*, December 5, 2013, http://www.c3sindia.org/japan/3801

2

Legacy that Abe Left Behind

The book was conceptualised to examine and analyse the India-Japan relationship during the long tenures of Prime Ministers Narendra Modi in India and Abe Shinzo in Japan. Though bilateral relations would follow the same traction during Abe's successors Yoshihide Suga and Fumio Kishida's tenures, it would do justice to examine the factors that led Abe to leave office and what legacy he left behind for his successive governments. Even when the Opposition was in power for a short time, there was no deviation from the chosen route, and bilateral relations thrived regardless of whose party was in control. The same is true in case of India.

So, what legacy did Abe leave behind, what were his accomplishments and where did he, if at all, err? It would be helpful then to evaluate how his successors, Suga and Kishida, are different. However, though the thrust and nuances could differ to some extent, the basic tenor and spirit remain intact. The brief tenures of Suga and Kishida indicate that there shall be more continuity than change in India-Japan relationship. In fact, the consolidation and deepening of ties are strengthened further.

The sudden departure of Abe Shinzo as Japan's Prime Minister and from Japan's political firmament in September 2020 shocked not only the Japanese people but numerous of his admirers across the globe, including India. Despite that his popularity rate had somewhat plummeted owing to how his administration handled the coronavirus pandemic, the overall admiration of him as a political leader to lead the country and carve out the nation's destiny never diminished. Assessing his tenure as the longest-serving prime minister is indeed a herculean task.[1] In fact, there could never be finality in evaluating the performance of such a towering personality as there would be admirers as well as detractors in any society and system. But objectively speaking, any comparative evaluation vis-à-vis with any of his contemporary counterparts would place Abe at a much higher pedestal.

By the time Abe resigned from office on September 16, 2020, he had become the longest-serving prime minister, having headed the government for 3,188 days in total, and 2,822 consecutive days since the start of his second term in office. Both are prime ministerial records in the country's constitutional history. Abe's first tenure as prime minister began in September 2006, but he resigned after just one year due to health problems. He came back to the helm of the Liberal Democratic Party in September 2012, when the Democratic Party of Japan was still in power, and re-elected prime minister in December of that year after the LDP regained power in a House of Representatives election.

On August 24, 2020, Abe had led the government for 2,799 consecutive days, overtaking the record set by his great-uncle Satō Eisaku half a century earlier. However, just four days later, he announced his resignation due to the recurrence of health issues. The top four longest-serving prime ministers—Abe Shinzō, Katsura Tarō, Satō Eisaku, and Itō Hirobumi—are all from Yamaguchi Prefecture. Until the end of the Edo period (1603-1868), Yamaguchi was known as Chōshū, the feudal domain that was a driving force in the movement to topple the Tokugawa shogunate that culminated in the 1868 Meiji Restoration. Many politicians active under the new Meiji government hailed from Chōshū.

Since the beginning of the Heisei era (1989-2019), Japan has had 17 prime ministers, including Suga Yoshihide, with only four serving for more than two years.

Apart from Abe, only Koizumi Jun'ichirō, with 1,980 days, makes the top 10 list of longest-serving prime ministers.

It may be useful to take stock of Abe's long tenure and see where he scored more and where he scored less. Abe was humble enough to say that the most important thing in politics is to give results, and that during his tenure of seven years and eight months he had worked hard to achieve those results. Now it is for the analysts to evaluate what were his objectives, what he achieved and where he fell short in an unattached, dispassionate and objective manner.

Going by the past trends, when Abe announced his decision to leave office, the old rumour of political stability revived, with the coinage of "revolving prime ministers" haunting public imagination and gained currency when Japan saw six prime ministers in six years.[2]

During the years Abe was at the helm, he had to deal with a host of critical issues such as overseeing the country's recovery from a devastating earthquake, tsunami and nuclear disaster, restoring some semblance of economic health, and dealing reasonably well with an unpredictable American President Donald J Trump. How did he fare in domestic and foreign policies? Objectively seen, his tenure was punctuated by success, failures and missed opportunities.[3]

On the domestic front, his success rate was relatively tricky as he was unable to revise Article 9 of the Japanese constitution, which was imposed by the occupation forces. His economic policy measures dubbed as Abenomics, an economic strategy that included a mixture of quantitative easing, fiscal stimulus through government spending and structural reforms, saw moderate results, but his decision to raise the consumption tax twice in 2014 and 2019 became controversial. This led to the loss of momentum of his Abenomics as people started doubting his lack of commitment to structural reform. The problem was further compounded by Trump's protectionist policies and the trade war with China. The outbreak of the pandemic further exacerbated Japan's economic decline, undermining the nation's recovery despite the massive stimulus package.

His second tenure also saw influence-peddling scandals, but he overcame them and rode out numerous elections. Unable to amend Article 9, he achieved some of his objectives when he pushed through contentious security legislation in 2015 that permitted Japanese troops to engage in overseas combat missions alongside allied forces, as part of collective self-defence.

According to a 2019 Goldman Sachs report,[4] empowering women and bringing them to the labour force, known as Womenomics, led to a "record female labour participation (71 per cent) surpassing the US and Europe, generous parental leave benefits, improved gender transparency, and labour reforms". However, the same report saw some deficiency too and noted "a dearth of female leaders, gender pay gaps, inflexible labor contracts, tax disincentives, insufficient care-giving capacity, and unconscious biases". These were not fully addressed by Abe's policies. Further, with few cabinet members and just 10 per cent women serving as law makers in the Lower House, it was seen that gender inequality persisted.

On the foreign policy front, again the results were mixed. He reinforced ties with the US despite the fact that unpredictable American President Donald Trump attempted to grab his pound of flesh from Japan by demanding a larger share of the security burden.

His endeavours to strengthen ties with ASEAN and India were commendable. Ties with Vietnam were taken to top gear. Relations between India and Japan scaled to new heights. Trade, investment, joint ventures, ODA grew. Defence cooperation was too deepened. Both sides signed an "Acquisition and Cross-Servicing Agreement" (ACSA) on September 9, 2020. Such an agreement would enable the Quad countries (the U.S., India, Japan and Australia) for logistic sharing bound by a shared strategic outlook.[5] The Agreement would allow the militaries of the two countries to exchange supplies and services on a reciprocal basis during exercises in which both participate, U.N. and humanitarian assistance operations, as well as visits to each other's ports. Japan becomes the sixth country with which India has such an arrangement, after the United States, France, Singapore, South Korea, and Australia. Both Modi and Abe concurred that the Agreement will further enhance the depth of defence cooperation between the two countries, and also contribute to peace and security in the Indo-Pacific region. Since 2015, Japan has participated in the US-India Malabar naval exercises, which have become considerably more sophisticated over the years.

There were some failures too on the foreign policy front. He was unable to resolve the territorial disputes with Russia that prevented the signing of a peace treaty to officially end World War II. The same problem has also continued during his successors' tenure.[6] He was also unable to resolve the abduction issue of Japanese nationals by North Korea in the 1970s, despite promises he had made to the families of the abductees. He failed to have a summit meeting with North Korean dictator Kim Jong Un, though Kim had summit meetings with Trump, South Korean President Moon Jae-in, Russia's Vladimir Putin and China's Xi Jinping. His administration was also embroiled in a bitter spat with South Korea and could not resolve the 'comfort women' issue, which impacted economic relations. The chill continued during Suga's administration.[7]

Initially, there was speculation about his possible successor and who was in a position to fill up the huge political vacuum. In the interim, a consensus candidate from the party was chosen to lead the government until the party held a leadership election. Abe's term was set to expire in September 2021. The leading candidates to replace Abe included Taro Aso, the long-serving deputy prime minister and a former prime minister; Yoshihide Suga, the chief cabinet secretary to Abe; Shigeru Ishiba, a former defence minister who once ran against Abe for party leader; Fumio Kishida, a former foreign minister; and Taro Kono, the current defence minister. As it transpired, with many competent leaders, and a weak opposition, the succession issue was resolved smoothly, and Suga was chosen to take up the mantle from Abe. From the first indication, bilateral ties between India and Japan will remain unchanged.

Why did Abe Resign?

The ulcerative colitis that Abe was carrying was controlled with treatment. This medical condition aggravated over time. Speculation over his health issue grew in August 2020 when he visited a Tokyo hospital two weeks in a row for unspecified health check-ups.

It soon became clear that he was undergoing a new treatment that required IV injections. Despite being stabilised, there was no certainty that his illness would be cured, prompting him to take the rare decision of resigning with a little more than a year remaining on his tenure.

One great contribution that he made to the country's political culture and system was that he secured political stability after a short spell of political instability. He ensured a new dimension of political stability when he took office in 2012 and remained at the helm for close to eight consecutive years.

Many people were dismayed by his decision to step down one year before his tenure, which was supposed to last until September 2021. He agreed to remain as a member of the Lower House of the Japanese Diet, or the Japanese Parliament.

His family's political lineage is quite long. His grandfather Nobusuke Kishi was Prime Minister (1957-60). His father Shintaro Abe was Foreign Minister (1982-86). Then Abe became Japan's longest-serving Prime Minister by consecutive days in office, overtaking the record of Eisaku Sato, his great-uncle, who served 2,798 days during 1964-72. It is a strange coincidence that Abe served two terms, first in 2006-07 and the second from 2012 till August 2020, and both times resigned due to medical conditions. When Abe left office in 2007, he came under fire for leaving after only one year in office.

Assessing Abe's Domestic Policies

What were his key domestic policy decisions over the years? As previously stated, his report card may be a mixed bag of success and failure, but it is full of innovation, hope, and hence admiration. In general, he had to deal with a number of critical issues, including overseeing the country's recovery from the March 2011 devastating earthquake, tsunami and nuclear disaster—the triple disaster—and restored a semblance of economic health, and dealt reasonably well with an unpredictable American President Donald J. Trump.

Objectively seen, his tenure was punctuated by both success and failure, as well as missed opportunities. His economic policy measures dubbed as Abenomics, was an economic strategy aimed at reviving a stagnant Japanese economy. Abenomics had three "arrows" that included a mixture of quantitative easing monetary policy, fiscal stimulus through government spending and most importantly structural reforms like corporate reform and labour liberalisation. Though the first two "arrows" saw moderate results, structural reforms never happened. Abenomics over-leveraged the economy to the point of sovereign bankruptcy, leading to the erosion of confidence in capital markets. While corporations and hedge fund managers did reasonably well, the common man was deprived to get any economic rent that was to accrue from the government measures. His decision to raise the consumption tax twice in 2014 (from 5 to 8%) and in 2019 (from 8 to 10%), sparked controversy and resulted in lower consumer spending.[8] This slowed the pace of his Abenomics, as people began to mistrust his commitment to structural reform. The problem was exacerbated by American President Donald Trump's protectionist policies and trade war against China. The epidemic exacerbated Japan's economic decline, denting the nation's recovery despite the massive stimulus package.

Scandals

The Abe administration could not escape dealing with some scandals during his long tenure, and saw influence-peddling scandals. But he successfully overcame and rode out numerous elections, though some were deadlocked for some time over vital issues, both politically and in terms of policy-making due to arrogance and complacency, leading to a drop in his popularity rating. Even in 2020, during ordinary Diet session, Abe was roundly criticized for hosting an annual cherry-blossom viewing party, which critics saw as an attempt to serve his personal interest.

A notorious scandal over the dubious sale of state-owned land to Moritomo Gakuen, an Osaka-based school operator linked to Abe's wife, Akie, came under renewed scrutiny in the aftermath of the suicide of a former Finance Ministry official who became embroiled in the scandal.[9] His widow published notes left by her late husband concerning how he was effectively forced to rewrite official documents related to the land sale.[10]

A massive vote-buying scandal involving Lower House lawmaker Katsuyuki Kawai, a former justice minister, and his wife, Anri, a rookie member of the Upper House, also damaged the reputation of the Abe administration. The allegations were that funds were made available to support Anri's possibly unlawful election campaign.[11] Another controversial issue was on his alleged attempt to revise the Public Prosecutors Office Law to extend the legal retirement ages of top public prosecutors. Following strong public opposition and criticism that it would threaten the independence and neutrality of prosecutors, Abe was forced to abandon his idea.[12]

Womenomics

Another significant policy decision taken by Abe during his long tenure was on women empowerment and promoting equality in the Japanese society. Such a position received admiration from Noriko Horiuchi, a member of his party, who credited Abe's championing of women's advancement as a factor in "the beginning of a new era in female success".[13] It may be prudent to analyse whether Abe's efforts to empower women can withstand examination, as detractors are inevitable in a democratic system. Like his economic policies dubbed as Abenomics, his policies to get more women in the workforce was termed as 'Womenomics' to describe this aspect of his politics. However, Abe's measures did not entirely address some inadequacies identified in the 2019 Goldman Sachs report, such as "a dearth of female leaders, gender pay gaps, inflexible labour contracts, tax disincentives, insufficient care-giving capacity, and unconscious biases" were not fully addressed by Abe's policies. Further, with few Cabinet members and just 10 per cent women as law makers in the Lower House, gender inequality continued to exist.

In 2014, Abe boasted that he had achieved the highest number of female Cabinet ministers ever in Japanese history (7 out of 10), but his 20-member Cabinet when he demitted office had only two women in it—Justice minister Yoko Kamikawa and Seiko Noda, whose briefs covered internal affairs, women's empowerment, and social security. Only 47 out of 465 lawmakers in the Lower House were women. In percentage terms, this was the lowest level in the G-8, and also lagged behind other countries in the region like South Korea, Indonesia and China.

Even in the World Economic Forum's (WEF) global ranking of the gender gap,[14] it dropped from 111th in 2016 to 114 in 2017. A decade ago, it ranked 80. The main criteria for ranking were to measure women's participation and opportunity. Atsuko Muraki, visiting professor at Tsuda University and a former vice-minister for Health, Labour and Welfare, opines that female employment in Japan improved in quantity but not in quality. According to WEF figures, only 12.4 per cent legislators, senior officials and managers were females.

Attempt to Amend Article 9 of the Constitution

Another significant aim that Abe wanted to achieve remained unrealised: amending the peace clause Article 9 in the war-renouncing Constitution imposed by the Occupation forces after the end of World War II.[15] Article 9 reads as follows: "Aspiring sincerely to an international peace based on justice and order, the Japanese people forever renounce war as a sovereign right of the nation and the threat or use of force as means of settling international disputes.

In order to accomplish the aim of the preceding paragraph, land, sea, and air forces will never be maintained. The right of belligerency of the state will not be recognised".

As it transpires from the clause, under the provision, Japan is not allowed to maintain an army, air force or navy for any purpose other than self-defence. Abe established a National Security Council and other institutions dealing with defence issues. The Constitution's text being hard to revise, he pursued a different strategy, to revise it by reinterpretation. On May 15, 2014, a committee set up by Abe (the Advisory Panel on Reconstruction of the Legal Basis for Security) recommended that collective security should be permitted under certain conditions. These included:

1. That a close partner to Japan (read 'US') should be under illegal attack.
2. That such use of force posed a clear threat to Japanese security.
3. That a request from the partner had been received, even if Japan was not directly attacked.
4. That taking action should not undermine trust in the Japan-US alliance.
5. That Japan had permission from other states to transit their territory if necessary.
6. That the use of collective defence was approved by Parliament.
7. That the level of use of force was judged by the National Security Council as necessary and proportionate, given that collective self-defence was a right, not an obligation.

In response to the region's changing geopolitical landscape, Abe felt compelled to solve the country's security concerns without relying heavily on external support. With this goal in mind, he sought to amend the post war Constitution to transform Japan into a 'normal country' capable of projecting military strength beyond its borders. However, his biggest obstacle was Article 96 of the Constitution, which makes it difficult to revise (though not as difficult as revising the US Constitution). A two-thirds majority of members of the House of Representatives, a two-thirds majority of members of the House of Councillors and a simple majority in a referendum of the people were required. At one stage, the idea was to revise Article 96 to make its conditions easier, and then go for a substantive amendment proposal, but this was dropped after parliamentary arithmetic suggested that a two-thirds majority in Parliament could have been feasible, but public opinion polls indicated that reaching a simple majority in a referendum would have been problematic. Moreover, the Buddhist-based Kōmeitō, junior partner in the Abe coalition government, was ambiguous in its views on revision. In his first administration, however, Abe steered a bill through Parliament that established procedures for a popular referendum, showing his commitment to revising the Constitution.

Abe welcomed the report, and promised to boost military capacity to deal with 'grey zone' situations, including a possible armed landing on the disputed Senkaku/Diaoyu islands. He also pledged to "defend the peace ideal (heiwashugi) proclaimed by the Constitution", and argued that "by increasing deterrent power, conflict can be avoided and the prospects of Japan becoming involved in war will be lessened".[16] When on July 1, 2014, a bill was adopted by the Cabinet to allow collective defence, the opponents, as expected, were dismayed.

Abe had to labour hard to dissipate the fear that by engaging in collective security with the US, Japan might be dragged into a war not of its own making. The contrast between the six decades of peace and prosperity since 1945 and regular large-scale warfare from the 1860s to 1945, ending in colossal destruction, the fire-bombing of major cities and nuclear bombing of Hiroshima and Nagasaki, are all etched deeply into the

Japanese consciousness. A poll in the *Asahi* newspaper in April 2014 showed 63 per cent of those polled opposed collective defence.

Analysing dispassionately, Abe's moves need to be viewed from the perspective of tightest rules and regulations (read imposed) by a foreign power on any military in the world to be understood and distinguished from 1930s militarism, where warfare was "built into the very ethos of the state". What Abe wanted was to avoid some of the constitutional constraints on the use of the SDFs in cooperation with the US, which must not be confused with Abe's so-called perceived ultra-nationalist policies by his detractors. Abe was convinced, and rightfully so, that collective security, or the freedom to cooperate fully with the US in deterrence against China, was much needed.

This appears to be a highly debated argument. It is unclear whether the collective defence of what Abe meant by participating in war beyond the country would inevitably improve Japan's ability to defend itself. As a result, Japan may be drawn into a conflict that may otherwise have been avoided. Furthermore, Abe and Obama were not always on the same page regarding security issues.

Ironically, though the United States was instrumental in disbanding the army after defeating Japan and then imposing a Constitution with a war-renouncing clause, the United States was again instrumental in creating the Self-Defence Forces in the wake of the Korean War, as some of the American Occupation forces in Japan had to be deployed to the Korean War front. Despite the fact that the SDF exists as defined in the Constitution, it is in reality a de facto military force, without official legitimacy. Abe intended to remove this uncertainty, and he was completely justified in doing so because the regional geopolitical environment had shifted radically, and new threats had appeared, necessitating a nation's defence of its territory, sovereignty and national interests. In view of this, despite the constitutional constraints, Japan today possesses the largest defence budgets in the world. What Abe wanted to do was to correct this historical wrong.[17]

His successor government headed by Yoshihide Suga, also sought a record defence budget of 5.5 trillion yen ($55 billion) amid regional threats, as well as more purchases of costly American stealth fighters to expand Japan's capability to counter possible cyber and outer space threats. This budget request was the first under Suga and would be an 8 per cent increase over the previous year. Japan's defence spending rose for eight consecutive years since 2013, a year after Abe took office. These increases in defence spending were consistent with Abe's pursuance to accord the Self-Defense Forces a greater international role and beef up the capability amid increasing threats from China and North Korea.[18]

Realising that amending Article 9 was too complicated and unfeasible, Abe created a different technique to construe the Constitution, allowing him to achieve some of his goals without really altering the peace clause. So, in 2015, he skirted Japanese rules to grant the SDF more power. This important move raised eyebrows in the neighbouring countries such as South Korea, North Korea and China who were victims of Japan's brutality in World War II. No wonder, they opposed the move but without success. Abe also faced criticism at home, as the Japanese people had a strong anti-militaristic sentiment stemming from their experiences when Japan was defeated in the World War II and two cities—Hiroshima and Nagasaki—were bombed by nuclear weapons for the first time in human history. Abe also faced opposition from his political rivals.[19] Abe had to find a middle path by pushing through contentious security legislation that permitted Japanese troops to engage in overseas combat missions alongside allied forces, as part of "collective self-defense". This in some limited way enabled Abe to achieving some of his objectives.[20]

COVID-19 Policy

The year 2020 turned out to be the most challenging for Abe. First, the country as also the world faced an unexpected difficulty in dealing with the coronavirus, which required an out-of-the-box solution. Abe's policy attempts to combat the virus received both praise and criticism. However, Abe's sincerity in alleviating the economic difficulties of the people cannot be faulted.[21] As the economy suffered greatly, he devised a large economic stimulus package to help it recover. As ties with China, where the virus originated, nosedived over the Senkaku issue, not only did the Chinese President's scheduled visit to Japan in April 2020 have to be postponed due to the epidemic, but many Japanese companies decided to relocate their manufacturing sites from China. Abe earmarked some money in his stimulus package to such companies to protect their interests.[22] Yet, Abe was criticised in various ways, including his handling of masks.

In April, Abe enacted an ambitious plan addressing various aspects of COVID-19 prevention and recovery, which included the delivery of fabric masks to all households in Japan, but was widely criticized online and in the media because of delays, the small size of the masks and other logistical hiccups. However, Abe defended his position by quoting COVID-19 fatality statistics. Japan's death rate compared to most countries was the standard by which he defended his position. Viewed from this perspective, his policy could be cautiously considered a success.[23] The total number of COVID-19 cases in Japan reached 744,487 on June 1, 2021, with 12,967 deaths since the start of the pandemic.[24]

Postponement of the Tokyo Olympic

Abe deserves credit for negotiating to bring the 2020 Olympics and Paralympics to Tokyo. Unfortunately, despite best efforts to keep the event on schedule in July 2020, the event had to be postponed until July 2021. Abe must be disappointed, but he could do little about it. The economic costs for the postponement were quite heavy for Japan[25] as it had already invested substantial amount of money in the preparation and infrastructure development and was expected to recover some of it by hosting the games.[26] Having decided to demit office, he offered to guide his successor to ensure a smooth transition and on the future of the Olympics. In view of the surge in the number of cases and increasing fatalities, the public demanded for the cancellation of the Games.[27] As it transpired, subsequently, the Games were held, albeit without spectators and many restrictions.

There are other issues that Abe dealt with during his long tenure that do not merit consideration in evaluating his competence. The issues mentioned and explained above are adequate to determine his success/failure rate, albeit it is difficult to assign a specific percentage point to each of the issues under consideration for evaluation. Overall, if one takes an objective and dispassionate stance, despite numerous failures, his domestic programmes cannot be considered a failure because no prime minister can deliver all that the people expect.

Assessing Abe's Foreign Policy

In the foreign and security policy arena, Abe's prolonged rule contributed, in a way, to strengthening his personal ties with some key foreign leaders. But his signature diplomatic initiatives, staged with a vow to settle Japan's unresolved post-World War II diplomatic issues once and for all, fell through.

Like on the domestic issues, in the foreign policy front, results were also mixed. He strengthened ties with the US despite that a mercurial American President tried to extract his pound of flesh from Japan to share a larger part of the security burden. His endeavours to strengthen ties with the ASEAN and India were commendable. As mentioned earlier, ties with Vietnam were intensified, while relations between India and Japan scaled to new heights. Trade, investment, joint ventures, ODA grew. Then came the signing of the ACSA in a virtual summit with Modi on November 9, 2020, Abe's last major engagement, enabling the Quad countries for logistic sharing bound by a shared strategic outlook, was path-breaking.[28]

There were some failures too in the foreign policy front. He was unable to resolve the territorial disputes with Russia that prevented the signing of a peace treaty to officially end the World War II. He was also unable to resolve the abduction issue of Japanese nationals in the 1970s and 1980s by North Korea, a promise he had made to the families of the abductees. He failed to have a summit meeting with North Korea's dictator Kim Jong-un, even though Kim had two summit meetings with Trump, three with South Korean President Moon Jae-in, Russia's Vladimir Putin and China's Xi Jinping. His administration was also embroiled in a bitter spat with South Korea and could not resolve the 'comfort women' issue, which spilt over into court cases including demands for compensation for Korean labour used during the War in Japanese companies in Japan, affecting economic relations. These are in brief the major foreign policy issues chosen for evaluating Abe's credit card. Though these issues have been discussed in previous pages of this Chapter, let me elaborate each of these further.

A charismatic leader like his predecessor Junichiro Koizumi and often projected as a nationalist, Abe represented stability both at home and abroad and took up the task of resurrecting a liberal order in Asia that the US President had abandoned.[29] And in doing so, he had the assurance and support of Indian Prime Minister Narendra Modi with whom he had already established a close bonhomie.

Failure to Resolve the Abduction Issue

As previously said, he could not keep the promise made to the families to bring back those abducted by North Korea in the 1970s and 1980s. Abe was modest enough to admit his failure at the press conference where he announced his decision to demit office and expressed regret for failing achieving some key goals during his tenure. The unresolved abduction issue with North Korea must have pained him that he had made it one of his top priorities as prime minister. He raised this issue with President Trump who mentioned during his summits with Kim Jong-un. It yielded no outcome. While expressing disappointment over Abe's decision to demit office, the chairman of the National Association for the Rescue of Japanese Kidnapped by North Korea (NARKN) remarked that the country needed Abe to do more to take the issue forward towards achieving a solution. Abe's consistent effort to raise the issue elicited broad international support.

Northern Territories

Abe also mentioned the unresolved northern territories issue in his August 28 press conference, expressing regret despite efforts. This festering territorial issue has prevented both the countries to conclude a peace treaty. The sticking point with Russia concerns the dispute over Japan's Northern Territories off the coast of Hokkaido, which were forcibly occupied by Russia at the end of World War II. This dispute has been brought up repeatedly in international negotiations by the Japanese government, but has never produced a tangible peace treaty to return the islands to Japan. His negotiations with Russian President Vladimir Putin to resolve the long-running Northern Territories reached an impasse. The issue was left for Abe's successors, Suga and Kishida, to seek a solution to the long-standing impasse.[30]

Ties with the ASEAN

During his long tenure, Japan's relations with the ASEAN bloc deepened both in economic and security/strategic domains. In particular, bilateral ties with Vietnam scaled new heights. Cooperation with the ASEAN bloc on securing the global commons, especially to deal with China's assertiveness and island-building activities in the much contested South China Sea was and shall remain a key focus in Japan's foreign policy agenda.

Bill Emmott observes that "at times, he has pursued a slavishly close relationship with Trump"[31]. On the issues of negotiating trade deal with countries and blocs, Abe chose a rather independent course. After President Trump withdrew from the 12-country Trans-Pacific Partnership in 2017, Abe led the efforts to salvage the trade deal but with limited success. His sincerity on the issue of negotiating the Regional Comprehensive Economic Partnership agreement, from which India decided to stay away, also received praise. During his tenure, Japan also negotiated a bilateral free trade arrangement with the European Union. Subsequently, Japan also signed a parallel deal with the United Kingdom in October 2020, the negotiations of which were completed during Abe's tenure.[32] This marked a historic moment as the UK's first major trade deal as an independent trading nation, and offering a glimpse of Global Britain's potential. Other agreements that Abe successfully negotiated and signed include multilateral trade agreements in the Pacific (the CPTPP) and the Atlantic (the Japan-EU Economic Partnership Agreement) and the Australia-Japan-US Trilateral Infrastructural Partnership.

India-Japan Relations

Consolidating and taking India-Japan ties to a much higher gear was one of Abe's most outstanding contribution and left an indelible mark in the history of India-Japan relations. Bilateral relations saw great strides after Modi came to power and established a close friendship with Abe. After a prolonged period and many rounds of negotiations, the civil nuclear energy deal was finally clinched during Modi's visit to Japan in September 2017. That time, Abe promised to invest 3.5 trillion yen in investment. Modi had already established a "Japan Plus" office in the Ministry of Commerce as a "one-stop" location for resolving problems faced by Japanese companies in India. Keeping China in mind and as mentioned earlier, a key military logistic pact, Acquisition and Cross Servicing Agreement (ACSA) was signed before Abe officially demitted office.

Some may be concerned that Abe's retirement from politics could jeopardise the Quad's efforts to construct a rules-based system for a free and open Indo-Pacific. Such concerns would be unwarranted, as the complementarities between the two countries are so strong that regardless of whatever party wins power in either country, bilateral ties will remain strong and add greater strength in the future. Indeed, if China intensifies tensions through muscle-flexing actions, it will only strengthen not only India-Japan relations, but also the coalition of democracies that share common principles.

Abe's remarks at the hall of Indian Parliament during his brief first tenure in August 2007, wherein he boldly re-imagined the shared geography by unveiling his vision on the "confluence of two seas"—now the Indo-Pacific—widened Tokyo's geographic horizons to include the Indian Ocean and invited India to reclaim its large strategic potential in the Pacific Ocean.[33] The visionary Abe also first called for the construction of a coalition of four Asian democracies in partnership with Australia and the US. Abe's concept of Quad that remained dormant during his first term gathered steam in his second term as geopolitical and geostrategic dynamics in the Indo-Pacific underwent a dramatic change and also embraced maritime security issue.

During his two tenures, Abe visited India four times (August 2007 during first term), thrice in second term (January 2014, December 2015, September 2017), the most visits by any Japanese Prime Minister, during which many important agreements were signed. He also was the first Japanese Prime Minister to be the Chief Guest at the Republic Day parade in 2014. He was wooed both by the UPA and the NDA government, reflecting that India saw him always as a true and trustworthy friend. While the foundation for "Global Partnership between India and Japan" was laid in 2001, and annual bilateral summits were agreed in 2005, it goes to the credit of Abe that he accelerated the pace of ties since 1012. But after Modi came to power, both sides agreed to upgrade the bilateral relationship to "Special Strategic and Global Partnership" when Modi chose Japan for his first bilateral visit outside the neighbourhood. Bilateral ties assumed multidimensional perspective encompassing civilian nuclear energy, maritime security, shinkansen project, infrastructure development, Act East Policy, collaboration to develop India's Northeast region, and Indo-Pacific strategy. It was indeed touching when Abe announced his decision to step down on health grounds, Prime Minister Modi tweeted "pained to hear about your ill health, my dear friend", thereby reflecting the sentiment and feelings of a 1.3 billion people.

Abe's Legacy

Seen for a long time as an economic giant but a political pigmy, Abe catapulted Japan for an Asian leadership role at a time when the US under Trump was seen to be abdicating the responsibility of securing Asian security in the wake of China asserting its muscular power. India and Japan, under Modi and Abe, were well positioned to reorient and carve a new course amid the tectonic shift in great power politics. Modi and Abe realised that in the changing Asian geopolitical dynamics, where certain Asian countries are assertively trying to reorder Asia in ways that are beneficial to their own national interests but detrimental to the interests of others, Asian nations needed to get out of the comfort zone under the American shadow and carve out their own course to defend and protect the security interests of the region. With Abe's departure, that strategy could face some roadblocks, but not insurmountable. Indirectly, this situation throws up new challenges to the Indian Prime Minister, and with the understanding he has developed with many Asian nations, the road is laid for Modi to leave his own footprints in the foreign policy domain in style. Abe's departure from the Asia's political firmament presented a new opportunity for Modi to activate his foreign policy serving both national and regional interests. Other specific issues such as economic, security/defence, and cultural are discussed in detail in subsequent chapters to present the India-Japan relations in a comprehensive manner for the benefits of students, scholars, policy makers and common readers.

In Retrospect

In the context of assessing Abe's performance and legacy, it is pertinent to take note of what Professor J.A.A. Stockwin, an eminent expert on Japanese domestic politics from Oxford University observed in his keynote address at The European Conference on Politics, Economics and Law (ECPEL) 2014, in association with the IAFOR Japan Research Institute (JRI), in Brighton, UK, on July 4, 2014, wherein he spoke about the new directions that Japan is likely to pursue under the Abe government, with specific focus on constitution, defence and nationalism. In 1979, Harvard scholar Ezra Vogel (he passed away in December 2020 at the age of 90) published a book entitled *Japan as Number One: Lessons for America*,[34] arguing that Japan is a country for the future with huge potential to emerge as an economic superpower that the US must watch out for. This observation was made following the astounding economic growth that Japan registered in the 1960s and early 1970s. But Vogel proved wrong. All Japanese economic activities came crashing down at the beginning of the 1990s with the collapse of a monstrous asset bubble, leading to two lost decades.

Not only has the country's economy stagnated and struggled to recover during the last three decades, but there have also been other sociological changes that the country has had to deal with. With a dwindling population and a rise in longevity, Japan has demographic concerns and related immigration issues, as its strict immigration policy is under fire. Abe attempted to address some of these issues by increasing the number of women in the labour force through his womenomics policy, paternity leave, incentives to increase birth rates, and other related policy measures. However, a conservative Japan was unwilling to adopt such drastic changes, so Abe's initiatives did not meet the intended results. These have already been discussed in the preceding pages.

Externally, Japan is also facing new challenges. Besides security threats emanating from China with increasing assertiveness on its territorial claims, while China's economy has surged, that of Japan has been sinking. For example, in 1990 Chinese GDP was around 25 per cent that of Japan. More than a decade ago, China pushed the economy of Japan from second to third place in world ranking. The gap is widening further. As India's economy continues to surge despite the pandemic, Japan could be pushed to the fourth place soon. At a time when Japanese women have gone on a 'birth strike', China has reversed its one-child formula with a view to boost population in response to the fear of an increase in elderly population to meet with the future workforce demands. A democratic nation like Japan cannot coerce women to give birth to more kids, but an authoritarian country such as China can adopt tough measures to meet its goals, as it did when it implemented the one-child formula with coercive measures.[35]

Some 18 months after Abe was in office, Stockwin expressed disquiet on some of Abe's intended policy measures. He was worried about Abe's radical policies that aimed to rewrite some of the established norms. Here, Stockwin could be wrong as Abe's policies were aimed only at responding to the changing geopolitical challenges that had emerged, and Japan needed to direct its policies to cope with such challenges. However, Stockwin endorsed 'Abenomics', though as expected met with limited results.

Yasukuni Shrine: Why it is Important and Controversial?

As if to open historical wounds as perceived by China and South Korea, Abe infuriated these two countries by visiting the Yasukuni Shrine that honours Japan's war dead, including some convicted war criminals on December 26, 2013, claiming that it was an anti-war gesture. China called the visit "absolutely unacceptable to the Chinese people, and Seoul expressed "regret and anger".[36] Both China and South Korea see Yasukuni as a symbol of Tokyo's aggression during World War II, when Japan occupied parts of China and the entire Korean Peninsula. The US embassy in Tokyo also issued a statement expressing disappointment and feared that Abe's actions would "exacerbate tensions" with Japan's neighbours.[37] This statement registered high in the internationally understood scale of diplomatic protest language.

It was the first visit to Yasukuni by a serving prime minister since Junichiro Koizumi went in 2006. Women and children who have died in 150 years are among 2.5 million people honoured. The enshrining of hundreds of World War II criminals in the 1970s made the shrine hugely controversial. The justification that Abe visited the shrine in his private capacity and not representing the government did not assuage the feeling of hurt in China and South Korea. China argued that Japan made an unwritten agreement with it in the 1970s that serving leaders would not visit the shrine and by visiting the shrine Abe seemed to have broken that deal. Earlier in August the same year, Abe sent a ritual offering to the shrine but was not among a group of dozens of Japanese politicians who visited Yasukuni.

Yasukuni is neither a functional equivalent of the Cenotaph, the Imperial War Museum in London, or the Arlington cemetery in Washington D.C., and therefore is controversial. Yasukuni includes a war museum, known as the Yashukan, whose displays give a largely benign, even enthusiastic, picture of the Japanese war effort between 1937 and 1945 and plays down the sufferings of Japan's wartime opponents. In contrast, the Atomic Bomb Museum in Hiroshima, though it has occasionally been criticised for deploying a "Japan as victim" message, makes a genuine and convincing effort to put the tragedy of the bombing into a balanced historical context.

Yasukuni Shrine was first established in 1869 as a memorial to those who had fallen in wars since 1853, including the Boshin war, fought between embattled elements of the former Tokugawa regime and armies of the rebellion that had overthrown it and were setting up a new modernising order at the Meiji Restoration of 1868. The names of those enshrined also includes those who had fallen in the Seinan War, the Sino-Japanese and Russo-Japanese wars, World War I, the Manchurian Incident, the China Incident and World War II, known in Japan as the Greater East Asian War.[38] In short, Yasukuni's status has been that of a national institution to glorify the souls of servicemen who had fallen in successive wars up to 1945. The Allied Occupation post-Japan's surrender insisted this should be revised, in line with the disestablishment of the Shinto religion seen as the fulcrum of Japanese nationalism up to the end of the war.

In 1978, the head priest of the Yasukuni Shrine secretly enshrined the souls of 14 class-A war criminals as well as over 1,000 lesser war criminals—all of whom were designated by the Tokyo trials after the war. When this news became public political controversy erupted almost overnight. While the right wing elements accused the war crime trials as sham deliverance of justice, thereby elevating Justice Pal to iconic status because of his thundering dissenting judgement, moderates in Japan, as well as governments in China, Korea and elsewhere, were disappointed by Japanese politicians' use of the Shrine to promote revisionist nationalism. Since then, official trips to the Shrine by top politicians, especially prime ministers, have continued to infuriate Japan's neighbours, especially China and Korea. It may be noted that after the 1978 enshrinement of war criminals, the Showa Emperor refused to visit the Yasukuni Shrine, and his grandson, the present Emperor Naruhito, who became the Emperor after his father Akihito abdicated, has also consistently refused to do so. The Heishi Emperor (Akihito) too refrained from visiting the Yasukuni Shrine during his tenure. Sadly, China and South Korea have overlooked this vital feature of the Yasukuni Shrine. After all, the Showa Emperor, in his greater wisdom, saw greater virtue in proclaiming Japan's surrender following the bombings of Hiroshima and Nagasaki, preventing further suffering for the Japanese people and symbolising and thus signifying the futility of war.

Concluding Observations

Did Abe achieve what he intended when he assumed his second term? Did he learn any lesson from his first term, albeit short one, so that he could improve in his long second tenure? Given the complexities of Japanese politics and the constitutional constraints, it was not possible for the Prime Minister, let alone Abe, to claim his aspirations were met. But Abe does deserve credit for trying and achieving moderate results. While he benefitted in his first term from the disillusionment with the Democratic Party, his second term saw an upsurge in his obsession to further his nationalistic agenda, but with limited success. In India he is remembered for good reasons for his famous speech in the Indian parliament in August 2007, wherein he articulated his Indo-Pacific concept in his Confluence between two Seas. The seeds of the Quad were sown at that time. Related to this, his push for collective self-defence, which aimed to weaken the peace clause, caused consternation in the region, which failed to see it as a legitimate response from a sovereign state seeking to secure its security, as well as in the region, whose strategic situation had changed noticeably. The question of whether Abe's decision threatened to undermine Japan's peace commitment entrenched in Article 9 of the Constitution, even though it mirrored his ideological mentality and so exacerbated tensions with surrounding countries, remains upto interpretations. Opinions could differ. One would agree with Stockwin when he observes that "Japan was the future once, and could be again" but there are "dark clouds on the horizon". That is how Abe's legacy in Japanese politics may be summarised and explained with potentials of uncertainties along the way.

Notes

1. "Japan's Longest-Serving Prime Ministers", November 20, 2019, https://www.nippon.com/en/features/h00296/japan%E2%80%99s-longest-serving-prime-ministers.html
2. See, Rajaram Panda, "Abe Shinzo: A giant departs Japanese politics", August 29, 2020, https://www.rediff.com/news/column/abe-shinzo-a-giant-departs-japanese-politics/20200829.htm
3. Ibid.
4. Kathy Matsui, "Op-Ed in the Financial Times: Why Gender Diversity Matters for Japan's Economy", *The Financial Times*, April 23, 2019, https://www.goldmansachs.com/media-relations/in-the-news/archive/matsui-womenomics-ft-2019.html
5. Abhijnan Rej, "India and Japan Sign Military Logistics Agreement for All to See", *The Diplomat*, September 12, 2020, https://thediplomat.com/2020/09/india-and-japan-sign-military-logistics-agreement-for-all-to-see/#:~:text=On%20September%209%2C%20India%20and%20Japan%20signed%20an
6. See, Rajaram Panda, "How is Suga Crafting Japan's Policies towards Russia?", December 15, 2020, https://www.vifindia.org/article/2020/december/15/how-is-suga-crafting-japan-s-policies-towards-russia
7. See, Rajaram Panda, "Japan and South Korea talk but Old Issues Continue to Figure", May 14, 2021, https://www.vifindia.org/article/2021/may/14/japan-and-south-korea-talk-but-old-issues-continue-to-figure
8. The consumption tax rate in Japan increased from 8% to 10% starting at midnight on October 1, 2019. Consumption tax was first introduced in Japan in April 1989 at 3% and was increased to 5% then 8% in April 1997 and April 2014, respectively. This was the third time that the consumption tax was increased.
9. Reiji Yoshida "Suicide note reignites Moritomo scandal that rocked Abe administration", *The Japan Times*, March 18, 2020, https://www.japantimes.co.jp/news/2020/03/18/national/suicide-note-reignites-moritomo-gakuen-cronyism-scandal-abe/
10. Eric Johnston, "With suicide note and lawsuit, Moritomo scandal back to haunt Abe", *The Japan Times*, April 2, 2020, https://www.japantimes.co.jp/news/2020/04/02/reference/moritomo-gakuen-back-to-haunt-abe/

11. "Ex-Japan justice minister, lawmaker wife charged over vote buying", July 8, 2020, https://english.kyodonews.net/news/2020/07/01547c4c74d5-update1-ex-justice-minister-wife-indicted-over-election-voting-scandal.html
12. "Kurokawa's resignation does not let Abe off the hook for fiasco", *Asahi Shimbun*, editorial, May 22, 2020, http://www.asahi.com/ajw/articles/13394244
13. "Reality Check: Has Shinzo Abe's 'womenomics' worked in Japan?", February 17, 2018, https://www.bbc.com/news/world-asia-42993519
14. http://www3.weforum.org/docs/WEF_GGGR_2020.pdf
15. Article 9 reads as: "Aspiring sincerely to an international peace based on justice and order, the Japanese people forever renounce war as a sovereign right of the nation and the threat or use of force as a means of settling international disputes."
16. See, *Asahi Shimbun*, May 16, 2014.
17. Rajaram Panda, "Can Article 9 of the Japanese Constitution be ever Amended", May 25, 2021, https://www.vifindia.org/article/2021/may/25/can-article-9-of-the-japanese-constitution-be-ever-amended
18. *The Times of India*, October 1, 2020.
19. Neha Banka, "Shinzo Abe resigns: A look back at the Japan PM's tenure, and what happens next", *Indian Express*, September 1, 2020, https://indianexpress.com/article/explained/shinzo-abe-resigns-japan-prime-minister-6573454/
20. See, Rajaram Panda, "Debate on Collective Self-Defence and Constitutional Revision in Japan", *Reitaku Journal of Interdisciplinary Studies*, vol. 26, 2018, pp. 1-19. https://reitaku.repo.nii.ac.jp/index.php?action=pages_view_main&active_action=repository_view_main_item_snippet&index_id=476&pn=1&count=20&order=17&lang=japanese&page_id=13&block_id=29
21. See, Rajaram Panda, "Abe Combats Covid-19", *The Nationalist* (New Delhi), May 2020, pp. 32-34. https://www.spmrf.org/wp-content/uploads/2020/05/The-Nationalist-May-2020.pdf
22. See Rajaram Panda, "Fallout from Covid-19: Japanese, S. Korean & US Companies likely to Relocate Production Bases from China to India", *Japan SPOTLIGHT* (Tokyo), July-August 2020, pp. 68-69. https://www.jef.or.jp/journal/pdf/232nd_Readers_Response.pdf
23. Arielle Busetto, "Shinzo Abe on His 8 Years as Prime Minister: 'Many Challenges, But Also Successes'", August 29, 2020, https://japan-forward.com/shinzo-abe-on-his-8-years-as-prime-minister-many-challenges-but-also-successes/
24. https://www.worldometers.info/coronavirus/country/japan/
25. The Abe administration had made a pre-Olympic stimulus package for construction, development design and for other services. The total costs had risen beyond $12 billion. Separately, Tokyo city was expected to spend another $7.4 billion on projects, directly and indirectly related to the games such as installing barrier-free facilities for the Paralympics, training programme for volunteers, and advertising and tourism plans. It is estimated that the total cost that Japan would have incurred is to the tune of $28 billion, almost quadruple of the $7.4 billion declared when Tokyo won the bid in 2013. Of these, only $5.6 billion of operating costs were covered with

revenues from sponsors, ticket sales, marketing, and IOC contributions. The Games were postponed till next year. Had they been cancelled altogether, it would have been disastrous for Japan.

26. Rajaram Panda, "What Olympics Postponement will Cost Japan", April 4, 2020, https://www.rediff.com/news/column/coronavirus-what-olympics-postponement-will-cost-japan/20200404.htm. Also see, Rajaram Panda, "Olympics Postponed: What Economic Costs Japan Face?", January-March 2020, https://usiofindia.org/publication/cs3-strategic-perspectives/olympics-postponed-what-economic-costs-japan-face/
27. Rajaram Panda, "CANCEL Tokyo Olympics!", May 28, 2021, https://www.rediff.com/sports/column/rajaram-panda-cancel-tokyo-olympics/20210528.htm
28. Rajaram Panda, "Abe Shinzo: A Giants Departs Japanese Politics", August 29, 2020, https://www.rediff.com/news/column/abe-shinzo-a-giant-departs-japanese-politics/20200829.htm
29. Swasti Rao, "Shinzo Abe's élan, his resolute foreign policy in disturbed international times shall be missed", *Indian Express,* September 1, 2020, https://indianexpress.com/article/opinion/columns/shinzo-abe-japan-his-last-bow-6577922/
30. Rajaram Panda, "How is Suga Crafting Japan's Policies towards Russia?", December 15, 2020, https://www.vifindia.org/article/2020/december/15/how-is-suga-crafting-japan-s-policies-towards-russia
31. Bill Emmott, "The Japan that Shinzo Abe has left behind", *The Japan Times*, August 29, 2010, https://www.japantimes.co.jp/opinion/2020/08/29/commentary/japan-commentary/japan-shinzo-abe-resignation/
32. "UK and Japan sign free trade agreement", October 23, 2020, https://www.gov.uk/government/news/uk-and-japan-sign-free-trade-agreement
33. https://www.mofa.go.jp/region/asia-paci/pmv0708/speech-2.html
34. See, Ezra F. Vogel, *Japan as Number one: Lessons for America* (Harvard: Harvard University Press, 1979), p. 272.
35. J.A.A. Stockwin, "New Directions in Japan under the Abe government: Constitution, Defence and Nationalism", July 18, 2018, https://think.iafor.org/new-directions-in-japan-under-the-abe-government-constitution-defence-and-nationalism/
36. For the background, see Rajaram Panda, "Japan and South Korea: Prisoners of History", *IIC Quarterly*, vol. Summer 2021, vol. 48, no. 1, pp. 111-121.
37. "Japan's PM Shinzo Abe visits Yasukuni WW2 shrine", December 26, 2013, https://www.bbc.com/news/world-asia-25517205
38. See https://www.historyhit.com/locations/yasukuni-shrine/.

3

Sculpting a New Economic Partnership

Introduction

In the economic realm, both India and Japan have experienced lost opportunities owing to contrasting policies, which came in the way of honing their potentials, despite the fact that India laid a favourable political foundation after Japan's surrender in the World War II. That aspect has already been explained in the Introduction of this book and needs no reiteration. To put briefly, Japan needed to obtain rare raw resources from overseas that its industries required during the post-war economic rebirth. A resource-deficient country had no other option but to import these from overseas countries wherever those were available for export. In the initial years of economic rebuilding phase in the 1960s, the focus was on heavy industries such as ship-building, steel, heavy equipment, large machine tools, large-scale infrastructure and many more. Heavy industry required higher capital intensity than light industry, and therefore heavily cynical in investment and employment.

Indeed, transportation and construction, as well as accompanying supply businesses have been the bulk of heavy industry throughout the industrial age, along with some capital-intensive manufacturing. Traditional examples from the mid-nineteenth to early twentieth centuries included steelmaking, artillery production, locomotive manufacturing, machine building, and the heavier types of mining. From the late nineteenth century to the mid-twentieth century, as the chemical industry and electrical industry developed, they involved components of both heavy industry and light industry, which was soon also true for the automotive industry and the aircraft industry. Modern shipbuilding (since steel replaced wood) is considered heavy industry. Large systems are often characteristic of heavy industry such as the construction of skyscrapers and large dams during the post–World War II era, and the manufacture/deployment of large rockets and giant wind turbines through the 21st century. Large components such as ship turbochargers are also characteristic of heavy industry.

During the period of economic revival from the ruins of the War, Japan focused recovery from the ruins of the war and concentrated on developing the country's heavy industries. Japan sourced precious resources from imports to meet the expanding demands of its industry. Other East Asian countries, particularly South Korea, began to follow Japan's lead in emphasising heavy industries. This reliance on heavy industries was often a result of government economic policies. Many Japanese and Korean firms with "heavy industry" in their names also manufacture aerospace products and serve as defence contractors to their respective governments, such as Japan's Fuji Heavy Industries and Korea's Hyundai Rotem, a joint project of Hyundai Heavy Industries and Daewoo Heavy Industries.

In the 20th-century communist states, the planning of the economy often focused on heavy industry as an area for large investments, even to the extent of painful opportunity costs on the production-possibility frontier. This was motivated by fears of failing to maintain military parity with foreign capitalist powers. For example, the Soviet Union's industrialization in the 1930s, with heavy industry as the favoured emphasis, sought to bring its ability to produce trucks, tanks, artillery, aircraft, and warships up to a level that would make the country a great power. China under Mao Zedong pursued a similar strategy, eventually culminating in the Great Leap Forward of 1958–1960, an attempt to rapidly industrialize and collectivise.

India positioned itself differently in terms of economic and foreign policy. It did not choose either the socialist or capitalist models. Instead, it carved out a new paradigm of non-alignment in its foreign policy, suggesting that it would not be perceived as linked with either of the two groupings that split the world: the capitalist group led by the United States and the socialist camp led by the Soviet Union. While these two camps were tied by alliances, India led the non-alignment group, which included four other countries. This was in the post-colonial world. The leaders of the non-aligned organisation did not want to risk losing their hard-earned independence from the colonial masters again after years of struggle. In the economic realm, the state took upon itself to develop major economic activities, with little space for private players.

This brief background explanation is necessary to contextualise how both India and Japan failed to capitalise their complementarities after Japan's defeat and India's independence, despite the abundance of political and cultural goodwill. In the meantime, Japan's post-War policies and political system were crafted by the US, which continued after the Occupation forces left, following the signing of the San Francisco Treaty. In short, while Japan chose to pursue an export-oriented economic strategy as development goals, India chose the policy of import-substitution with self-sustaining goals and less dependence on exports to fuel domestic growth. These basic contrasting strategies prevented both India and Japan from honing their potentials for mutual benefit. This equation changed after India decided to liberalise its economy in 1991, and there has been no looking back since then.

Importance of Iron Ore and how it Lost its Lustre

During the 1950s and half of the 1960s, the bulk of Japan' iron ore requirements were obtained from Asian countries such as Malaysia, the Philippines and India. By the early 1970s, the share held by the Asian sources considerably declined after other exporting countries such as Australia and Brazil emerged as stiff competitors. In 1960, Asian sources supplied nearly 71 per cent of Japan's total iron ore requirements. India alone accounted for 27.8 per cent. A decade later, the share of Asian sources declined to 23.4 per cent, with India contributing a mere 15.8 per cent. By 1973, it further shrunk to 16.4 per cent, with India's share remaining at 14 per cent.

By 1977, while the total Asian share was a mere 16.1 per cent, India's share remained at 13.6 per cent. On the other hand, Australia's share jumped from nothing in 1960 to 47.8 per cent in 1977. In 1968, Australia supplanted India as the chief supplier. The main reason for India's declining share was the development of triangular trade and the emergence of other suppliers in Australia, Brazil and Africa, which were in possession of excess capacity and able to sell to Japan at competitive prices as well as in bulk vis-à-vis India. However, whilst the average quality 'Fe' content of the Indian ore was 65.14 per cent and commanded the highest price of $24.4 per ton in the Japanese market, that of Australia was 64 per cent and $20.2 and of Brazil was 65 per cent and $19.97.[1] Japan used to take nearly 70 to 80 per cent of India's total iron ore exports and was India's major source of foreign exchange earnings. However, while demand for iron ore in Japan increased, the quantity available for export in Australia and Brazil commensurately increased. On the other hand, growth in production of iron ore in India did not remain consistent with the rise in demand in Japan. The loss of its share to Australia and Brazil was because of the small size of her iron ore available for export to Japan. While the Japanese demand for iron ore increased six fold between 1960 and 1978, India's production registered a lower growth rate vis-à-vis Australia and Brazil.

There were other reasons for this too. In the first place, India's iron ore industry was not export-oriented, as that of Australia and Brazil whose economies were then and even today basically are external-oriented.[2] This trend was not unnatural as India's economy was more or less self-sustaining, like that of the US, and did not depend on foreign trade like Japan, Australia and Brazil. Secondly, about half of the total production used to be consumed domestically and the rest was available for export. In 1976, about 55.8 per cent of the total production was exported of which about 70 per cent went to Japan. However, the size of the Australian iron ore available for export was about 4 times more, and that of Brazil was about 2.8 times more than that of India. Though India was able to negotiate better prices for its iron ore because of its quality, the quantity available or export did not increase substantially, thereby losing substantial market share in Japan. Thirdly, the inadequate harbour facilities inhibited introduction of big carriers. In contrast, the development of very large carriers was a major factor in the development of Australian and Brazilian iron ore industries. Big carriers lowered the transport cost so that distant sourced which were inaccessible earlier because of high transport costs became accessible easily. Fourthly, there was a lack of capital investment in the development of infrastructure like railroad and transportation from mining points to the loading point. Moreover, unfavourable investment climate for overseas investors prevailing in India then did not provide adequate inducement to potential investors to develop interest in the Indian mines. The relative cost involved for Japan to buy iron ore from India vis-à-vis Australia and Brazil, combined with the massive capital investment required to develop the deposits and the Indian government's restrictive policy towards foreign capital, resulted in a stagnation of India-Japan iron ore trade. Finally, the disincentive to install modern facilities in mines for projected production due to workforce issues harmed any chance of enhanced production. With a socialist worldview and social welfare objectives, workers were granted the freedom to protest under the labour laws in effect at the time.

In fact this remained as the most vexing issue in India-Japan talks, with the Japanese side consistently demanding major labour reforms so that Japanese companies can aim for result-oriented approach in the post-liberalisation era. At that time, it was feared that introducing modern machinery would result in many people losing their jobs, exacerbating the already serious unemployment crisis. When Japan received assurances of secure supplies of its bulk demand from Australia and Brazil without considerable development, it lost interest and appeal to Indian resources that required heavy capital investment. At that time, Australian policy aimed to expand and tap its export market. Therefore, country risk for Japan in Australia was virtually nil, which explains why Japan was reluctant to commit to India.

The truism is that compared to Australia and Brazil, India is a resource-poor country. With a huge population and large size, its domestic needs are also immense. Even in the post-liberalisation era, its exportable resources had limitations and therefore its competitive edge remained weak when faced with other suppliers with exportable surplus. In its path to industrialise its economy in quick time after the War, it was a part of Japan's global commercial strategy. Procuring critical resources from newfound sources such as Australia and Brazil to feed its industries became the new development mantra.

This new Japan-Australia trade in minerals and raw materials that affected India's trade ties with Japan has an interesting tale. Before and during the War, Japan was seen as a potential invader from the viewpoint of the Australian Government.[3] In 1936, the Nippon Mining Company invested about 450,000 pound in the Yampi Sound Mining Company to develop the Koolan Island ore deposits in Western Australia.[4] This was the first Japanese direct investment in mining in Australia. Japanese firms were to take delivery of the ore at Koolan Island and then to be shipped to Japan in vessels of the Nippon Yusen Kaisha. The trade war between Japan and the Commonwealth caused no hitch to the arrangements. Production was expected to commence before the end of 1938. Japanese steel interests were guaranteed 500,000 tons of iron ore during 1938 and the minimum of one million tons per annum thereafter. The first shipment was expected during September 1938. This amount represented a minimum of 15-20 per cent of Japan's total iron ore requirements from this single source.

These hopes were frustrated in May 1938, when the Australian government applied a total embargo on exports on iron ore as it felt the deposits were inadequate and must be kept for domestic needs. Though the decision of the government was questioned widely domestically, there were other considerations as well. At the time, Japan was viewed as a potential invader, and the government considered Yampi as a Japanese scheme to monopolise Australian mining riches, which was only part of a larger plan to merge Australia's northwestern frontiers.

During the post-war years, as Australia discovered huge amount of raw materials and minerals, it looked for export markets. As Japan had begun to rebuild its economy from the devastations of the War, it presented itself as an attractive market for the Australian resources. This trend continued throughout the 1960s and 1970s, until Japanese economy started contracting, leading to fall in demand. This corresponded with the start of China's economic expansion, and Australia's focus began to move towards China. One notable development during this time period was talks between India, Japan, and Australia to pursue trilateral economic cooperation. Three visionaries—C. Subramaniam from India, Saburo Okita from Japan and Sir John Crawford from Australia—got together to discuss how these three countries can cooperate for the well-being of their economies and leverage the potentials for mutual benefits. To explore the idea further and hammer out to the possibilities, the Australian National University hosted an international conference in Canberra and gathered academic inputs. The proceedings soon came out in the form of an edited volume.[5] Nothing moved beyond this. With differing economic approaches of the three countries, not much headway for a trilateral economic cooperation could be possible. While India was left to itself with declining share of its main export of iron ore, Japan and Australia built up a strong economic partnership until eclipsed by China and when Japan started entering the Lost Decades.[6]

Economic and Trade Relations until the 1990

Despite cordial relations and abundant goodwill that was generated in the aftermath of the War, and backed by civilizational linkages, trade and economic relations remained low-key throughout the Cold War years. Despite the ease of travel provided by air connectivity and economic complementarities, there remained hesitation and psychological distance in the perceptions of the peoples on both sides. This narrative has dramatically changed in recent years. As China's economic and military clout has shown ascendance in a global scale, Japan's global profile has diminished to some extent. This has provided strategic space to both India and Japan to play a larger role in regional and global levels. Seen from this larger perspective, there has been a paradigm shift in the bilateral ties in coping with the challenges. Both are seeking geopolitical partnerships in multiple directions to serve their individual national interests as well as that of the region. In this construct, while security and strategic ties assumed a stronger spine, the economic relations have also expanded in multiple directions. The impetus has also been received as fellow democracies without hegemonic intentions unlike certain powers in the region, both seek ways to achieve peaceful resolution of conflicts and engaging economically with other friendly countries of Asia.

Bilateral ties remained dormant and relatively inactive in the 1960s to 1980s. A study by the New Delhi-based think tank, the ICRIER, described the trade and economic relations during this period as such: "During the Cold War era, if India was guilty of dismissing Japan as a camp follower of the US, the Japanese in turn perceived India as a chaotic, dysfunctional, desperately poor country and not as a potential partner; the persistence of poverty in India and the successful drive for prosperity in Japan had changed the bilateral relationship. With the end of the Cold War, India began its "Look East" policy in the early 1990s that dovetailed with the opening up and liberalization of its economy."[7]

When things were looking up, bilateral ties nosedived when India conducted the nuclear test in 1998, marking a low point in the relationship. This aspect is already discussed in Chapter I and therefore needs no further elaboration. A turnaround in ties started when Prime Minister Yoshiro Mori visited India in August 2000. A new chapter opened. Today, the prolonged economic slump in Japan and the re-emergence of India as an economic power are, among other things, once again redefining bilateral relations. Thus, now one can see a paradigmatic shift in India-Japan relations on a range of areas, including the new strategic and global partnership.

The Role of ODA

Japanese Official Development Assistance (ODA) to India is a critical component in India-Japan economic cooperation and it has helped India's economic progress. Japan began offering bilateral loans and grants to India in 1958 and has since become India's top bilateral contributor. Japanese ODA supports India's attempts to expedite economic growth, notably in critical areas such as power, transportation, environmental initiatives, and basic human necessities.. The Ahmedabad-Mumbai High Speed Rail, the Western Dedicated Freight Corridor (DFC), the Delhi-Mumbai Industrial Corridor (DMIC) with twelve new industrial townships, the Chennai-Bengaluru Industrial Corridor (CBIC) are all mega projects which, when completed, will transform India in the next decade. Japanese ODA in the Delhi Metro Project is a stand-alone example that has revolutionalized the transportation network in the capital city and is one of the most successful examples of Japanese cooperation through the utilisation of ODA.

In the post-Cold War era (since the 1990s), Japanese ODA to India increased substantially. In the initial years of post-Cold War years, Japanese ODA were mostly directed towards China and Indonesia. When security and strategic considerations surfaced concerns arose and geopolitical developments occurred as a result of China's assertive foreign policy, Japan's opinion of India as a potential response to the perceived threat from China shifted. Japan's thinking about ODA allotment also changed.[8] In fiscal 2006, Japan granted India with approximately ¥184.89 billion in loans. The commitment was an increase of 18.9 per cent over the previous year, and was the highest ever amount of yen loans to India. Since 2003 India has been the largest recipient of Japanese ODA. The cumulative amount of Japan's loan to India adds up to approximately ¥2,817 billion. Until 2006, the cumulative amount of grant aid provided by Japan to India amounted to ¥86.69 billion and loan assistance amounted to ¥2817.166 billion.

The Japanese help in the development of the Delhi-Mumbai industrial corridor, among other big projects, demonstrates a purposeful effort to strengthen the economic connection.

The focus areas of Japan's ODA to India have been as follows: development of physical infrastructure, mainly in the areas of power and transportation; poverty reduction through agricultural and rural development; environmental protection, through afforestation and improvement of water quality; and assisting improvements in health and medical care. Japan's Country Assistance Program for India was formulated in May 2006 with the following priority areas: (i) promotion of economic growth (power and transportation, etc.), (ii) improvement in poverty issues (health and sanitation, local development, disaster prevention, development of tourism, etc.), (iii) improvement in environmental issues (water supply and sewerage systems, forestry, renewable energy and energy saving, and urban environment), and (iv) expansion of human resource development and people-to-people exchange. The Japan-India Joint Statement issued in April 2005 stated the resumption of the Japan Overseas Cooperation Volunteers (JOCV) programme that had remained suspended since 1979 due to policy changes by the Government of India in 1978. In April 2006, after a gap of 30 years, a JOCV group was sent to India to teach the Japanese language.

Since the primary objective of the Japanese ODA is to help the recipient country's economy grow, it is frequently linked to technological know-how and other restrictions, such as ensuring that the project is completed by a Japanese company. This frequently garnered criticism, thus Japan had to adjust its policy for spreading ODA more equitably. In the initial years of the ODA disbursement when such aids were tied, Japanese businesses got opportunities to get involved in the projects where the ODA was targeted. Even during the pre-liberalization era, when the ODA was often tied, the projects that received the ODA money qualitatively changed the development pattern. Projects such as the Bombay High Deep Sea Drilling Project, which received Japanese ODA funding, resulted in the development of the first offshore pick-up drilling rig, and its success helped to reduce India's reliance on oil. As a result, multiple fertiliser initiatives funded by ODA have the potential to significantly modify the Green Revolution programme, allowing India to become self-sufficient in food grain production. The Vishakhapatnam Outer Harbour Project and Cochin Shipyard Project, which facilitated sea logistics, are other projects where ODA money contributed a lot.

Three types of aid come under Japanese ODA—Yen loan, Grant Aid Cooperation and Technical Cooperation. All the three categories address to meet India's basic human needs. Focus is on the area of health, one of key MDGs. Yen loan is the most common form of aid from Japan and grant-in-aid and technical aid form only a miniscule part of the aid basket. Grant aid of 1.16 billion yen provided in fiscal 2010 took the total assistance to 89.654 billion yen since Japan began extending grant aid to India in 1977. Grant aid projects approved in fiscal 2010 included Strengthening Electronic Media Production Centre at Indira Gandhi National Open University (IGNOU) (787 million yen). The purpose was to improve the Centre's educational materials and equipment. IGNOU is a leading institution in developing and offering distance learning programmes to the citizens of India.[9]

The other two projects were for the Eradication of Poliomyelitis (192 million yen), and Grant Assistance for Grass-Roots Projects. Under the first category, Japan has provided a total of approximately 8.2 billion yen since 1996 for the procurement of polio vaccine and necessary equipment through UNICEF. Japan's assistance has contributed to significantly reduce sporadic polio cases in India from 5,881 in 1994 to 774 in 2009. Under the second category, a total of 20 projects totaling 169 million yen and the Cultural Grass-Roots Assistance in the amount of over 10 million yen were extended.

Under the Technical Cooperation category, India received in fiscal 2009, a total of 1,855 million yen including development studies. The total amount of cooperation through fiscal 2009 is 29.351 billion yen, 5,689 trainees were received by Japan and 971 experts were sent to India. In the next fiscal 2010, two projects, "Information Network for Natural Disaster Mitigation and Recovery in India" and "Project for Research Partnership for the Application of Low Carbon Technology for Sustainable Development", were initiated under the scheme of Science and Technology Cooperation on Global Issues, or SATREPS.

As mentioned, the Japan Overseas Cooperation Volunteers (JOCV) Program was suspended in 1979 following the policy change of the Government of India in 1978. After an agreement in the Japan-India Joint Statement issued in April 2005, the Notes were exchanged regarding the resumption of the JOCV programme. In April 2006, the first JOCV, Japanese language instructor, in 30 years was despatched. As of April 2011, 14 JOCVs work across the country.[10]

One trend in the Japanese ODA disbursements to India over the past few years demonstrates that while the grant aid is decreasing, technical help is increasing. This aligns with India's developmental strategy since the inclusion of fresh knowledge and understanding of skill development, in which Japan excels, can help India maximise its gains.

There is another perspective to the role of the ODA. Any strategic connection must include an economic dimension for the complementarities to be fully developed. The Japanese ODA can also be seen from this perspective. While the economic dimension of the bilateral relationship took some time to take stronger roots owing to factors already mentioned, the current economic engagement between the two continues to be low-key if measured in terms of overall bilateral trade which totalled a meagre $17.63

billion in 2017, demonstrating that the inherent complementarities between the two have not been exploited to their full potentials.

Seen differently, the overall economic relationships between the two countries have steadily expanded and deepened. In 2019, India was the 21st largest trading partner for Japan, while Japan was the 12th largest trading partner for India. Also, direct investment from Japan to India has been increased, and Japan was the 4th largest investor for India in fiscal 2019. Japanese private-sector's interest in India is rising, and, currently, about 1,454 Japanese companies have branches in India. At the 2016 summit between Modi and Abe in Tokyo, the two leaders reconfirmed commitment to synergising India's demographic dividend and Japan's capital and technology to realise the true potential of the Japan-India economic partnership for a prosperous future. In this regard, two leaders welcomed the agreement to conclude a Bilateral Swap Arrangement of $75 billion, the launching of a comprehensive Japan-India Digital Partnership, and other cooperation and initiatives.[11] The indicators of a close economic relationship between the two countries to strengthen the strategic dimension can be examined in terms of Japanese foreign direct investment (FDI), Official Development Assistance (ODA), and bilateral trade.

As indicated, ODA is an important instrument in Japan's economic diplomacy. For five successive years since fiscal 2003, India has been the largest recipient country for Japanese ODA loan.[12] Japan provides support to India for improvement of economic and social infrastructure such as electricity and transport for the trade and investment climate, as well as water and sewerage.

A key element of Japanese ODA in Asia is to use the aid amount as an instrument of fostering economic and political security in Asia. Japanese ODA has mostly focused on infrastructure and human resource development. ODA has also helped to facilitate private sector investment and trade through large-scale projects lending. Recently, these economic cooperation relationships are being institutionalized. As a consequence, Japan has been signing economic partnership agreements (CEPAs) with many Asian countries. South Asia and India have begun to emerge as priority in Japan's ODA radar more recently and there are big programmes underway.[13]

According to the Ministry, Economy Trade and Industry (METI), there are four prioritized fields in Japan's global economic strategy and economic foreign policy. These are: (a) domestic and foreign integrated economic measures; (b) promotion of innovation in the "volume zones"; (c) global development of the low carbon revolution; (d) and multi-layer cooperation including industrial cooperation with countries rich in natural resources.[14]

Adding to domestic demand expansion, Japan wants to promote domestic and foreign integrated economic measures aiming to grow with Asia by promoting expansion of domestic growth of Asia, the "Growth center in the world". Three big growth zones in South and Southeast Asia have been identified in which Japan is committing substantial economic cooperation funding to support Asian development.[15] These three projects are: (a) Delhi-Mumbai Industrial Corridor (DMIC), (b) Mekong River Valley Synthesis Development; and (c) BIMP Wide areas coordinated development.[16] The thrust is towards achieving doubling the size of Asia's economy. Japan wants to achieve this aim by (a) fostering cooperation in maintenance of the large area of infrastructure and the social security system, etc., to expand domestic demand of Asia; and (b) promoting economic cooperation with Asia such as promoting system sharing by utilizing APEC 2010 in Japan. Many of Japan's aid programmes are open to international tender through aid recipient agencies. For the purpose of the present study, only the DMIC is discussed at length.

In the on-going ODA projects, on February 28, 2023, India and Japan exchanged notes for Mumbai Trans-Harbour Link Project of 30.755 billion yen (Rs. 1728 crore approx) and Project for the Establishment of Mizoram State Super Specialty Cancer and Research Centre of 9.918 billion Yen (Rs. 560 crore approx).[17] The Mumbai-Trans-Harbour Link Project aims to improve connectivity in Mumbai Metropolitan Region by connecting Mumbai with Navi Mumbai, thereby contributing to migration of traffic congestion, and promoting regional economic development. This is Trance-III loan for the project.

The Project for the Establishment of Mizoram State Super Specialty Cancer and Research Centre aims to improve access to cancer prevention, detection, and treatment as well as human resource development and research that support cancer control system, thereby contributing to achieving Universal Health Coverage through strengthening the healthcare system pertaining to cancer in the state.[18] As mentioned earlier, India and Japan have had a long and fruitful history of bilateral development cooperation since 1958. In the last few years, the economic cooperation between the two countries has steadily progressed. This further consolidates and strengthens the Strategic and Global Partnership between the two countries.

Delhi-Mumbai Industrial Corridor

The DMIC project was launched in pursuance of an MOU signed between the Government of India and the Government of Japan in December 2006 during the visit of the Indian Prime Minister to Japan to promote investments and explore opportunities for mutual cooperation. Indian government accorded 'in principle' approval to the project outline of the DMIC Project in August 2007.[19] DMIC Development Corporation (DMICDC) incorporated in January 2008, is the implementing agency for the project. The DMICDC is tasked with project development, coordination and implementation of the numerous projects. DMICDC has been registered as a company with 49 per cent equity of Government of India with an authorised Capital of Rs. 10 crore, 26 per cent equity of the JBIC and the remaining held by government financial institutions and private entities. The Japanese Government had also announced financial support the DMIC project in the first phase of $4.5 billion for projects with Japanese participation that involve involving cutting edge technology.

In pursuance of the Cabinet decision dated 15 September, 2011, the equity held in DMICDC by IL&FS (41%) and IDFC (10%) were taken over by IIFCL (41%) and LIC (10%) respectively. The Authorized Capital of DMICDC was increased from Rs. 10 crore to Rs. 100 crore. Secretary, Department of Industrial Policy & Promotion (DIPP) is the ex officio Chairman of DMICDC. The Chief Executive Officer of DMICDC is appointed on the recommendation of a Search Committee headed by the

Cabinet Secretary. In pursuance of the Cabinet decision in August, 2012, equity structure of DMICDC was revised whereby Government of India's equity is retained at 49 per cent, JBIC's (Japan Bank for International Cooperation) equity at 26 per cent, HUDCO at 19.9 per cent, IIFCL at 4.1 per cent and LIC at 1 per cent.[20]

The project spans the states of Uttar Pradesh, Haryana, Rajasthan, Madhya Pradesh, Gujarat and Maharashtra along the Western Dedicated Freight Corridor (DFC) of the railway. Initially, 8 nodes/cities in the six DMIC states were chosen for development. The DMIC is proposed to be developed on either side along the alignment of the 1483 kilometres long Western Dedicated Rail Freight Corridor between Dadri (UP) and Jawaharlal Nehru Port Trust (JNPT), Navi Mumbai. The project seeks to create a strong economic base with a globally competitive environment and state-of-the-art infrastructure to activate local commerce, enhance investments and attain sustainable development. A model Industrial Corridor of international standards is proposed to be developed with emphasis on expanding the manufacturing and services base and creating a "Global Manufacturing and Trading Hub". Majority of projects in DMIC are envisaged to be implemented through Public Private Partnership.[21]

In the initial phase, Special Purpose Vehicles (SPVs) were constituted in Five DMIC projects. Four DMIC projects were identified to be launched. The details of the projects are:[22]

- Ahmedabad-Dholera Special Investment Region in Gujarat
- Shendra-Bidkin Industrial Park in Maharashtra
- Integrated Industrial Township Project in Greater Noida, Uttar Pradesh
- Integrated Industrial Township Project in Vikram Udyogpuri in Ujjain, Madhya Pradesh.

The requisite land was transferred to the SPVs by the respective state governments. DMIC trust released matching equity to the SPVs. Master planning, environmental clearance, and a legislative framework granting authority to SPVs have been accomplished. Work on Trunk Infrastructure packages which includes Common Effluent Treatment Plant (CETP), Administrative Business Centre (ABC), Water Treatment Plant (WTP),

Sewage Treatment Plant (STP) and Roads and Services are ready to commence after finalization of tenders which have already been floated.

What was the Proposed Development?

The Cabinet in its meeting held in August, 2007 approved development of 24 investment regions/industrial areas under the project. Following six Investment Regions and six Industrial Areas were approved to be developed in Phase I of the project. The following are the investment regions:

- Dadri-Noida—Ghaziabad Region in Uttar Pradesh as General Manufacturing Investment Region;
- Manesar-Bawal Region in Haryana as Auto Component/Automobile Investment Region;
- Kushkhera-Bhiwadi-Neemrana Region in Rajasthan as General Manufacturing/Automobile/Auto Component Investment Region;
- Bharuch-Dahej Region in Gujarat as Petroleum, Chemical and Petro-Chemical Investment Region (PCPIR);
- Igatpuri-Nashik-Sinnar Region in Maharashtra as General Manufacturing Investment Region;
- Pitampura-Dhar-Mhow in Madhya Pradesh as General Manufacturing Investment Region.

Below is the List of the Industrial Areas:

- Meerut-Muzaffarnagar Zone in Uttar Pradesh as Engineering & Manufacturing Industrial Area;
- Faridabad-Palwal Zone in Haryana as Engineering & Manufacturing Industrial Area;
- Jaipur-Dausa Zone in Rajasthan as Marble/Leather/Textile Industrial Area; (Subsequently, Government of Rajasthan requested to replace this IA with Kishangarh, Ajmer);
- Vadodara-Ankleshwar Zone in Gujarat as General Manufacturing Industrial Area;
- Industrial Area with Greenfield Port at Dighi in Maharashtra;
- Nimach-Nayagaon in Madhya Pradesh as Engineering and Agro-Processing Industrial Area.

Following 12 investment regions/industrial areas identified tentatively for development in Phase II of the project:

- Kundli – Sonepat Investment Region
- Ajmer-Kishangarh Investment Region
- Bharuch-Dahej Investment Region
- Dhule-Nardhana Investment Region
- Ratlam-Nagda Investment Region

The identified industrial areas are:

- Rewari-Hissar Industrial Area
- Rajsamand-Bhilwara Industrial Area
- Pali-Marwar Industrial Area
- Surat-Navsari Industrial Area
- Valsad-Umbergaon Industrial Area
- Pune-Khed Industrial Area
- Shajhapur-Dewas Industrial Area

Initially, the following eight investment regions/industrial areas were taken up for development as Industrial Cities:

- Ahmedabad-Dholera Investment Region, Gujarat
- Shendra-Bidkin Industrial Park city near Aurangabad, Maharashtra
- Manesar-Bawal Investment Region, Haryana
- Khushkhera-Bhiwadi-Neemrana Investment Region, Rajasthan
- Pithampur-Dhar-Mhow Investment Region, Madhya Pradesh
- Dadri-Noida-Ghaziabad Investment Region, Uttar Pradesh and
- Dighi Port Industrial Area, Maharashtra
- Jodhpur-Pali-Marwar Industrial Area, Rajasthan

In the third meeting held on 18-19 March, 2013, the following investment proposals were considered and approved:

- Model Solar Power Project Neemrana, Rajasthan
- Water Desalination Project at Dahej, Gujarat
- Logistic Data Bank Project

The following six investment proposals worth Rs. 2215.03 Crore were considered in the fourth meeting of DMIC trust which was held on September 10, 2013:

- Vikram Udyogpuri, Ujjain, Madhya Pradesh
- Integrated Industrial Township at Greater Noida, UP
- Multi Modal Logistics Hub at Greater Noida near Dadri
- Improvement of Water Supply System to Pithampur Industrial Area and Phase-1 of Pithampur-Dhar-Mhow Investment Region, Madhya Pradesh
- Integrated multimodal Logistics Hub, Rewari Haryana
- Construction of New Rail Line from Bhimnath to Dholera Special Investment Region in Gujarat.

The Trust granted in-principle approval in the case of (ii) and (v), and approved the rest.

At its meeting on January 20, 2014, the CCEA approved the projects of Integrated Industrial Township Project at Vikram Udyogpuri near Ujjain, Madhya Pradesh and Integrated Industrial Township Project, Greater Noida. It was also decided that the Model Solar Project in Neemrana, Rajasthan will be operated and influenced by a 100 per cent subsidiary of DMICDC. The SPV in respect of Integrated Industrial Township Project, Greater Noida and the Model Solar Project in Neemrana, Rajasthan, has been formed and the implementation of the project is in progress.

A proposal for transfer of land at Sector 25 and Sector 26 in Dwarka, New Delhi, to DIPP for the development of a world class state-of-the-art Exhibition cum Convention Centre (ECC) and Integrated Freight Complex (Air Cargo Complex) is under consideration.

As regards financial assistance, during the 11th Five Year Plan, after appraisal and approval by competent authorities, an amount of Rs. 219.00 crore was released to the DMICDC for carrying out project development activities.

- During 12th Five Year Plan (2012-2017), an amount of Rs. 7546 crore was allocated for DMIC Project.

- During 2013-14, an amount of Rs. 303.80 crore (Rs. 302.99 crore for project implementation and Rs. 0.81 crore for grant–in-aid for project development related activities) was released to DMIC Project Implementation Trust Fund.
- During 2014-15, an amount of Rs. 693.00 crore was allocated during Budget Estimates 2014-15 for Project Implementation including Exhibition cum Convention Centre Project in Dwarka, New Delhi.
- During 2014-15, an amount of Rs. 214.00 crore was released so far to DMIC Project Implementation Trust Fund for project implementation activities.
- A proposal for utilization of Japanese Assistance Under Japan International Cooperation Agency (JICA) through Special Terms for Economic Partnership (STEP) Loan for DMIC Project was approved by CCEA at its meeting held on January 20, 2014, and further action is in progress.[23]

The Cabinet in its meeting held in August 2007 approved development of 24 investment regions/industrial areas under the project. Six Investment Regions and six Industrial Areas were approved to be developed in Phase I of the project.

Thus, it transpires that the DMIC is a huge ambitious development project on either side of the Western Dedicated Freight Corridor (DFC) of the Indian Ministry of Railways with a band of 150-200 kilometres. It was conceptualized as a global investment and manufacturing destination with emphasis on expanding the manufacturing and services base and establish DMIC as the 'Global Manufacturing and Trading Hub'. This project is going to catapult the bilateral relations to a level that will be the envy of other nations in Asia. The project aims at doubling the employment potential, tripling industrial output and quadrupling exports from the region, in its first five years.

Both India and Japan agreed to set up a project development fund. The initial size of the Fund was agreed upon to be Rs. 1,000 crore (about $212 million). Both the Japanese and Indian governments contributed equally.[24]

The fund will initially finance the preparations of overall development and feasibility studies for the 1483 kilometres DMIC. The corridor would include six mega-investment regions of 200-square-kilometres each and will run through seven states. Each investment region would have a combination of production units, public utilities, logistics, environmental protection facilities, residential area, social infrastructure and administrative services. The first phase of the project was completed by 2012, with an estimated $90 billion (Rs. 4,23,000 crore) invested to develop infrastructure in the investment regions.[25] The minimum processing area in the specifically delineated investment regions will be 40 per cent of the total designated area, which may or may not be contiguous. In addition to the investment regions, the DMIC will also have six industrial areas of 100 square km each. A steering authority, headed by the Finance Minister, is overseeing the project.

Japanese commitment comes from soft funding. Japan has a strategic interest in increasing investment in India. In fact, during the visit of Prime Minister Manmohan Singh to Japan in October 2008, the Joint Statement defined the roadmap for the advancement of Strategic and Global Partnership between the two countries.[26] DMIC is a unique application of the Public Private Partnership (PPP) approach to infrastructural development in India.

In the joint statement, both the prime ministers reaffirmed their commitment to the realisation of the Western corridor of the DFC project, as the flagship project of India-Japan cooperation, with the Japanese ODA loan utilizing Japan's Special Terms of Economic Partnership (STEP) scheme and confirmed their readiness to jointly initiate the first phase (Rewari-Vadodara sector) of the project. India commissioned the Western Corridor of the DFC with electric traction system. The assistance began with an ODA Loan for Engineering Services, with the overall loan volume for the first phase being roughly Yen 450 billion based on the provisional project design.

Indeed, the DMIC, which is linked to the Western Corridor of DFC Project, has the potential to transform the dynamics of the India-Japan economic engagement. In the unique application of the PPP approach, the

Japan Bank for International Cooperation (JBIC) and India Infrastructure Finance Company Ltd. (IIFCDC)/Delhi Mumbai Industrial Corridor Development Corporation (DMICDC) worked together closely for the joint establishment of a Project Development Fund. Japanese companies agreed to participate in the five early bird projects in DMIC region in the areas of logistics, human resource development, power generation and enclave development. The DMICDC agreed to take up select projects for early implementation in the Project States alongside the master planning exercise.

During Prime Minister Yukio Hatoyama's visit to India in December 2009, two MoUs were signed. The first MoU assured collaboration between DMICDC and the Japanese External Trade Organisation on two-dozen industry-based communities, while also promising environmental efficiency. The second MoU established a project development fund, which served as the financial common-ground between the two partners.[27] The $75 million will be paid back to the JBIC in about 18 years.

Differences on CEPA and How those were Resolved

As was with the nuclear issue, there existed differences on the conclusion of a Comprehensive Economic Partnership Agreement (CEPA).[28] Even after twelve rounds of negotiations, a number of issues in the proposed India-Japan CEPA remained unresolved, including items in the negative list of products to be protected from tariff-cuts and quality control norms for import of farm goods. As a result, reducing existing non-tariff barriers (NTBs) was a critical factor in increasing market access for Indian products in Japan.

Japan retains strong technical barriers to trade (TBT), and also maintains stringent sanitary and phytosanitary measures (SPS). These act as NTBs to Indian export items such as pharmaceuticals, chemicals, biotechnology, and cosmetic sector goods. Indian pharmaceutical companies felt deterred by the stringent SPS, TBT and environmental norms. Japan is the world's second-largest drug market, but a potential Indian pharmaceutical exporter had to wait up to 5 to 7 years after filing his application before receiving the legal documents to start his export business. While India insisted that both the parties agree to a mutual recognition agreement in pharmaceutical sector and recommended the application of the same testing norms set by the US Food and Drug Administration (FDA), Japan contended that these are not stringent enough and preferred to push its own testing measures. This was one major reason the CEPA was delayed.

Even in the automobile sector where Japan has already made a major market penetration in India, the Indian industry continued to seek greater protection in these items. Therefore, joint collaboration proved to be a success story. Japan is known for its frustratingly prolonged process of decision-making in any business activity and the delay is much more in sensitive sector such as market access in agricultural and dairy sectors. The implementation norms of SPS are so stringent that it took 15 years for India to get clearance to market access for its mango. Rules of origin, which lay down how much of an imported item should be allowed under the CEPA norms, was another contentious area. No wonder, the best quality of Indian mango, Alphanso for example, sells at an exorbitant price in the Japanese market as market access is restricted in terms of quantity.

Even in the service sector, differences exist. Both took time to agree to accept foreign professionals with degrees and diplomas to join the workforce, confronting a significant demographic issue, resulting in an expanding senior population, exacerbated by a dropping birth rate, and maintaining a rigorous immigration system. In a globalised economy, this exclusivist strategy contradicts the forward-looking policy. Japan must implement serious structural adjustments in this area. Japan also charges a 15 per cent withholding tax (the portion of a payment withheld by the paying party for taxes), which was a major barrier to Indian professionals working in Japan. Japan needed to look into it in the long-term interest of bilateral relations. The integration process was delayed when such irritants were not addressed on time.

What is CEPA?

CEPA is a market access agreement between two countries to enter each other's markets for their products on the terms agreed upon in the agreement. After several rounds of negotiations, India's then commerce minister Anand Sharma informed at a function organised by the FICCI, USIBC and Archam Negotiations on CEPA that the negotiations on CEPA were concluded during then-Prime Minister Manmohan Singh's visit to Japan in December 2012, and that the market-opening pact would be signed in a month.[29] However, as it transpired, the CEPA between the two countries came into force in August 2011.[30] Despite the agreement, bilateral trade stood at measly $16 billion as compared to Sino-Indian trade amounting to $70 billion and Sino-Japanese trade at a whopping of $343 billion in 2014.[31]

The agreement had two major concerns, namely: the infrastructure in India, and non-tariff barriers in Japan. On the infrastructure front, the two countries reached an agreement in August 2011 collaborating on the huge, $90-billion Delhi–Mumbai Industrial Corridor (DMIC) project. The project agreement appeared highly promising in the environment of the new manufacturing policy whereby India was positioned to target to increase the share of manufacturing in GDP to 25 per cent within a decade, potentially creating 100 million jobs.

Japan had invested in dedicated freight corridor west project, strategic port facility in Chennai, and the development of strategic assets including highways and dams in North East Region where India's immediate neighbour is eyeing for territorial expansion. Japan has set up multi-product SEZ and clusters, custom-free and warehousing zones (in Neemrana in Rajasthan), leading to greater economic integration in Asia. In 2014 Kyoto-Kashi pact was signed between two countries, and Kashi became known as the 'city of ten-thousand shrines' in the 'land of rising sun'. Under this agreement Kyoto and Kashi would prepare a detailed roadmap for making Kashi a 'smart city', retaining its rich culture, tradition and heritage.

India's *Economic Times* reported that the CEPA will bring immediate gains to exporters of textiles, seafood and spices to Japan as duties on these products would be eliminated on the first day of elimination. It would ultimately result in removal of duties on almost 90 per cent of products traded between the two countries. Other sectors that were expected to gain from the CEPA through lower duties included agricultural products such as mangoes, citrus fruit, spices, instant tea, most spirits, petrochemical and chemical products, cement and jewellery.

The CEPA signed in February in 2011 was expected to boost trade to $25 billion by 2014 from $10.36 billion in 2009-10. That did not happen even till 2021. Bilateral trade between the two countries totalled $21.98 during fiscal 2023 While the Indian automobile and automobile parts industry were largely shielded from tariff cuts by their inclusion in the negative list of items, India agreed to reduce tariffs on auto parts made of steel, which is a major gain for the Japanese industry. Japan was also expected to increase exports of consumer durables, such as electronics, which were cheaper in India, but India's tariff reductions occurred in stages over 10 years. The Indian textile business benefits significantly since Japan imposes tariffs of up to 15 per cent on the item, compared to an average import duty of less than 5 per cent. So, what was expected at the time the agreement was signed has not been realised.

Despite several rounds of negotiations and agreement, there are hurdles at the implementation stage. For example, tariff and non-tariff barriers do still exist. Japan continues to impose import prohibitions and quantitative restrictions on imports from India, for example, on fish and silk items. Also, as mentioned briefly earlier, Japan's Sanitary and Phytosanitary Measures (SPS) are major barriers to Indian exports of poultry, meat, shrimps and fruits like mangoes and grapes. This issue highlights the need of sharing and facilitating the exchange of technology under the agreement to promote Indian exports to Japan.

Since India is the biggest recipient of Japanese ODA, engaging Japan economically is always important for India. India is also a premium destination for foreign direct investment from Japan. Attracting Japanese investment, technology and business is crucial for transforming India into Asia's new production line. India's economic involvement with Japan has a strategic rationale. India is far more comfortable with Japanese businesses investing in the development of strategic infrastructure assets, whereas Chinese investment in infrastructure is viewed with caution and suspicion due to security concerns and mistrust, even if such investment can help India address some of its trade imbalance with China.

For Japan economic partnership is shaped by realpolitik too. Japanese investment was very vital for Chinese miracle, as China was the highest recipient of Japanese aid between 1980 and 2003. Greater economic integration with China has not translated into political trust between the two countries, hence disputes over Senkaku islands escalated. There was no such irritant with India. During the Indian Prime Minister's visit to Japan in 2014, the two countries announced 'India-Japan Investment Promotion Partnership'. Japan promised to invest more than $35 billion in India. ODA and private investment is biggest foreign investment by any single country into India. Substantial contract on export of rare earth minerals from India to Japan is on anvil, which would offset Japan's reliance on China for supply. Both India and Japan are concerned that their growing economic interdependence on China might make the Indian and Japanese economies more vulnerable to Beijing's economic coercion. Secondly, both the nations are exasperated by China's strategy of deploying surrogates in East and South Asia, primarily North Korea and Pakistan, to wear them down. One example is the China-Pakistan Economic Corridor (CPEC), a $45 billion project that runs along India's very sensitive Karakoram border.

The Shinkansen Project

India-Japan bilateral relations scaled new heights following a slew of agreements in the economic and defence fields reached by Prime Minister Narendra Modi and Japanese Prime Minister Abe Shinzo during the latter's visit to India in December 2015. Over a dozen agreements were inked of which three stands out: introduction of the big-ticket agreement on Japan's High Speed Railways (HSR) technologies (the Shinkansen system or the Bullet train) to the Mumbai-Ahmedabad route, civil nuclear cooperation and transfer of defence equipment and technology cooperation. Among the other concrete outcomes was a reaffirmation of the commitment made by Abe in 2014 during Modi's visit to Japan to inject a massive $34 billion over the next five years.

But for the Japanese firms to follow through with the investment commitment made by Abe, they need a predictable tax and regulatory regime to which Modi was committed. Like most businesses in the West, the Japanese seek certainty and predictability. Moreover, the Japanese businesses are very cautious and take a lot of time in the negotiation process and conducting numerous risk analyses of the project in question. This could be frustrating to the other party, raising doubt about the commitment and sincerity of the Japanese companies. One needs to understand, therefore, the negotiating style and business practices of the Japanese for a proper understanding of the business proposal. For example, lack of proper labour reforms for a long time in India was a major complaint by the Japanese companies as these wanted a free hand in dealing with the labour engaged in the project. Many of such bottlenecks hindering participation of Japanese companies in Indian projects have now been removed, though certain grey areas do still remain. The Goods and Services Tax legislation which was stuck in parliamentary logjam but adopted subsequently further shall facilitate a smooth entry for Japanese firms in the Indian business market.

The Shinkansen project is a 508-kilometres high speed railway agreed for construction between Indian economic centre of Mumbai and the western city of Ahmedabad at a top speed of 320 km/h (200 mph) along western coast. The plan is to build a standard gauge using Shinkansen technology. Japan will cover 80 per cent of the Rs. 98,000 crore (equivalent to 1.2 trillion Japanese yen or $16 billion in 2019) project cost through a soft loan. The project is planned to carry passengers between the two cities in just three hours, with ticket prices pegged between Rs. 2,500 to Rs. 3,000, cheaper than airfare. The targeted completion is around 2027-2028.

Indeed, Japan's high-speed train, the Shinkansen, with its promise of speed, reliability and safety is going to be a significant milestone and game changer in India-Japan ties.[32] At the moment, India does not have high speed rail lines operating at over 200 km/h (120 mph) under the definition of the International Union of Railways (UIC), the international rail transport industry body. As of 2021, the fastest train services operating in India is Gatimaan Express, with a top speed of 160 km/h (99 mph).[33] At the 2014 general elections, the BJP announced its desire to build the Diamond Quadrilateral high speed rail project, which was to connect the cities of Chennai, Delhi, Kolkata and Mumbai via high-speed rail. After the party came to power, the project was approved as a priority for the new government in the President's speech. It was estimated at the time that the construction of one kilometer of high-speed railway track would cost between Rs. 100 crore ($14 million) and Rs. 140 crore ($20 million), which was 1014 times higher than the constructing a standard railway.

As per the plan, India would have two types of gauges for high-speed rail. The new high-speed rail lines with Japanese technology were to be in standard gauge, while older tracks upgraded to high-speed rail standard were to be 5' and 6" in broad gauge. Thus, there was no interchangeability between newly laid tracks and the older upgraded tracks for passenger and cargo traffic.

The story of India's desire to introduce high-speed train date back to the mid-1980s when then Railway Minister Madhavrao Scindia mooted the proposal for the first time. A high-speed rail line between Delhi and Kanpur via Agra was proposed. An internal study found the proposal not viable due to the high cost of construction and the inability of passengers to bear higher fares than those for normal trains. Instead, the railways introduced Shatabdi trains that ran at 140 km/h. The Ministry of Railways set up the National High-Speed Rail Corporation Ltd. as a government company on February 12, 2016 to promote high-speed rail corridors.

On July 25, 2013, the Rail Vikas Nigam Limited (RVNL) set up a corporation called High Speed Rail Corporation of India Lt (HSRC) to deal with the proposed high-speed rail corridor projects. As a wholly owned subsidiary of the RVNL, the corporation was tasked to handle tendering, pre-feasibility studies, awarding of contracts, and execution of the project. The corporation comprises four members, all of whom are railway officials. All high-speed rail lines are to be implemented as public-private partnerships (PPP) on a Design, Build, Finance, Operate, and Transfer (DBFOT) basis. The corporation was officially formed on October 29, 2013.

The Mumbai-Ahmedabad Shinkansen project, India's first high-speed rail corridor, started construction in 2017 and is expected to be completed by 2027. The foundation stone was placed in a ceremony held on September 14, 2017, when Japanese Prime Minister Abe Shinzo and the Indian Prime Minister Narendra Modi flagged off the construction work in Ahmedabad. The JR East/Hitachi E5 Series Shinkansen trains will be used in this line.

It has a maximum operational speed of 320 km/h and an average speed of 260 km/h. The Shinkansen trains are envisaged to run on elevated corridors to isolate high-speed train tracks and thereby prevent trespassing by animals or people. The current conventional lines between Amritsar-New Delhi, and Ahmedabad-Mumbai runs through suburban and rural areas, which are flat and have no tunnels. The Ahmedabad-Mumbai line runs near the coast and therefore, has more bridges, and parts of it are in backwaters or forests. The 1987 RDSO/JICA feasibility study found the Mumbai-Ahmedabad line to be the most promising.

In commitment to its friendship, Japan made an extraordinary package and technical assistance on easy terms. The project can also be seen from the prism of strategic perspective. The project also symbolises strengthening of relations between Asia's second and third largest economies as Modi and Abe sought to balance China's rise as the dominant Asian power. The India-Japan Shinkansen deal took a lead over China, which was also conducting feasibility studies for high-speed trains on other parts of India's dilapidated rail network.

Modi observed: "This enterprise will launch a revolution in Indian railways and speed up India's journey into the future. It will become an engine of economic transformation in India."[34] Japan was gracious to offer "highly concessional loan" of over Rs. 78,000 crore at an interest rate of 0.1 per cent rate with repayment over 50 years and moratorium for 15 years. A bullet train between the two cities will cut travel time from eight hours to around three. The issue of repayment of the loan remains somewhat unclear. What if the ticket collections all short of expectations for complete loan repayment because the operational costs of a high-speed queue are considerable, leaving only a fraction of the ticket revenues to pay down the original debt—these are issues that remain unclear.

The decision to introduce the Shinkansen rail system was based on the recommendation of a panel headed by then NITI Aayog Vice-Chairman Arvind Panagariya, which chose the low-cost funding proposed by Japan International Cooperation Agency (JICA) at less than one per cent interest rate apart from a commitment for technology transfer and local manufacturing for a specified period. Indeed, the Shinkansen system of bullet trains had the best safety record, with no fatalities and delays of less than a minute.

Earlier, India's hopes from bullet trains were marred by the experience of Taiwan, which has been operating the high-speed train service based on Japan's Shinkansen bullet train system since 2007. Saddled with huge losses owing to high depreciation and interest payments and low ridership numbers, the operator sought a bailout by the government to turnaround the troubled business.

The project received the approval of the Cabinet and will be executed under the provisions of the existing Railway Act, 1989. This excused the Railways from having to go to Parliament to adopt a law for high-speed trains, saving the project from potential delays due to parliamentary procedures. Furthermore, it was recognised that granting governments a stake in the project was critical to its success. A new organisation, formed from a Centre-state joint venture like the DMRC, is charged with carrying out the project with Japan's aid. Following consultations with the Japanese, a three-member empowered committee, consisting of the chairman of the Railway Board and secretaries from the Departments of Industrial Policy and Promotion and Expenditure, will make the required decisions.

This model of execution will serve as a pattern for all future bullet-train corridors in the Diamond Quadrilateral.

Not only is Japan providing 81 per cent of the $18 billion project at a mere 0.1 per cent, but railway negotiators have assured that the arrangement is far sweeter than the Dedicated Freight Corridor, which had several restrictions for India. Aside from being less expensive, the bullet train loan allows India to carry out civil construction without Japanese participation, which is critical for ensuring timely tender award and implementation, as opposed to the DFC. For the first time, Japan has agreed to distinguish between civil and system contracts. System contracts are those involving installation of signalling system, key safety apparatus, rolling stock, etc. India will buy the entire rolling stock from Japan—the new version of the Shinkansen—while Japan insisted that certain "prime contractors" from Japan are a must in the system contracts which are crucial for safety features like the Shinkansen. These features of the assistance significantly lower the monetary impact of the clause that 30 per cent of the sourcing should be done from Japan. The grace period of the 50-year loan is 15 years and Japan has agreed to partner in areas like setting up technical training centres for skills upgrade. Around $13 billion is the cost of construction, while around $1 million has been worked out as eventual cost of rolling stock (the trains).

India and the Regional Comprehensive Economic Partnership (RCEP)

At the East Asia Summit meeting that ended in early November 2019 in Bangkok, where the issue of concluding the much-hyped Regional Comprehensive Economic Partnership (RCEP) agreement was at centre stage, India ultimately decided to opt out, saying its key concerns were not addressed. Making a forceful argument in his address at the summit, Indian Prime Minister Narendra Modi said: "The present form of the RCEP Agreement does not fully reflect the basic spirit and the agreed guiding principles of RCEP." Elaborating, he said: "It also does not address satisfactorily India's outstanding issues and concerns. In such a situation, it is not possible for India to join [the] RCEP Agreement."[35]

What is RCEP and why was it Important for India?

It is a proposed free-trade agreement between the 10 member states of the Association of Southeast Asian Nations (ASEAN)—Brunei, Cambodia, Indonesia, Laos, Malaysia, Myanmar, the Philippines, Singapore, Thailand, Vietnam—and what is now five FTA partners—China, Japan, South Korea, Australia and New Zealand. India, the sixth partner, quit the pact at the November Bangkok summit. In response, China announced that India would still be welcome to join RCEP whenever it is ready.

RCEP negotiations were formally launched in November 2012 at the ASEAN Summit in Cambodia. In 2017, the 16 prospective signatories accounted for a population of 3.4 billion people with a total gross domestic product (GDP) of $49.5 trillion, approximately 39 per cent of the world's GDP. Had this mega-FTA been concluded in Bangkok, it may have been the world's large move in the right direction. It has given enough elbow room to India to handle bilaterally issues with other countries. The onus is now on other members. If they are unable to resolve India's concerns, India will remain out of the trade deal.

The Stance of Industry and Dairy Farmers

Domestic industry and dairy farmers had strong reservations about the trade pact. India's trade deficit with RCEP nations is $105 billion, with China alone accounting for $53.5 billion. The main worry was over Chinese manufactured goods and dairy products from New Zealand flooding Indian markets.

He trade pact was also viewed as damaging to the government's Make in India initiative. India sought strict rules of origin to guarantee that the pact was not misused by non-partner countries, as well as an auto-trigger mechanism to safeguard itself against a surge in imports. E-commerce and trade remedies were among other key areas of concern that were not satisfactorily addressed. New Delhi had proposed different levels of tariff concessions for China to safeguard its domestic industry from cheap imports. On the other hand, India did not get any credible assurance on market access and non-tariff barriers. India was also worried about keeping 2014 as the base year for tariff reductions.

India had been consistent about raising these issues from the start of RCEP negotiations. Many of its earlier trade agreements had been lopsided and hurt domestic industry, and New Delhi was keen not to make the same mistakes again. The Modi government felt that previous governments engaged in poor negotiations in reaching free-trade agreements, which is why it wanted to review its trade pacts with South Korea and ASEAN. India is now expected to pursue separate trade agreements with some of the countries that will be part of the bloc, such as Australia and New Zealand, as well as those with which negotiations have not made substantial progress in recent years, such as the European Union.

The decision to stay away from the mega-trade deal resulted in a political blame game between the ruling party and the party it ousted from power, Congress. It was the United Progressive Alliance led by the Congress Party that agreed to explore an India-China FTA in 2007 and join RCEP negotiations with 2011-12. The Modi government now blames the UPA for negotiating a lopsided deal. The impact of these decisions resulted in India's trade deficit with RCEP nations increasing from US$7 billion in 2004 to US$78 billion in 2014, leaving domestic industry reeling under the impact of those decisions. Therefore, India made a strong case at the RCEP summit for an outcome that would be favourable to all countries and all sectors. In 2018-19, while India's total imports from RCEP countries was $172.9 billion, its exports accounted for only $67.8 billion, leaving it with a deficit of $105.1 billion. Briefly put, the balance of trade for India with all 15 nations in the RCEP group is unfavourable.

Modi said that "when I measure the RCEP Agreement with respect to the interests of all Indians, I do not get a positive answer" and "therefore, neither the talisman of Gandhiji nor my own conscience permit me to join RCEP." It was a strong rebuttal to the position of the other 15 states. Modi also said that in the last seven years of RCEP negotiations, many things, including global economic and trade scenarios, had changed, and India cannot overlook this. Indeed, India had been proactively, constructively and meaningfully engaged in the RCEP negotiations since their inception and had worked for the "cherished objective of striking a balance, in the spirit of give and take."

The Confederation of Indian Industry (CII) said it will continue to support and work with the government in its endeavour to integrate with the global economy through mutually beneficial trade agreements. While welcoming the RCEP leaders' joint statement acknowledging India's legitimate concerns, it hoped that the concerns would be addressed soon to the mutual satisfaction of all RCEP countries.

Dairy farmers welcomed the RCEP news along with small businesses, micro and small entrepreneurs, copper producers, bicycle manufacturers, e-commerce players, data service providers and others. Besides laying down the template for future trade negotiations, the RCEP decision also underscored the need to make the country's exports more competitive. India has already convinced ASEAN countries to review the FTA with India, and it made similar requests to Japan and South Korea. It is also simultaneously negotiating a trade pact with the US and an FTA with the European Union. Both of these jurisdictions are seeking similar concessions as those deliberated in RCEP, which includes free flow of data, integration of the agriculture market, and so on. India finds both the US and China to be among the most difficult jurisdictions regarding market access. So, will India concede? In view of the ongoing trade war between the US and China, it remains unclear what India's stance would be.

Arguments For and Against

Some have argued that RCEP may have created opportunities in the manufacturing sector associated to the global value chain (GVC). Others, however, argue that this would also have been neutralised due to India's lack of infrastructure. GVC manufacturing enables multinational firms to employ several nations, reaping the benefits of lower labour costs. With labour prices rising in China, firms are going to newer jurisdictions such as Indonesia, Vietnam, Thailand, and India to manufacture products. However, India was concerned that Chinese enterprises would take advantage of this opportunity to dump a large number of their products in the country. Over the last three years, India has imposed the highest anti-dumping duties on Chinese companies.

Although India refused to concede space in the RCEP negotiations for policy-making aimed at local data storage and processing, its domestic responsibilities are obvious. To increase export competitiveness, India will need to speed up reforms. The Bangkok choice was influenced in large part by the fact that Indian manufacturing is not competitive enough. Policymakers are also concerned that a deluge of imports from RCEP partner countries could wipe out many Indian players. As mentioned, out of the 15 other countries in RCEP, India has a total trade deficit of more than $105 billion. Understandably, India sought safeguard processes such as an automatic trigger safeguard mechanism (ATSM)—a process that automatically increases levies once imports cross a given threshold—which the negotiating partners considered an irritant.[36]

Before expecting the 15 RCEP countries to soften their stance on India's concerns, India ought to keep its own house in order. This includes round-the-clock quality electricity, cheap and efficient logistics, and access to cheaper and high quality capital. India's export-to-GDP ratio dipped from 25.3 per cent in 2012-13 to 19.7 per cent by the end of 2017-18. The list also includes the reforms required to push the micro, small and medium enterprise (MSME) segment. The RCEP countries are aware of limits and have left a window open for India to return for the agreement's signature in February 2020. That did not happen, therefore India's position remained unchanged.

In an op-ed article in *The Economic Times* on 8 November 2019, Columbia University Professor of Economics Arvind Panagariya made a strong argument for India to reconsider its exit, because staying out would not be in India's economic interest.[37] He questioned the wide range of claims made by pundits that India's previous trade deals had hurt its economy and that the RCEP would make things even worse.

He also rebutted arguments that demand a return to the inglorious days of "self-sufficiency" and insisted that the withdrawal reflected the weakness of the government against the efforts of protectionist lobbies. Panagariya writes: "During 2000-11, India signed 14 preferential trade agreements (PTAs), 10 of which were bilateral agreements with individual countries (which included Japan, South Korea, Malaysia and Singapore) and four were plurilateral agreements (including with the Association of Southeast Asian Nations ... and the Southern Common Market, Mercosur, in South America). What will likely come as a surprise to most is the fact that the effects of these agreements on trade have been modest. Thus, while India's imports from its 10 bilateral partners added up to 13.3 per cent of its overall imports in 2007, that number actually fell slightly to 11.8 per cent in 2017. Similarly, exports to these 10 partners added up to 13.7 per cent in 2007, and stayed nearly the same at 14 per cent in 2017. India's imports under the ASEAN pact, its most significant plurilateral agreement, inched up from 9.6 per cent in 2007 to 10.2 per cent in 2017, while exports expanded modestly faster from 9.5 per cent to 12 per cent."[38]

He examined the share of the trade deficit contributed by India's agreements and found that India actually improved its bilateral positions with FTA partners during 2007-17. He further found from data that large parts of the Indian economy had not come under stress because of intensified import competition under these agreements, but found that during 2007-17, the sectors in which imports under trade agreements had grown faster than overall imports from all trading partners by even 25 per cent accounted for only 6-7 per cent of overall imports.

Taking a micro view and considering the larger scope of RCEP—over three billion people and roughly 40 per cent of global GDP—Panagariya argued that access to this market on a "frictionless", duty-free basis would have provided tremendous advantages to India's exports. He further observed that "in the absence of trade barriers on its imports (imposed by itself) and its exports (imposed by partner countries), India would have had an excellent opportunity to integrate itself into regional and global value-chains, where India's participation has been low. India would have been more easily able to attract foreign direct investment (FDI) and to also take over production in sectors that China is now vacating."

How might an RCEP deal vary from proposed agreements with the United States or the EU? Agreements like the Trans-Pacific Partnership (TPP) presented a greater challenge. The TPP demanded concessions on several contentious non-trade issues, including environmental and labour rules, intellectual property (IP) protection, and the operations of state-owned firms. In contrast, RCEP prioritised trade liberalisation.

True, India runs a huge trade deficit with China, accounting for about 40 per cent of its overall deficit, but had it signed the pact, India could have negotiated hard for expansion of access to the Chinese market in areas of its comparative strength, such as pharmaceuticals and IT services. On the import side, it could have sought exclusions of especially sensitive sectors and a more gradual liberalization schedule. This would have allowed India to simultaneously exploit greater market integration with Asia, while allowing it time and economic space to adjust.

To India's satisfaction and according to government data, its trade deficit with China reduced significantly from over $53 billion in the fiscal 2018-19 to $48.66 billion in fiscal 2019-2020 owing to a reduction in imports on account of imports decline,[39] after it had reached nearly $50 billion, even without a trade agreement. The trade deficit between the two countries stood at $63 billion in the financial year 2017-18.[40] A trade deficit is an amount by which the cost of a country's imports exceeds the cost of its exports.

India has an adverse balance of trade with not just Japan but also South Korea as well in the North East Asia. For example, Korean auto giants Hyundai and Kia have cost India billions of dollars in trade deficit as free trade agreements allowed them to import indiscriminately. The same applies to Japan as well. Both Japan and South Korean business entities are highly nationalistic and they prefer to buy from the local market even at a higher cost, which profit-oriented Indian business unfortunately lack. While Japanese and Korean governments do not stop any steel export from India to their countries, India is unable to do so even a ton of steel in both these two countries due to their highly nationalist spirit. Japan and Korea prefer to buy steel from their domestic market even if it costs a hundred dollars a ton more, but will not allow an Indian firm to become their supplier.[41] This was one of the reasons why India stayed out of the RCEP.

India's main import items from China included clocks and watches, musical instruments, toys, sports goods, furniture, mattresses, plastics, electrical machinery, electronic equipment, chemicals, iron and steel items, fertilisers, mineral fuel and metals. In view of the ever widening trade deficit, New Delhi time and again raised concerns and took steps as framing technical regulations and quality norms for several products to cut dependence on China for imports. India also imposed anti-dumping duties on several goods that were dumped in Indian market at below the average prices from China with a view to guard domestic players from cheap imports. As many as 371 products were identified for technical regulations and 150 products worth about $47 billion of imports came under this purview.

Over 50 quality control orders (QCOs) and other technical regulations were notified including on electronic goods, toys, air conditioners, bicycle parts, chemicals, safety glass, pressure cooker, items of steel, electrical items such as cables. China accounts for about 14 per cent of India's imports and is a major supplier for sectors like mobile phones, telecom, power, plastic toys, and critical pharma ingredients. Similarly, foreign direct investment (FDI) from China into India also dipped to $163.78 million in 2019-20 from $229 million in the previous fiscal. India's position on the RCEP can be deciphered from its concern over unfavourable trade balance with many RCEP member countries. However, there are other opinions as well.

For example, writing for *The Hindu*, Biswajit Dhar remarked that after the RCEP opt-out, now is the time for a shake-up.[42] He argued that India must shed its defensive mindset in trade deals and, instead, work on creating globally competitive sectors. In an editorial, *The Hindu* observed that "India must not take the easiest way out on the trade deal and walk out of talks.[43] *The Times of India* was a bit more critical of India's decision to stay out. Commenting in an editorial dated 7 November 2019, it said "isolationism is not an option." Making a forceful argument, it observed: "From a practical standpoint, it's not realistic to turn inwards in the search for efficiency before opening up again. Being plugged into the global economy through trade agreements and enhancing domestic competitiveness are interrelated. Therefore, [the] government must pursue domestic reforms simultaneously with negotiations to expand India's basket of trade agreements."[44]

Indeed, in line with global norms, India has trade agreements with about 54 countries, of which many are WTO members. These trade agreements cover more than half of international trade. Taking a critical view of the Modi government's decision to stay out of the pact, the editorial observed: "Given this backdrop, India's decision-making should be guided by a major feature of international trade: regional trade agreements can lead to trade diversion. To illustrate, even if India is the most efficient exporter of a certain kind of apparel, a new regional trade agreement which excludes India can lead to a diversion of our exports to a less efficient producer. Consequently, sitting on the sidelines is not an option."

Now that India is wary of a surge in Chinese exports, if it remains outside of the pact, it should look into alternative partners with whom it has economic complementarity, such as the EU, the US or Australia, all of which share strategic interests with India. In contrast, rules and decision-making in China are opaque, and market access is typically granted based on strategic considerations.

In order to cope with the changing times and new situations, the Modi government needs to shore up its sagging competitiveness through domestic reforms aimed at enhancing long-term economic strength and unshackling rigid markets while at the same time accelerating negotiations on other trade agreements. With a clear majority, the government should not feel diffident about making major decisions that would be in India's medium—and long-term economic interests.

In this context, the political blame game must stop forthright. Though the preceding Congress-led UPA government had made a case for joining RCEP in November 2012, it was not oblivious to a possible surge in Chinese imports and was mindful of adequate safeguards. Therefore, staying out of RCEP is not an option for India. It is necessary that India remains engaged actively so that the agenda and pace of negotiations address India's concerns. The good thing is that India has not withdrawn acrimoniously. The door is still open. It is unlikely that the Modi government would walk away from its "Act East" policy and leave India wholly disadvantaged.

For the time being, India is not ready, which is why industry and trade experts backed India's decision not to join the RCEP agreement. India wants stringent rules of origin for all imports under the pact. It wants safeguard mechanisms to prevent import surges to protect the interests of domestic industry. Trade experts say the government must have a clear strategy going forward on trade pacts.

The situation on India's stance on the RCEP may change and potentially toughen under the new situation, as COVID-19 has forced a major reassessment of many of the country's policy concerns. India has historically relied on free trade agreements (FTAs) to expand its trading reach. However, it turned out that these agreements were arranged in such a way that they were harming rather than helping the Indian economy. Experts believe that the manner these FTAs were drafted has damaged, rather than benefited, the country's commercial relations.

They say that as vaccination increased and the threat of COVID-19 ebbed around the world, the spotlight now will firmly be on economic growth. According to experts, there could be compelling reasons for India to revive trade links with the neighbouring countries but not on the strength of the FTAs.[45]

In the meantime, Cambodia's Ministry of Commerce expects the RCEP agreement signed by 15 countries in November 2020 could be ratified on January 1, 2022, and then enters into force.[46] Heavily dependent on external trade, Japan was quick to ratify the mega pact on June 25, 2021. Tokyo deposited its ratification instrument with the ASEAN Secretariat, making it the third member to do so toward the possible enforcement of the 15-nation RCEP by the end of 2021.[47] The ASEAN Secretariat processes operating procedures on behalf of the pact, whose members account for about 30 per cent of the world's output, trade and population.

Japan's Economy, Trade and Industry Minister Hiroshi Kajiyama expressed optimism that the "deal will strengthen the link between Japan and the (Asia-Pacific) region, which is the world's growth center". The pact will be Japan's first trade deal involving both China and South Korea, its biggest and third-biggest trade partners, respectively. The Japanese government estimates that the trade treaty could lift the gross domestic product of the world's third-largest economy by about 2.7 per cent.

The trade deal is designed to remove tariffs on 91 per cent of goods, and standardize rules on investment, intellectual property and e-commerce among other trade practices. It also aims to promote optimization of the supply chains within the free trade zone. The pact will enter into effect 60 days after it is ratified by at least six ASEAN members and three other signatory countries.[48] Singapore and China are among the signatories to have completed the ratification process.

The signatory countries expect that ratification of the trade deal is expected to open up more new markets as well as upgrade value chains and integrate them within the region and beyond. To recapitulate, the world's largest regional trade deal was initiated in November 2012 at the 21st ASEAN Summit in Phnom Penh, but it was not endorsed until November 15, due to the complexity of negotiations. Leaders of the 10 ASEAN states, as well as Australia, China, Japan, New Zealand and South Korea witnessed the signing of the agreement via video link following the conclusion of the 4th RCEP Summit on the same day.

The chief purpose of the deal was to promote trade between the 15 signatory Asia-Pacific countries. The 15 signatory countries feel that the RCEP will establish a modern, comprehensive and high-quality partnership framework as well as mutual economic benefits that will facilitate the expansion of supply chains, trade and investment in the region.[49]

It is expected that the RCEP would provide the world a symbol of support for a multilateral free trade system based on the rule of law, and in particular, its rapid contribution to the economic recovery in the region from the COVID-19 crisis. As per the 2019 data, the RCEP has a combined gross domestic product (GDP) to the tune of $26.2 trillion, or 30 per cent of global GDP, and engages 2.2 billion people, or 30 per cent of the world's population. For example, Jakarta-based Economic Research Institute for ASEAN and East Asia (ERIA) found that the RCEP would boost Cambodia's gross domestic product (GDP) an additional 2 per cent, increase exports by an extra 7.3 per cent and raise investment by an added 23.4 per cent.[50]

Way Out

China is responsive to India's concerns. A day after India opted out of RCEP, China, taking a more accommodative stance, said it would follow the principle of "mutual understanding and accommodation" to resolve the outstanding issues raised by India.[51] China also said it would welcome India joining the deal at an early date. Chinese Foreign Ministry spokesman Geng Shuang said that "RCEP is open", adding, "If it is signed and put into implementation, it is conducive for the Indian goods entry into China and other participating countries. In the same vein, it will also help Chinese goods to enter the markets of India and other participating countries." India has been cautious in its response, and is not easily buying China's arguments.

The Confederation of Indian Industry (CII) argues that opting out of RCEP will harm India's exports and future investment flow. CII's main concern is if India is not a part of RCEP, it would hinder India's efforts to increase its integration into regional and global value chains, as preferential and comprehensive agreements facilitate investments and foster the growth of value chains. The CII feels that "not being part of the bloc is tantamount to not having an even footing in terms of preferential access and losing export competitiveness."

The bottom line is that FTAs must be considered for their long-term impact, both on the domestic market and the access they provide. Indian industry is now more focused domestically, but in about a decade's time, it would like to have greater access to the vibrant region outside of it. Thus far, it has done the impact analysis of FTAs only bilaterally, ignoring how these have been integrated into global supply chains. The problem is Indian industry never looked towards RCEP as an opportunity to gain additional market access and to become integrated into a robust regional value chain.

So far, Indian discourse has centred on defensive interests and protection from China. It's time to shift this narrative. Before launching ambitions to integrate its economy with the region, India must conduct due diligence on urgent changes. Delays in this attempt would result in India missing the bus.[52]

The situation on India's stance on the RCEP could further change and might even toughen in the new situation when the COVID-19 has forced a major reassessment of many of the country's policy concerns. India has historically relied on free trade agreements (FTAs) to expand its trading reach. However, it turned out that these agreements were arranged in such a way that they were harming rather than helping the Indian economy. Experts believe that the way these FTAs were framed, the country's trade ties have weakened, rather than strengthening. They say that as vaccination increased and the threat of COVID-19 ebbed around the world, the spotlight will firmly be on economic growth. According to experts, there could be compelling reasons for India to revive trade links with the neighbouring countries but not on the strength of the FTAs.[53]

There is another perspective regarding the RCEP that is worth evaluating. This perspective takes the position that RCEP sans India would be rudderless.[54] The new trading bloc signed by 15 nations on November 15, 2019, would cover 210 crore people, with the member states' combined GDP of $26.2 trillion accounting for around 30 per cent of the global GDP. The finalisation of the deal comes around a year after India announced its decision not to join the grouping, mainly because the terms are skewed in China's favour. The deal would have allowed Chinese goods to flood Indian markets, threatening domestic industries. The pact is also a milestone in China's ambition of becoming a trade lynch-pin.

Among the 15 signatory countries, Japan would be disappointed that India opted to stay out. These 15 countries expect that the agreement will progressively lower tariffs across many areas in the coming years. The pact was first proposed in 2012, and it makes up nearly a third of the world's population and accounts for 29 per cent of global gross domestic product. It aims to lower tariffs, open up trade in services and promote investment to help emerging economies catch up with the rest of the world. While Malaysia's trade minister Mohamed Azmin remarked that eight years of negotiating with blood, sweat and tears have come now to fruition, Singapore Prime Minister Lee Hsien Loong hailed the signing of the RCEP as a "major milestone". Over past eight years, there were 46 negotiating meetings and 19 ministerial meetings to ink the pact, which was hailed as a major step forward for the world at a time when multilateralism was losing ground and global growth slowing.

The RCEP will come into force when six ASEAN countries and three non-ASEAN countries have ratified it. The 15-signatory nations see RCEP showing diversity and how free and open trade and investment is in the common interest of all economies, regardless of their development stages. Realising that their prosperity and success are interlinked, the 15 nations hope that deeper integration and a more interdependent world will ultimately lead to a safer and more prosperous world.

Though India was involved in the negotiations for the past eight years, India pulled out of talks in November 2019, worried that the elimination of tariffs would open its markets to a flood of imports that could harm local producers. Membership to the group would not be open for a while, with the exception of India which could join at its will. Should India decide to join in the future, it would have to re-apply for membership negotiation.

Given the deep economic relations of most ASEAN countries, these countries hope RCEP will allow many of the Chinese companies to invest in the regional markets while they expect to enjoy access to the huge Chinese market. The ASEAN nations also hope that RCEP will help attract investors beyond the region as the Chinese and regional markets will be seen as an "integrated market", making exports much more competitive for the rest of the world.

After the RCEP, at least 65 per cent of the services sectors will be open to foreign participation, with increased foreign shareholding limits.

It is also expected that at least 50 sub-sectors will be open for 51 per cent foreign equity across sectors such as telecommunications, financial services, computer-related services, professional services, and distribution and logistics services. Emerging trade fields including e-commerce, competition policy and intellectual property (IP) rights are also pursued under the RCEP.

Despite RCEP's historic size, it falls short of other major trade deals in the level of market access. The deal will eliminate tariffs on 91 per cent of goods, less than the revised TPP or Japan's economic partnership agreement with the European Union. Japan will eliminate 61 per cent of tariffs on agriculture imports from ASEAN nations, Australia and New Zealand, 56 per cent for China, and 49 per cent for South Korea, while maintaining tariffs on five product categories—rice, wheat, dairy products, sugar, and beef and pork—to protect domestic farmers. Meanwhile, the other 14 countries will cut tariffs on 92 per cent of Japanese industrial exports, including automobile parts and steel products.

Did India miss out by opting out of the massive trade agreement? The response is a strong no. India made a principled decision to withdraw because it believed the RCEP failed to address its outstanding issues and concerns. Though the RCEP has provided an opportunity for India to participate if it so desires, India's position is unlikely to change as long as China remains the elephant in the room. India was concerned that the accord might become a free trade agreement with China through the back door, possibly through other nations, which is why New Delhi is currently considering a number of regional free trade agreements (FTAs).

Had India joined, it would have led to Chinese goods flooding the domestic Indian markets once tariff are lowered on about 80 per cent of the imports. India also feared lowering tariffs would exacerbate the trade deficits India has with 11 of the 15 RCEP signatory countries. India was also irked that the groupings were reticent on allowing the flow of Indian labour for services, on which India's specialisation is high. There was also domestic opposition to the deal over fears that would adversely affect Indian agricultural and dairy sectors.

Besides the geo-economic considerations, India was also wary about geo-political issues where China is displaying its vulgar military muscle while disregarding the sensitivities of other nations. There is no denying the fact that RCEP will cement China's clout in the Asia-Pacific. The interplay of geo-economics and geopolitics in this cannot be overlooked.

Unexpectedly, Chinese state media commented that India committed a "strategic blunder" and "missed the bus". That is absolutely rubbish. India must make an informed judgement about its growing trade deficit with China. China forgot that a joint statement was issued in Thailand in November 2019, at the end of RCEP negotiations, that acknowledged India's concerns. That was not addressed, and China has no right to comment on what India as a sovereign nation decides.

Deepening of Ties during COVID-19 times

A crisis situation of any nature in any friendly country presents an opportunity for rendering material, financial and moral help. The COVID-19 pandemic provided an opportunity for mutual aid, similar to Justice Pal's dissenting judgement at the Tokyo trial exonerating Japanese leaders of war crime that boosted the morals of the Japanese people to signing of a separate peace treaty and not joining the San Francisco Peace Treaty, thereby according recognition to Japan as a sovereign independent country and refusing to demand any reparation. Even earlier, when in the early 1990s India faced critical foreign exchange crisis and was on the verge of becoming a defaulter to international lending agencies, it was Japan that bailed out India by providing financial assistance, thereby demonstrating mutual trust.

The balance of payment crisis had resulted because of poor economic policies, inefficient public sector units, resulting in trade deficit.

The World Bank and the IMF withdrew their help after India's credit ratings were downgraded, leaving the government with no choice but to mortgage the country's gold to avoid defaulting on payments. As a friend to come to India's rescue, Japan extended a soft loan of $150 million with a further commitment of $350 million. The crisis, in turn, paved the way for the liberalisation of the Indian economy.[55]

Similarly, when Japan was struck by the triple disaster—earthquake, tsunami and nuclear meltdown—in Fukushima in March 2011, the timely assistance of India's National Disaster Management Force in the restoration efforts received admiration from Japan. There are several other examples of one coming to the other's rescue when faced with a crisis.

The latest in this narrative was the timely Japanese aid to India in response to battling the COVID. When India was faced with the second wave and a panic gripped the county, Japan together with other countries, decided on May 28, 2021, to extend an Emergency Grant Aid of approximately $14.8 million.[56] On April 30, Japan announced its decision to provide 300 oxygen concentrators and 300 ventilators to India. This was followed by Foreign Minister Motegi informing his Indian counterpart on May 5, that Japan was ready to provide additional grant assistance of up to $50 million, based on India's needs. Then on May 14, Japan announced the assistance to transport the 300 ventilators announced on April 30 through the United Nations Office for Project Services (UNOPS), as well as to provide additional 500 ventilators and 500 oxygen concentrators to India through UNOPS. In total, Japan provided to India with 1,800 ventilators and 2,800 oxygen concentrators.

As part of the $50 million aid announced on May 5, 2021, UNOPS provided India with additional 1,000 ventilators and 2,000 oxygen concentrators. As a result, 1,800 ventilators and 2,800 oxygen concentrators in total were provided to India through a series of Japanese assistance. This shows that Japan stands with India as a friend and partner in its fight against the COVID-19 pandemic. Japan hoped that such emergency assistance shall contribute to alleviating and containing the COVID-19 situation in India.

At this time of national crisis, Japan's ambassador in India Satoshi Suzuki showed his pro-activism by staying in constant touch with the Indian authorities to coordinate what medical aid and other assistance from Japan could alleviate India's sufferings, so that he shall make efforts to procure such requirements. Reiterating that India needs Japan at this critical time, Suzuki assured that "Japan stands with India", an observation comforting to India. In an interview with *The Statesman* on June 5, 2021, Suzuki spoke extensively on the emergency supplies sent by Japan, Quad's proposal to ramp up the manufacture of Covid vaccine and the possibility of the India-Japan annual summit in late 2021, among other issues.[57]

Indeed, after ramping up medical aid and related assistance, Japan also made other effective interventions such as collaborating with the United Nations Development Program (UNDP) to set up eight Pressure Swing Absorption (OSA) oxygen generation plants in India's North-Eastern states of Meghalaya, Nagaland and Tripura. This announcement was made on May 10, 2021, when the second wave of the pandemic was at its peak. Japan was concerned that India's healthcare system was stressed and acute shortage of medical oxygen was one of the key challenges. The hospitals, with a capacity of approximately 1,300 beds in total, were identified in the region for these oxygen generation plants. Plans were afoot to distribute the excess oxygen among other health facilities in the hospitals' vicinity. The installation sites were prepared to fast track oxygen production. Satoshi remarked that "Japan stands with India, our friend and partner, in her efforts to fight against COVID-19 pandemic in this critical time." Indeed, North East occupies a special place for Japan-India relations. In addition to this, UNDP has started initiative to support the Ministry of Health and Family Welfare with digitization of supply chain of vaccines and tracking beneficiaries across states to ensure better access and coverage. It also helped build capacities of 820,500 frontline workers across the country to support the 'world's largest vaccination drive'.[58]

After dealing with the pandemic, the focus shifted to developing policies for economic recovery. The path to accomplishing this will be within the framework and mandate of Prime Minister Modi's ideals of 'Make in India' and 'Atmanirbhar Bharat', ensuring that supply chains remain resilient, dependable, and results-oriented. The greater purpose is to keep the region free and open, as defined by rules and norms, to maintain safety and prosperity of the people.

In times of crises, sharing each other's experiences and expertise is always helpful. India and Japan realised this before the pandemic started ravaging the world and therefore launched the Healthcare Joint Committee in 2018. Since then both have been promoting exchange of medical doctors and professionals. Under the pandemic situation, the focus was on containment of the pandemic. Though India claims to be "the pharmacy of the world" and a leader in vaccine production, the laxity following the first wave proved to be a fundamental fault in mitigating the pandemic when the second wave hit harder. In terms of medical cooperation, there is still room for both India and Japan to work together to create vaccines to combat COVID-19, such as partnering and combining aid for last-mile solutions in their respective and other nations.

Economic and Commercial Cooperation

In the broad rubric of economic relations, several areas of cooperation are envisaged. Trade, investment, joint collaboration, joint collaboration in third country projects, ODA and several others cover economic cooperation. A brief analysis of each category can put the India-Japan economic partnership in perspective.

Trade and Investment

The picture of trade ties during the immediate post-War years has already been explained. How the prospect for a new beginning in economic ties to take off following the liberalization of the Indian economy was abruptly halted when India conducted nuclear tests in 1998 and Japan reacted strongly on India's move has also been analysed in details. It took another two years when then Prime Minister Mori decided to visit India in August 2000 signalling a fresh beginning. The background of the timing of Mori's decision to visit India and break the logjam has also been explained in Chapter I. There has been no stopping after that.

It has now transpired that the recent developments would strengthen India-Japan relations economically, politically and strategically in Asia and beyond. Japanese investment that remained lukewarm began to pick up. For the first time, Japanese investment overtook, bolstered by the two big deals—the Tata-DoCoMo tie up and the Daiichi Sankyo deal with Ranbaxy. However, soon the Daiichi-Ranbaxy deal went sour, when the former owners of Ranbaxy Laboratories Ltd., two Singh brothers—Malvinder and Shivinder—were ordered by a Singapore arbitration tribunal to pay $385 million to Japanese pharma company Daiichi Sankya Co. Ltd, which had bought the firm in 2008. Daiichi accused the brothers of misrepresenting the problems facing Ranbaxy when it acquired the firm.

In 2008, Daiichi had bought the Singh brothers' 34.82 per cent stake for $2.4 billion. The total deal value was $4.6 billion. Problems emerged soon after the acquisition, when Ranbaxy's plants came under scrutiny by the US Food and Drug Administration (FDA). In 2014, Sun Pharma acquired Ranbaxy. This failed business deal offered many valuable lessons for future similar deals.[59]

Notwithstanding this hiccup, the number of Japanese affiliated companies in India has grown significantly in recent years. As per the list prepared by the Japanese Embassy, Consulate General of Japan in India, the JETRO and in cooperation with the Japanese chambers of commerce and industries in India, the total number of Japanese business establishments registered in India is 1,455 as of March 2021, same as the previous year (1,454 in October 2019). The total number of Japanese business establishments in India is 4,948, with a decrease of 74 establishments (1.5% decline) as compared to 5,022 in October 2019.[60] Manufacturing firms accounted for half of this total number. This shows that the number of Japanese companies investing in India more than doubled from 267 in 2006 to 627 in 2009[61] and further to 1,455 in March 2021. Similarly the number of Indian companies working in Japan has also increased with the number crossing more than 100. Indian investment in Japan in the first quarter of 2018 was $384.8 million with total investment crossing $1 billion.[62]

When India launched its Look East Policy, Japan was a late responder, but South Korea was not. Despite India's concerted measures to attract Japanese participation through foreign direct investment, the response from Japan was rather subdued. India's "Look East" policy did not attract the attention of potential Japanese investors.[63] As regards the reluctance of Japanese investors, they not only seek economic ties but also commitment and trustworthiness. They also tend to test the waters by assigning limited work involving unachievable targets to their overseas partners.

The tepid response of the Japanese private sector to investments in and trade with India is attributed to the procedural bottlenecks that plague the domestic business climate. Among the reasons often cited are infrastructural and institutional hurdles, regulations and legal impediments, difficulty in land acquisition to set up industries, stringent taxation and subsidies issues, procedural delays, political instability, and legal matters. The case of Korean steel giant POSCO exiting from the big project (the single largest investment project) in Odisha after wait for years over land acquisition issue sent a wrong message to all potential investors from Japan and also other countries.

As compared to investment, bilateral trade continues to remain considerably low, though both the countries hoped to double the size to $20 billion by 2010 when compared with Japan-China trade or even India-China trade (respectively $237.193 and %37.931 billion in 2007-08). The total volume of Japan-China trade grew from $823 million in 1970 to $6.7 billion in 1979 and grew consistently in subsequent years. China is Japan's largest export destination country, and Japan remains China's second biggest trading partner, with trade volume between the neighbours reaching nearly $317.5 billion in 2020, a year-on-year rise of 0.8 per cent. Sino-Japan trade increased 23.5 per cent year on year in the five months of 2021.[64]

Like growth in the Japan-China trade ties, a similar trend was observed between India and China also. In the year 2019, India was the 12th largest trade partner of China, though total bilateral trade registered a reduction of 2.93 per cent year on year to reach $92.89 billion. India's exports to China increased by 4.55 per cent to $17.97 billion, and India's imports from China also witnessed a drop by 2.54 per cent to $74.92 billion.[65] Compared to the Japan-China and India-China trade, India-Japan bilateral trade volume remains relatively small. Japan's bilateral trade with India totalled $17.63 billion during 2018-19. Exports from Japan to India during this period were $12.77 billion and imports were $ 4.86 billion. Japan's exports to India were 2.48 per cent of India's total imports and India's exports to Japan were 1.47 per cent of India's total exports. This underlines that there remains a big potential.

India's primary exports to Japan have been petroleum products, chemicals, elements, compounds, non-metallic mineral ware, fish and fish preparations, metalliferous ores & scrap, clothing and accessories, iron and steel products, textile yarn, fabrics and machinery, etc. India's primary imports from Japan are machinery, electrical machinery, iron and steel products, plastic materials, non-ferrous metals, parts of motor vehicles, organic chemicals, manufactures of metals, etc.[66] Like China, Korean products also dominate India's white goods sector and have assumed high brand recognition in India in recent years.

The Japanese government realized this and augmented infrastructure projects so that Japanese investment can pick up. After investment from Japan gathered steam, there was a dramatic turnaround. This upswing can also be vulnerable to volatile capital markets, which is why investment still remains much lower than potentially possible.

The Japanese companies are known for making for internal business risk analyses, not once but several times, before committing investment or entering into partnership in a project. Once a decision is taken, the company sticks to the decision despite there could be initial teething problems. Also, the Japan Bank for International Cooperation (JBIC) conducts annual surveys on Overseas Business Operations by Japanese Manufacturing Companies and examines the outlook for Japanese FDI. For example, the 2008 survey projected India as the most favoured investment destination for long-term Japanese investment.[67]

In the survey, though China topped as the top position, companies also started viewing India, Brazil and Russia as promising.[68] The number of companies that viewed India as promising increased to a level on par with China. India continued to make gains, leaving it almost on par with China in terms of percentage shares.[69] "Growth potential of the local market" was listed as the top reason for India being a promising destination, revealing the hopes in the survey on the future growth of the Indian market, besides "inexpensive source of labour" and the most important "qualified human resources". However, deficiency in infrastructure remains a major factor deterring Japanese companies to commit to the Indian market. Since then, both the countries have been making assiduous efforts to develop the infrastructure by joint collaboration and the JICA has been playing a significant role in utilizing the ODA money to improve many infrastructure projects in India. With this, the message for the Japanese companies is loud and clear and India is now on the top of the radar where they can engage with their Indian counterparts for mutual beneficial partnership.

Taking the clue, Japanese multinationals have seen potentials of India's robust economic growth and therefore evinced interest to participate as partners with Indian corporate groups. The Confederation of Indian Industries (CII), the Federation of Indian Chamber of Commerce and Industry (FICCI), and the Associate Chamber of Commerce and Industry (ASOCHAM) are actively engaged with the task of facilitating Japanese involvement in Indian ventures. The strategic element in this evolving partnership can also not be overlooked as there is greater convergence of interests between the two countries in the political domains.[70]

Besides trade and investment cooperation, both have also been collaborating in the field of science and technology as well as culture. Both sides signed the Science and Technology Cooperation Agreement in 1985, which underpins the bilateral S&T cooperation. The India-Japan Science Council (IJSC) was established in 1993. As per the data by the Indian embassy in Tokyo, 19 annual meetings were held, 250 joint projects were supported, 1,600 exchange of visits by scientists took place, 65 joint seminars/ workshops, 9 Asian Academic seminars and 10 Raman-Mizushima lectures have been organized. In 2006, the Department of Science and Technology (DST) initiated a value based partnership working on the principles of 'reciprocity and co-funding with the Japan Society for the Promotion of Science (JSPS) and Japan Science and Technology Agency (JST) through MEXT (Ministry of Education, Culture, Sports, Science and Technology). Since then several Institutional Agreements/MoUs in the areas of life sciences, material sciences, high energy physics, ICT, biotechnology, healthcare, methane hydrate, robotics, alternative sources of energy, earth sciences, outer space, etc., have been signed between the science agencies of both countries. Since May 2015, about 250 students visited Japan under the annual "Japan-Asia Youth Exchange Program in Science" also known as the "SAKURA Exchange Program" implemented by DST and JST.

In the cultural domain, efforts to forge greater understanding through various programs and events have not remained wanting. The Japan Foundation in India and the Vivekananda Cultural Centre in Japan have remained active in showcasing various facets of cultures through programmes and events to forge mutual understanding at the people-to-people levels. A cultural agreement was signed between the two countries on October 29, 1956, which came into effect on May 24, 1957. In 1951, India established a scholarship system for young Japanese scholars to study in India. Prime Minister Rajiv Gandhi attended the April 1988 opening ceremony of the Festival of India. The Vivekananda Cultural Centre in Tokyo opened in September 2009. The Centre offers classes on Yoga, Tabla, Bharatanatyam, Odissi, Sambalpuri, Bollywood dances and Hindi and Bengali languages. The ICCR set up two Chairs on India studies at Ryukoku University, Kyoto and in Reitaku University, Chiba.[71] A year-long Festival of India in Japan 2014-15 was held from October 2014 to September 2015. The Embassy and the Consulate General in association with a number of partners organised various events marking the celebrations of 2nd International Day of Yoga on June 19, 2016. In pursuance of the MoU signed in 2015 between Yoga Organisation of Japan and the Quality Council of India for the promotion of Scheme for Voluntary Certification of Yoga, the first QCI examination outside India, was held in Japan at the Vivekananda Cultural Centre on April 23, 2016.

Similarly, the Japan Foundation in New Delhi has remained active in showcasing Japanese culture through various programs in Delhi and other cities of India since it was founded in 1993.[72] In recent years, promotion of Japanese language teaching has been the primary focus, though other programs remain in place.

A separate chapter will address how both sides employ soft power to promote mutual understanding.

Notes

1. W.R. Purcell, "The Nature and Extent of Japanese Commercial and Economic Interests in Australia, 1932-41, *Australia-Japan Economic Relations Research Project Research Paper no 53*, Canberra, October 1978, p. 14.
2. For a broader study on the export-oriented nature of the Brazilian industry, see Ippei Yamazawa and Kazutaka Kunimoto, "Minerals Trade and Economic Cooperation: The Case of Iron Ore", in Sir John Crawford and Saburo Okita, eds., *Australia and Japan: Issues in the Economic Relationship* (Canberra, 1979), pp. 75-87.
3. Though there is no recorded evidence to this plan, there could have been some truth to such suspicions because a 90+old man, whom the author met in Hiroshima in July 1979 over dinner, confided that it was indeed the plan of Japanese Army to invade Australia, annex it, make it its colony, and then foist a member of the Imperial family as the Emperor of Australia. And with this objective, the Japan's Imperial Navy had already made its presence in Port Darwin.

4. For a detailed history of the deposits and a brief account of the arrangement between Brasserts Co., the British firm and the Nippon Mining Company, see Commonwealth of Australia, Department of External Affairs, *Current Notes on International Affairs* (Canberra), vol. 2, no. 5, March 1, 1937
5. J.D.B. Miller, ed., *India, Japan, Australia: Partners in Asia* (Canberra), Australian National University Press, 1968
6. Hiroshi Yoshikawa, *Japan's Lost Decade* (Tokyo), I-House Press, 2002
7. P.G. Rajamohan, Dil Bahadur Rahut and Jabin T. Jacob, "Changing Paradigm of Indo-Japan Relations: Opportunities and Challenges", Working Papers No. 212, Indian Council for Research on International Economic Relations, 2008, https://icrier.org/pdf/Working_Paper_212.pdf
8. See, Lalima Verma, "Japan's Official Development Assistance to India: A Critical Appraisal", *India Quarterly* (New Delhi), vol. 65, no 3, July-September 2009, pp. 237-244., Available at https://www.jstor.org/stable/45072944?seq=1
9. https://www.mofa.go.jp/policy/oda/region/sw_asia/india_o.pdf
10. Ibid.
11. https://www.mofa.go.jp/region/asia-paci/india/data.html
12. Ministry of Foreign Affairs, Government of Japan, http://www.mofa.go.jp/policy,oda/white/2008/parts3-2-3.pdf
13. Ibid.
14. http://www.meti.go.jp/english/report/downloadfiles/2009WhitePaper/sumary.pdf
15. Ibid.
16. BIMP includes Brunei, Indonesia, Malaysia, and the Philippines.
17. H C Vanlalruata, "Centre, Japan ink loan deal for Cancer Centre in Mizoram", *Times of India*, February 28, 2023, https://timesofindia.indiatimes.com/city/guwahati/centre-japan-ink-loan-deal-for-cancer-centre-in-mizoram/articleshow/98291022.cms. For main ODA projects in India's North-East, see, https://www.in.emb-japan.go.jp/files/100365125.pdf
18. "Japan's Official Development Assistance (ODA) to India", February 28, 2023, https://www.newsmania.co.in/2023/02/28/japans-official-development-assistance-oda-to-india/
19. https://dipp.gov.in/programmes-and-schemes/delhi-mumbai-industrial-corridordmic
20. Ibid.
21. Ibid.
22. https://dipp.gov.in/japan-plus/delhi-mumbai-industrial-corridor-dmic
23. https://dipp.gov.in/programmes-and-schemes/delhi-mumbai-industrial-corridordmic
24. *The Hindustan Times,* December 29, 2009.
25. Ibid.
26. http://www.mofa.go.jp/region/asia-paci/india/pmv0810/joint_s.html
27. *The Indian Express*, 29 December 2009.

28. A Joint Study Group (JSG) was set up in April 2005 for a free trade agreement (FTA). In June 2006, the JSG submitted its report, in which it recommended that both the governments launch an inter-governmental negotiation to develop an Economic Partnership Agreement (EPA)/Comprehensive Economic Partnership Agreement (CEPA), within a reasonable period of time. See, "Report of the India-Japan Joint Study Group, June 2006", http://www.mofa.go.jp/region/asia-paci/india/report0606.pdf.
29. "India, Japan to sign CEPA in a month", January 21, 2013, https://www.business-standard.com/article/economy-policy/india-japan-to-sign-cepa-in-a-month-110111000079_1.html
30. "Comprehensive Economic Partnership Agreement (CEPA) between India and Japan comes into force", *The Economic Times*, August 1, 2011, https://economictimes.indiatimes.com/news/economy/foreign-trade/comprehensive-economic-partnership-agreementcepabetween-india-and-japan-comes-into-force/articleshow/9437145.cms
31. "India-Japan Relations", August 24, 2017, https://www.civilsdaily.com/india-japan-relations/
32. Rajaram Panda, "A Revolution in store for Indian Railways", February 10, 2016, https://www.indiaglobalbusiness.com/igb-archive/revolution-store-indian-railways
33. "High-speed rail in India", https://en.wikipedia.org/wiki/High-speed_rail_in_India
34. https://forums.bharat-rakshak.com/viewtopic.php?t=3086&start=3800
35. "India to stay out of RCEP in its present form", November 4, 2019, https://www.theweek.in/news/world/2019/11/04/india-to-stay-out-of-rcep-in-its-present-form.html
36. Rajaram Panda, "India Opts Out of RCEP: Cost-Benefit Analysis", *Mainstream,* November 30, 2019, Vol. LVII, No. 50, pp. 11-15; Rajaram Panda, "Is the RCEP China's gain and India's loss?", *China Brief: A Journal of Analysis and Information,* vol. 20, no. 22, December 23, 2020, pp. 26-31, https://jamestown.org/wp-content/uploads/2020/12/Read-the-12-23-2020-CB-Issue-in-PDF.pdf?x30227
37. Pravin Krishna & Arvind Panagariya, "View: Staying out of RCEP is not in India's economic interests", *The Economic Times*, November 8, 2019, https://economictimes.indiatimes.com/news/economy/foreign-trade/view-staying-out-of-rcep-is-not-in-indias-economic-interests/articleshow/71961145.cms
38. Ibid.
39. "India's trade deficit with China dips to $48.66 billion in FY20", *The Hindu*, July 2, 2020, https://www.thehindu.com/business/Economy/indias-trade-deficit-with-china-dips-to-4866-billion-in-fy20/article31973598.ece
40. Palak Agrawal, "India's Trade Deficit With China Reduces To $48.66 Billion For Year 2019-20", https://thelogicalindian.com/news/india-trade-deficit-with-china-reduces-to-4866-billion-in-fy20-22084
41. "Hyundai, Kia's FTA rise cost us billions in trade deficit: Goyal", *Times of India,* February 26, 2023.

42. Biswajit Dhar, "After RCEP opt-out, the challenge of a shape-up", *The Hindu*, November 7, 2019, https://www.thehindu.com/opinion/lead/after-rcep-opt-out-the-challenge-of-a-shape-up/article29902806.ece
43. "Stay with RCEP", August 21, 2018, *The Hindu,* editorial, www.thehindu.com/opinion/editorial/stay-with-rcep/article24739401.ece
44. "Export and reform: If RCEP failed, look to other trading blocs. Isolationism is not an option", *The Times of India,* November 7, 2019, editorial, https://timesofindia.indiatimes.com/blogs/toi-editorials/export-and-reform-if-rcep-failed-look-to-other-trading-blocs-isolationism-is-not-an-option/
45. "India's free trade agreements are hurting domestic firms". Here's is formula for FTAs to work, *The Economic Times,* June 24, 2021, https://economictimes.indiatimes.com/small-biz/trade/exports/insights/indias-free-trade-agreements-are-hurting-domestic-firms-heres-the-formula-to make-ftas-work/articleshow/83798683.cms
46. Hin Pisei, "RCEP could be ratified on Jan 1: ministry", June 22, 2021, https://www.phnompenhpost.com/business/rcep-could-be-ratified-jan-1-ministry
47. "Japan ratifies world's biggest trade deal involving China, ASEAN", *Mainichi Daily News,* June 25, 2021, https://mainichi.jp/english/articles/20210625/p2g/00m/0bu/066000c
48. Ibid.
49. Rajaram Panda, "RCEP Minus India is a Lame Duck Trade Pact", *World Focus,* No. 480, December 2019, pp. 27-34.
50. Ibid.
51. "Will try to resolve India's outstanding issues: China on RCEP", *Indian Express,* November 5, 2019, https://indianexpress.com/article/world/will-follow-principle-of-mutual-understanding-accommodation-to-resolve-indias-issues-china-on-rcep-6104619/
52. Rajaram Panda, "A Step Too Far: Why India Opted Out of RCEP", *Global Asia,* Vol. 14, No. 4, December 2019, pp. 82-88. http://globalasia.org/v14no4/feature/a-step-too-far-why-india-opted-out-of-rcep_rajaram-panda
53. "India's free trade agreements are 'hurting domestic firms". Here's is formula for FTAs to work", *The Economic Times,* June 24, 2021, https://economictimes.indiatimes.com/small-biz/trade/exports/insights/indias-free-trade-agreements-are-hurting-domestic-firms-heres-the-formula-to-make-ftas-work/articleshow/83798683.cmsc
54. See, Rajaram Panda, "RECP and India", *The Statesman,* December 3, 2020.
55. See, A.K. Bhattacharya, "Two months that changed India", *Business Standard,* July 1, 2011, https://www.business-standard.com/article/beyond-business/two-months-that-changed-india-111070200041_1.html
56. "Emergency Grant Aid in Response to COVID-19 in India", May 28, 2021, https://www.mofa.go.jp/press/release/press23e_000032.html. Also see, https://www.mofa.go.jp/press/release/press1e_000198.html
57. "Japan stands with India", *The Statesman,* 5 June 2021, https://www.thestatesman.com/exclusive-interviews/saturday-interview-japan-stands-with-india-1502971050.html

58. "Government of Japan and UNDP have joined hands to boost oxygen supply in North Eastern Region in India", May 10, 2021, Embassy of Japan, New Delhi, Press Release, https://www.in.emb-japan.go.jp/files/100187212.pdf
59. Rajesh Shrivastav. "Six business lessons from the Daiichi–Ranbaxy deal fiasco", *The Mint,* 31 May 2016, https://www.livemint.com/Companies/ABxz5axWTnk7EmtdNF7GxN/Six-business-lessons-from-the-DaiichiRanbaxy-deal-fiasco.html
60. "Japanese Business Establishments in India", March 2021, Embassy of Japan, New Delhi, https://www.in.emb-japan.go.jp/PDF/2020_co_list_en.pdf
61. *The Indian Express*, December 26, 2009.
62. "India-Japan Economic Relations", Embassy of India, Tokyo, https://www.indembassy-tokyo.gov.in/eoityo_pages/NjA
63. See, Srabani Roy Choudhury, "Japan's Foreign Direct Investment Experiences in India: Lessons Learnt from Firm Level Surveys", *ICRIER Working Paper No. 243*, December 2009, New Delhi, p. 3.
64. www.xinhuanet.com, June 16, 2016.
65. "India-China Trade and Economic Relations", Embassy of India, Beijing, https://www.eoibeijing.gov.in/economic-and-trade-relation.php
66. See n. 59.
67. "Special Report on Overseas Business Operations by Japanese Manufacturing Companies Result of JBIC FY 2008 Survey: Outlook for Japanese Foreign Direct Investment" (20th Annual Survey), November 2008, Appendix 2, p. 33.
68. Ibid., p. 5.
69. Ibid., p. 7.
70. Geethanjali Nataraj, "Japan-India partnership: Focus squarely on strategic interests", *Financial Express,* April 18, 2018, https://www.financialexpress.com/opinion/japan-india-partnership-focus-squarely-on-strategic-interests/1136620/
71. The author was the holder of the ICCR Chair at the Reitaku University for two years till March 2018. The programme has been kept on hold since then owing to budgetary constraints by the University.
72. The author also worked at the Japan Foundation's New Delhi office for 15 years, from 1994 till 2009, and has deep insights into the office's operations and activities.

4

Indian Diaspora: The Case of Indians in Japan[1]

Introduction

The arrival of Indians in Japan started more visibly after the Meiji Restoration in 1868, ending the 200 years of self-imposed isolation by the Tokugawa Shogunate. Indians started arriving in Japan for business and commercial activities in the 1870s at the two major open ports of Yokohama and Kobe. More Indians as British colonial subjects entered Japan during World War I when Japanese products were sought to fill gaps in demand that war-torn Europe could not meet. The Anglo-Japanese alliance facilitated this process. Following the great Kanto Earthquake in 1923, most of the Indians in Yokohama relocated to the Kansai region (Osaka-Kobe) and the city hosted the largest migrant Indian population in Japan. Yokohama authorities offered special incentives to the Indian community after World War II to revive their old base in Kanto. The old Indian community in Japan focused on trading in textiles, commodities and electronics. With close linkages to India as well as connections in Hong Kong and Shanghai, they became major players in trading activities across Asia. A newer segment of the community is engaged in gems and jewellery.

In recent years, there has been a change in the composition of the Indian community with the arrival of a large number of professionals, including IT professionals and engineers working for Indian and Japanese firms as well as professionals in management, finance, education, and S&T research. The Nishi-Kasai area in Tokyo, 15-minutes from central Tokyo on the Tozai subway line has emerged as Japan's "Little India" as it is home to the largest Indian community in Japan. Their growing numbers had prompted the opening of three Indian schools in Tokyo and Yokohama. The community is actively engaged in events organized by the Embassy of India and their own groups. The Indian community lives harmoniously with the neighbours and has developed relations with local governments to become valuable members of the Japanese community. As per the latest information available, approximately 53,000 Indians live in Japan now. This figure is rather small compared with millions of Indians dispersed in Europe, Australia and other developed countries. The reason for this shall be discussed in the subsequent pages.

Background of the Indian Diaspora

Against the backdrop of an increasingly globalised society and the unparalleled pace that this process is experiencing, cross-border and cross-continental migration of people makes for an intriguing story in the academic community. The migration of people brings in its wake issues of cultural conflict, clash of interests, racism, economic domination, influence of political power, question of identity and so on. This phenomenon of demographic dispersal of people is not recent; it has been there for centuries and ages. Historians, scholars and analysts have tried to examine this phenomenon from different perspectives. Cultural theorists try to see this from the perspective of either cultural assertiveness, which perceives the domination of one culture over the other, or cultural refinement that stems from different cultures and towards refinement of a richer culture. Similarly, historians see this from different perspectives. For example, Samuel Huntington sees this as clash of civilizations. Similarly, political theorists have their own perspectives to evaluate such developments. The purpose here is not to indulge in such controversies. Nor does it aim to debunk one theory and extol the other. The basic hypothesis here is to say that migration is a global phenomenon, which has existed over centuries and it is in this context that the position of the Indian community in Japan and their role in Japan is being discussed and examined. It is presumed that this global human movement has contributed to the development of civilization and enrichment of human knowledge.

The international movement of people from one country to another and from one region to another is a time-tested development in human history.

People are increasingly migrating from undeveloped and impoverished countries to more developed ones in search of better opportunities and lifestyles. Throughout history, nations that were once wealthy have become impoverished, and vice versa. Thus, it is not just Indians who have relocated abroad and are now dispersed over the world. Japan, before becoming wealthy during the post-World War II period, also saw movement of its people outside its shores. For example, at present, there are a sizable number of Japanese settlers in countries such as Brazil and Peru.

In fact, in April 2008, Japanese and Brazilian officials celebrated the centennial of Japanese immigration to Brazil. In April 1908, 781 Japanese immigrants had departed Kobe aboard the Kasato Maru, bound for Brazil. The majority of the immigrants were farmers, and they arrived at the port of Santos, south of Sao Paulo, where they went on to work at coffee plantations. The number of Japanese immigrants to Brazil numbered 190,000 until the end of World War II. Today there are over 1.5 million Brazilians of Japanese ancestry currently living in Brazil, making it the largest Japanese-derived descendants outside Japan in the world. Called as Nikkejin (overseas people of Japanese descent), they are by far the world's largest group in this category. They have maintained a prominent "Japanese" minority identity.

The author had a chance to travel to Sao Paulo in August 2017 to deliver lectures at two universities and was hosted by a Professor of Japanese descent and got precious insights about Japanese migrating to Brazil in the early phase of Meiji period and settled there. The 1.5 million Brazilians of Japanese descent are mostly of third or fourth generations. Though some of the third generations of Japanese speak Japanese, most of the younger ones speak only Portuguese, Brazil's national language, and have little knowledge about Japan. Growing up in a Brazilian cultural milieu and having been disconnected with a major part of Japanese culture, some educated Brazilians of the third generation shared their experiences when they had chance to visit Japan either as tourists, or on business or for emotional connection, that they found difficult to adjust with the traditional Japanese culture. Since they look the same being from the same race, they are often looked with suspicion by the native Japanese as their mannerism and social etiquette or conduct of public life are based on Brazilian culture and therefore not in tune with Japanese culture. Since most are settled in their new settings in businesses or other professions, there is little incentive for them to return to Japan.

More than 60 per cent of the latest generations of Japanese-Brazilians are mixed as they are children of inter-racial couples. In Japan immigration and miscegenation are still a social issue which is often resisted. As the Professor shared with the author they are culturally more Brazilian than Japanese. They may have Japanese food, but due to generations of living in Brazil, they have lost touch with their cultural roots, and gradually became Brazilianised. It is natural for a group of immigrants to lose contact with their roots after living in a country for centuries, such as Brazil. Slowly, the barriers to interracial marriage also wither away.[2] Similar is the case with the case of interracial marriage among Japanese-Americans. According to a Pew Research Center Report, 64 per cent of newly wedded Japanese-Americans between 2008 and 2010 were married to Non-Japanese and 55 per cent of them married to non-Asians and 9 per cent married to non-Japanese Asians.[3]

Similarly, Japanese-Americans live in a similar reality that Japanese-Brazilians live in. Their families have lived in the US for generations, becoming increasingly Americanized and losing contact with their cultural roots. In Japan, immigration and intermarriage are social issues that are resisted in Japan because they are more to do with culture than race. The defensive attitude of Japanese back home is more to do with culture than race and this gets reflected in the country's immigration policy. They expect foreigners to respect their laws, values and customs. A foreigner who does these things has a lower cultural barrier to marrying a Japanese native.

Having Japanese blood does not mean Japanese people will immediately accept an outsider. Japanese people who have lived overseas for generations are aliens to most Japanese people as much as aliens with no Japanese heritage. To most Japanese people in Japan, Japanese Americans, Brazilians, and Peruvians are just Americans, Brazilians and Peruvians.

In contemporary times when Japan faced labour shortage but were no longer willing to do the types of work referred to as the three Ks – Kitanei, Kitsui and Kiken (dirty, hard, dangerous), the society had to find someone who can do such works. It was that at time, Japan gave the first preference to import diaspora Japanese from Brazil and Peru in attempt to solve their labour shortage. However, these migrants of Japanese background faced and still face many challenges. As a result, their integration into the Japanese society has been slow. And, this mindset of the Japanese also applies to all gaijins (foreigners) irrespective of nationality. Such perceived discrimination mixed with language barrier has resulted many of these South American migrants to create their own enclaves and stores, away from native Japanese population. Despite assimilation problems, as of today's count, around 250,000 Brazilian Japanese are living in Japan, making them the second largest foreign population in Japan.

Interestingly, it is not only the attitude of the native Japanese unwilling to culturally accept Brazilian Japanese but the latter too suffer from the same malaise. The Japanese Brazilian migrants do not often develop a transnational identity, a strong, positive feeling of attachment and belonging to the two nations. They do not characteristically surrender their old identity and adopt a new, transnational ethnic identity. Instead, their experiences in Japan tend to make Brazilian Japanese feel more Brazilian and less Japanese.[4]

Is the huge number of Brazilian Japanese in Japan, sometimes known as reverse migration, a win-win situation for both nations? The answer could perhaps be "Yes". This is because, despite the cultural assimilation issue, the Brazilian Japanese in Japan have addressed, to some extent, if not entirely, Japan's labour shortage issue, and Japanese Brazilian migrants are able to remit to Brazil around $2 billion per year, which is equivalent to approximately 6 per cent of Brazil's export trade. Such a contribution is quite important to the Brazilian economy.[5]

Notwithstanding the Japanese perception towards foreigners or Japanese of foreign origin, such as Brazilian Japanese or American Japanese or Peruvian Japanese, Japan seems to have a soft spot for Brazil and this is reflected in Japan's foreign policy. Brazil finds special focus in Japanese government's foreign policy. Sao Paulo was one of the first countries where the Japan Foundation's overseas office was established in 1975, within three years of its founding. In order to deepen ties and expand Japan's cultural presence, the Japanese ministry of foreign affairs decided to open Japan House, to have major Japanese activities such as exhibition hall, library, bank, theatre, restaurant, etc., all under one roof. Three countries—Brazil, Los Angeles and London—were selected and Sao Paulo in Brazil was the first city where Japan House was inaugurated in April 2017.

The Japan House is an overseas hub to showcase and communicate Japan to the international community as part of efforts to improve strategic global communication. Its goal is to explain Japan's numerous attractions, policies, and activities to a wide spectrum of individuals, including those who know little about the country, as well as to broaden the base of people who are interested in and knowledgeable about Japan. It provides a "one-stop service" where individuals can access a variety of information about Japan, as well as commercial venues such as restaurants, cafes, shops, and so on, which help to transfer information throughout Japan by proactively utilizing the commercial vibrancy and regional attractions.[6]

Japan House in the similar pattern in Los Angeles[7] and London[8] followed subsequently. The building in Sao Paulo looks quite impressive with modern architecture and showcasing various facets of Japanese culture under one roof. It was impressive to witness the large number of Brazilian students flocking the exhibition hall and listening with rapt attention to the leader explaining every exhibit. Even the new Japan Foundation office was quite impressive. The library also had a good selection of books on Japan in three languages—Japanese, English and Portuguese. The other country in South America where a large number of Japanese migrants settled is Peru.[9]

Historical Background of Indian diaspora

The term 'diaspora' is a word of Greek origin that means scattering or sowing of seeds. The term is used to refer to any people or ethnic population forced or induced to leave their traditional ethnic homelands, being dispersed throughout other parts of the world, and the ensuing developments in their dispersal and culture. Indian Diaspora is a generic term used for addressing people who have migrated from the territories that are currently within the borders of the Republic of India.

Those Indians who decided to leave their native lands to live in other parts of the world were driven by employment, business or any other purpose. The word 'diaspora' suggests the idea of dispersal and fragmentation. 'Indian Diaspora' would mean Indian population outside India, particularly those who have migrated to foreign lands and settled, thereby surrendering their Indian nationality. Broadly, Indian Diaspora would mean disparate elements from the Indian subcontinent settling overseas whereby the diaspora is expected to shed their regional, ethnic and linguistic identities and assume a more general identity of being Indian. In this definition, the plurality of India is supposed to disappear. The truism is that all human beings across continents and regions maintain multiple identities as propounded by the Nobel laureate Amartya Sen in his famous and much-quoted book *Identity and Violence: The Illusion of Destiny*.[10]

The Indian Diaspora is estimated to be over 30 million, and consists of Persons of Indian origin (PIO) and the Non-Resident Indians (NRIs) who have migrated ever since the colonial times and are one of the most dynamic and vibrant. Many Indians who decide to migrate to other countries for various reasons decide to surrender their Indian citizenship and assume the citizenship of the country of their adoption. This trend has been on the increase over the years. The Minister for External Affairs S. Jaishankar informed the Rajya Sabha on February 9, 2023 that more than 16 lakh surrendered their Indian citizenship since 2011, including 2,25,620 in 2022. The lowest number of people renouncing Indian citizenship during this period was 85,256 in 2020.[11] The Government of India recognises the importance of Indian Diaspora as it has brought economic, financial, and global benefits to India. The Indian Government recognises the importance of Indian Diaspora, who despite being away from India is making her shine on a global platform. The Indian Diaspora today constitutes an important, and in some respects unique, force in world culture. The government of India has brought about a "transformational change" in its engagement with the Indian diaspora around the world.[12]

While the early migration was in the form of indenture, kangani and maistry, the post-War migration segment by and large constitute professional category. It continues to grow in size and transnational presence with its invaluable contribution to countries not only they have adapted but also to the ancestral motherland, culturally, economically and politically. It is because of this fascinating phenomenon, the study of Indian diaspora has evolved as a rich and diverse area of multidisciplinary research interest, with scientists and scholars focusing on problems such as social adjustment, family change, religion, language, ethnicity and culture.

Indian emigration has been taking place for centuries, but India has never seen such huge movements of people from India to other areas of the world as it did in the nineteenth and twentieth centuries. Overseas Indians make up a large proportion of the immigrant population of various ethnicities. In terms of sheer numbers, they make the third largest group, next only to the British and the Chinese. The people of Indian origin with over 30 million population settled in 70 countries, constitute more than 40 per cent of the population in Fiji, Mauritius, Trinidad, Guyana and Surinam. They are smaller minorities in Malaysia, South Africa, Sri Lanka, Uganda, UK, USA and Canada. In UAE alone, about 50,000 people came to hear Rahul Gandhi when he visited. (This information could not be verified by official sources). So much so that the former late Australian Prime Minister Gough Whitlam, while speaking to the students and faculty at the School of International Studiers, Jawaharlal Nehru University, New Delhi, in late 1979, while replying to a question by the author, was provoked to refer to the India community overseas and sarcastically remarked that India is the greatest modern colonial power. He was referring to the large number of Indian natives who have migrated and settled in different corners of the world. That was an unfair assessment by the late Australian leader.

There are three broad patterns of overseas migration in terms of history and political economy: (a) emigration that began in the 1830s to the British, French and Dutch colonies; (b) emigration to the industrially developed countries during the post-World War II period; and (c) the recent emigration to West Asia and elsewhere.

In India the sacred Hindu scriptures prohibited crossing the seas. There was no large-scale migration until the nineteenth century. During the second half of the eighteenth century, some Indians migrated to the Philippines, USA and Indonesia to work as agricultural labourers. It was the European imperialist expansion during the nineteenth and twentieth centuries, which created conditions for emigration in large numbers.[13] New plantations, industrial and commercial ventures in European colonies created the need for large supplies of labour. With the abolition of slavery in the British, French and Dutch colonies in 1807, 1848 and 1863, respectively, there was a severe shortage of labourers working in sugar, tea, coffee, cocoa, rice and rubber plantations in the colonies. India and China became the obvious alternative sources of labour. By and large, there were two streams of Indian and Chinese emigrants to the colonies: unskilled labourers and small-scale entrepreneurs.

Indian labour emigration under the indenture system first started in 1834 to Mauritius, Uganda and Nigeria. Later, the labourers emigrated to Guyana (1838), New Zealand (1840), Hong Kong (1841), Trinidad and Tobago (1845) Malay (1845), Martinique and Guadeloupe (1954), Grenada, St. Lucia and St. Vincent (1856), Natal (1860), St. Kitts (1861), Japan and Surinam (1872), Jamaica (1873) Fiji (1879), Burma (1885), Canada (1904) and Thailand (1910). Under the indenture system, some 1.5 million persons migrated. On their arrival in the colony, the immigrants were assigned to the plantations to which they were bound for five or more years, where they lived in isolated and insulated lives. Most of these immigrants and their descendants did not return home, though the indentured system of labour was discontinued in 1917.

Emigration to the developed countries like Britain, USA, Canada, Australia and New Zealand is a post-World War II phenomenon. The first trickle of Indians to Britain occurred during the period of British Raj. However, a major influx of Indians took place only after India's independence in 1947. In contrast to the ex-indentured populations, the Indian migrants in the industrially developed countries have been able to maintain extensive ties with India because of their comparative affluence. Marriage arrangements, kinship networks, property and religious affiliations keep many migrants well linked to their place of origin, since a large number of Indians are still first-generation migrants.

Large-scale migration of Indians to the United States started only after the Immigration and Nationality Act in 1956 were modified several times, though not repealed. By 2001, there were about 1,500,000 Indians in the US. The Indians who migrated to the US belonged to the class of educated and professional elite such as engineers, mostly software, scientists and college teachers as well as accountants and businessmen. Their lifestyle and aspirations are similar, in general, to the American middle class. Language and religion have emerged as the most important identities among the Indian immigrants.

Recent emigration of the Indians to the West Asian countries was basically oriented to labour and servicing occupations on a contract basis. There were only 14,000 Indians in the Gulf in 1948 and 40,000 in 2001. Following the oil boom of the mid-1970s, the Middle East witnessed a massive induction of the South Asian workers. The population of Indian workers, which was 14,418 in 1975 rose to 599,500 in 1981 and to 1,150,000 in 1992. Presently there are about 3.6 million Indians in the Gulf countries.[14] However, the need for unskilled South Asian workers during the 1960s and early 1970s, was soon eclipsed by the requirement for skilled labour since the 1980s.

According to a report by India Spend,[15] more than 7 million Indians are currently living in six Gulf Cooperation Council (GCC) nations—Saudi Arabia, UAE, Oman, Qatar and Bahrain—and other West Asian countries. Every year thousands of Indians move to greener pastures in search of better jobs and employment opportunities. They are employed as nurses, engineers, semi-skilled workers such as craftsmen or artisans as well as unskilled labourers in construction sites, farmers, manning patrol pump, shops, stores and as household domestic workers. While the money, lifestyle and good opportunities definitely lure people towards gaining employment in these countries, there are always two sides to the story.[16]

The year 1973 experienced the beginning of the rapidly increasing demand for expatriate labour in oil exporting countries of the Gulf and

North Africa such as Saudi Arabia, Kuwait, the UAE, Bahrain, Qatar and Libya. These countries adopted a development strategy centred on infrastructure development, which created a demand for labour in unskilled manual jobs, particularly in the construction industry. With the completion of the first phase of infrastructure projects and the increased emphasis on industrialization in the Middle East, there has been a significant change in the structure of labour demand. Between 1975 and 1980, one million skilled workers had to be imported to manage and operate this new infrastructure.

The Indian diaspora today constitutes an important, and in some respects unique force in world culture. As the preceding paras demonstrate, the origins of the modern Indian diaspora lie mainly in the subjugation of India by the British and its incorporation in the British Empire. Over two million Indian men fought on behalf of the numerous wars, including the Boer war and the two World Wars, and some remained behind to claim the land on which they fought as their own.

The definition of the Indian diasporic community is a tricky one as Indians constitute diverse elements as South Asian Hong Kong Muslims, Canadian Sikhs, Punjabi Mexican Californians, Gujarati East Africans now settled in the US by way of England, South African Hindus, and so forth. The increasing number of the Indians in their countries of adoption in specific clusters that clearly distinguish them not only stands out because of their different cultural identity but also attract racial insults. The Indian woman in her native dress with the vermilion dot on her forehead, is easily seen as an embodiment of sheer "dot-busters", a gang of white teenagers that operated in New Jersey and were responsible for several violent crimes against Indian women. Similarly, Sikhs in England have insisted that they be exempt from the law that compels bicyclists and motorcyclists to wear helmets for such helmets cannot be worn over turbans, and their religious faith requires Sikhs to wear turbans. Similarly, the kirpan has been an issue of contention in California schools.

Irrespective of their diverse cultural identities, the Indian communities across the world maintain some sort of links with their motherland. Hindi feature films provide Hindi feature films offer the most prevalent cross-ethnic bonding opportunity. A phenomenon unique to the Indian diaspora is that what Hollywood is to Western Europe, Bombay's Bollywood is to the Middle East and East Africa. Even Indian Hindi films can be seen screened in groceries stores and video stores with Arabic or English subtitles.

It is worth noting that even a Tamil film titled Muthu with Japanese subtitles, starring Rajnikant, became a smash hit in Japan, although Indian population is rather low in comparison to other places. When an Indian film is shown at a theatre in Vietnam, there is often a long queue for tickets, demonstrating the popularity of Indian films in the country. The tradition of 'arranged marriage' still exists in Indian settlement regions, and any publications created by Indian communities include a section for matrimonial advertising. However, such distinctions raise serious problems concerning the concept of 'otherness'—the 'otherness' of Indians in relation to 'Americans' and the internal 'otherness' of certain Indians in relation to other Indians.

Indians in Japan—Historical Background

Indian presence in Japan is almost eight centuries old, when Buddhism and the Buddhist spirit of humanism travelled through China and Korea and finally reached Japanese soil. Historical factors such as Europe's imperial expansion in Asia, ending Japan's isolation and the subsequent impact of Japan's transformation and modernization on educated Indians, the encounter between poet Rabindranath Tagore and art historian Okakura Tenshin in search for a common Asian identity strengthened the foundations already laid by the mercantile community.[17] This aspect and other related issues have already been discussed in details in the author's recent Occasional Paper available in the NMML website and therefore needs no reiteration.[18]

According to the 2nd Imperial Great Japan statistics, under an account of British subjects in Japan, one Indian male was supposed to have been living in Yokohama in 1881. Statistically, this might have been the first Indian in Japan. After that the yearly almanac records the subjects of British Indian as 2 Government employees (1884), 1 in 1885 and 2 in 1887.

Before the Asia-Pacific war, Sindhis, Parsis, Gujaratis, Punjabis and other Indian merchants were actively engaged in foreign trade in Japan and other parts of the East Asia, but it was the Sindhis who were the most prominent, handling textile in particular. Sindhis preferred to deal in textiles, largely because these goods were imperishable and could be kept in stock for a long period. First, when the British brought different parts of the world under their control, Indian traders as British colonial subjects were able to expand their commerce in the colonial markets. Second, the revolution in transport and communications made the transportation of people and merchandise easier and cheaper. Third, the second half of the nineteenth and the early twentieth century witnessed a rapid development of modern textile industry particularly in Japan and India, and yarns and piece goods of cotton and silk began to play an increasingly important role in the expansion of the intra-Asian trade.[19]

The Sindhi merchants expanded their trading operations in two major directions: westward and eastward. In East Asia, Sindhi merchants expanded their trading operations from India to Singapore and further to other parts of Asia. According to Markovits, they began to expand into China in the late 1870s or early 1880s, and Japan in the 1890s.[20] In Japan, it was not Kobe, but Yokohama, where they first settled. As Japan's export of silk textiles greatly increased, the number of Indian merchants continued to rise. According to G.A. Chandru Advani, in 1912 there were some 25 Indian trading firms in Japan, most of which were based in Yokohama.[21] Although many of them left Japan when World War I broke out, they later returned to the country to resume their commercial activities,[22] and by that time the Sindhi commercial community had become more powerful than that of the Parsis in Yokohama. When the Great Kanto Earthquake occurred in 1923, however, all the commercial premises of the Indian traders in Yokohama were razed to the ground.[23] There were some 170 Indian residents in the port city, of which twenty-three died. Consequently, many of the Indian merchants with their families left Yokohama for Kobe to resume their trading activities.[24]

In the 1930s, Kobe rose to prominence as a key port for Indian traders. With a dramatic surge in demand for Japanese textiles in Southeast Asia, an increasing number of Indian merchants moved to Kobe in the second half of the 1930s. In fact, Indian trading firms outnumbered all other non-Japanese trading firms. As of December 1937, there were 259 non-Japanese trading enterprises, 130 of which were Indian. Also, Kobe has the highest concentration of Indian traders in Japan. As of December 1937, the country had 176 Indian trading enterprises, with 130 in Kobe, 34 in Yokohama, and 11 in Osaka. Twelve of these Indian enterprises in Kobe were incorporated, while the remaining 118 were unincorporated.

In response to the growing number of Indian merchants in Kobe, the Indian Chamber of Commerce was set up in 1937. As of January 1938, there were 128 members of the chamber. It is not surprising therefore that almost all the large textile manufacturers and wholesale merchants of Fukui and Kanazawa had branches or representative offices in Kobe, and went around the Indian merchant houses to take orders. Such commercial activities received a severe jolt when World War II intervened. But the versatility of the Indian trading networks can be measured when they started diversifying their activities in the post-War period. Some of the Indians returned to Japan after the War to resume their commercial activities in Kobe. The Indians in the port city rose in number from 151 in 1950 to 392 in 1955, and in the mid-1950s, they started shifting their business offices to Osaka where there were large numbers of Japanese textile manufacturers and wholesale merchants, while keeping their residences in Kobe. The Indian Chamber of Commerce was also moved to Osaka in 1957.

Thus it transpires that in the Far East, which emerged as a major source of supply for Sindwork merchants (also called Sindhi workies, Sindworkis or Sindworkies) during the first four decades of the twentieth century, their purchasing operations were concentrated in a few port cities where most foreign traders congregated. No precise indication about the beginning of the Sindworkie presence in Japan has come to light,[25] but commercial directories of the 1890s mention a few Sindwork firms as having branches in Kobe and Yokohama. As said earlier, the network expanded rapidly during the first two decades of the 20th century and a survey of British firms in Japan around 1920 in a British Consular document revealed the presence of almost 30 Sindwork firms, most of which were described as trading with India only.[26]

Yokohama was the major location of Sindwork firms in Japan. Actually in Yokohama, the Sindworkies represented the bulk of the Indian merchant community, while in Kobe they were only one of the communities (other communities represented were Parsis, Gujarati Hindus, Bohra, Khojas and Marwaris). The reason for this specific choice of location probably has to do with the fact that Yokohama, except for part of the 1920s, was the main centre of the Silk trade in Japan. Even after the 1923 earthquake in Yokohama, Kobe became for a few years the most important silk exporting port in Japan, exporting mostly the finer qualities of silk, while Yokohama specialized in the slightly coarser varieties, in which the Sindworkies tended to deal.

Thus, a few families of Indian businessmen, mainly Sindhis and Parsis, migrated to Japan and settled in Yokohama areas in around 1872-73 to carry out on their textile business. At around the same time, about 16 families, mostly Sindhis, landed in Okinawa. The number of Indians gradually grew to 1,000 by the beginning of World War I. During the War, about 60 per cent of them left for India but returned soon after the War was over. Most of the Indians at present are concentrated in Tokyo-Yokohama and in Osaka-Kobe regions, which now includes Rajasthanis and Gujaratis. Others are spread out in Nagoya, Okinawa, Sapporo, Sendai and Niigata.

The Indian community in Japan is financially stable and mostly engaged in the export of electronic goods, textiles, auto parts and jewellery, and imports of handicrafts, garments, precious stones and marine products from India.

Students, engineers, scholars participating in the exchange scheme, and Yoga practitioners make up the non-trading community, as do officials from the Indian government and public sector undertakings. The number of Indian engineers in Japan, particularly computer software experts, has grown significantly over the years, from 120 in 1993 to over 800 in 2000. There are approximately 60 academics and translators working at several universities. Over 1,000 Indian cooks work in the immensely popular Indian restaurants. There are almost 500 such restaurants in the Tokyo area alone. Most of these restaurants are owned and managed by the Japanese. While dining at an Indian restaurant in Nijibasumae area of Tokyo in 2017, the author was pleasantly surprised when told on inquiry that there were 28 persons from the district of Balesore in Odisha alone working in restaurants as chefs and workers in Tokyo area. There is a small Sindhi community in Okinawa providing services particularly tailoring to the American base.

Current Situation

The presence of the Indian community in Japan is negligible as compared to their presence in other countries in the Indo-Pacific region. The presence of the Indian community in Japan as compared to other regions such as Europe, UK, the US or more recently the Middle East is again incomparable. For example, the presence of the Indian community in Australia is just 1.02 per cent and that in New Zealand 1.45 per cent. In Japan, it is negligible. With a population of 126.6 million in Japan, Indian community accounted for only 10,000 (9,000 NRIs and 1,000 PIOs) in 2001.[27] According to the Annual report of statistics on legal migrants (2004) of the Ministry of Justice and published by the Foreign Press Center, Japan, the number of Indians in Japan totalled 14,234 as of December 2003. This number has substantially increased in the past few years as a result of expanding ties in almost all domains.

According to the available data, as of 2014, there were 28,047 Indian nationals living in Japan, of which roughly 60 per cent consisted of expatriate IT professionals and their families. The official statistics, however, say that the number of Indians in Japan rose from 7,478 in 1997 to 24,524 in December 2014. In the case of Japan, this increase might look substantial but in fact small if compared to the Indians living in the US, UK, Singapore and Malaysia, for example. As per the latest information available, the Indian population in Japan totals some 53,000. Even this figure is too small compared to Indians' presence in other countries. Why is this so?

The language remains a major challenge for many Indians in Japan. Though navigating one's way on day-to-day business may appear easy and manageable, there could be unexpected situations that arise, such as dealing with police or hospital cases where explanations with proper language communication could be found wanting. Education of children poses another challenge for Indian parents.[28] Good international schools are not affordable and choices for Indian schools are limited in terms of location, making it difficult for students to attend.

Despite these and other obstacles, Japan continues to be India's favourite country. Japanese characteristics such as punctuality, discipline, patience, and civic and social duty appeal to Indians positively. They realise that incorporating such qualities into Indian systems might make India's aim of establishing a clean India a reality. Though Japan's immigration laws apply to all nations, and while Chinese, Koreans, and Filipinos outnumber Indians, India remains reticent due to assimilation concerns, despite their appreciation for the country.

As has been elsewhere in the world and cutting across nationality, when peoples of one nationality have migrated into another place, they usually have formed their own social groupings as an expression of their own ethnic identity. No wonder, the Indians in Japan formed their own social organization way back in 1902 when the Indian students in Tokyo formed the Hindustan Association in Japan and the Oriental Young Men's Club in Kobe. The name of this club was changed later to India Club in 1913 and Parsee Club in 1923. In the same year, some Japanese who took an avid interest in India teamed up with some Indian residents in Tokyo to form the Japan-India Club.[29] This club was the beginning of the Indo-Japanese Association. The Association activities remained suspended following rupture of diplomatic relations between Japan and India in 1904 until 1906, when peace was restored. Elsewhere, the silk merchants formed the Silk Merchants Association in 1930 and the merchants also found a textile club with Sindhis as the main members constituting the club. Also the Indian Chamber of Commerce was established in the same year.

The Indian settlement in Japan comprises people of different ethnic groups. Thus, while the Sindhis are mainly in the textile and electronic business, the Gujaratis and Jains are usually in the pearl business. There are several Bengalis who are computer programmers and software writers. The Sikh community is mainly in the textile and engineering business and also actively involved in the auto parts industry. In addition, there are many Indians, who are in Japan via the US and work mostly on contractual basis with American firms.

More recently, Indians in Tokyo areas have founded their own association, the Indian Community Activities Tokyo (ICAT), to organise cultural events. It organises three primary events: the Holi Musical Evening, the Deepawali Get Together, and the Sakura Ladies Charity Bazaar. Over 2,500 Indian-born residents of Tokyo and surrounding areas attend the Deepawali celebration. The three active associations of the Indian community in Osaka-Kobe areas in Western Japan are the Indian Social Society, the Indian Club and the Indian Chamber of Commerce and Industry. Ramakrishna Mission has a Branch there. There is a Sathya Sai Centre in Tokyo. There is also a Gurudwara in the premises of Namaskar Indian Restaurant in Tokyo, where the Sikh devotees meet twice a month. Bengal and Marathi community have also set up their own cultural bodies. In 2005, the small Odia community in Tokyo found a patron in the Ambassador, who is also Odia and used to organise Oriya community gatherings in and around Tokyo on a regular basis. Manilal Tripathi, the ambassador, returned to India in April 2006 after reaching retirement age and died in December 2012. The Indian community has an abundance of in-house talent for classical, folk, and film music and dance, which is showcased at community events and gatherings. APS Mani, Hon. Convenor, ICAT, was commended by the Government of Japan for his distinguished services. The truism, however, is that not many Indians in Japan have a positive opinion of Mani, who is seen as the self-made president of ICAT, which the Indian diasporic community in Japan suspects is operated for profit. Diwali, the single community activity he organises every year, has been converted into a money-making event, and Indians in general dislike attending. Such unpleasant feelings, however, do not diminish the acknowledgment of the Indian community's altruistic and voluntary assistance during the Kobe earthquake in 1994 and the Great Eastern (Sendai) earthquake in March 2011, both of which were widely appreciated.

Prominent commercial organizations in Japan include Indian Merchants Association of Yokohama, Indian Chamber of Commerce and Industry, Japan-India Business Cooperation Committee and Standing Committee of the Japan-India Business Cooperation. A number of Indian Public Sector Undertakings have their offices in Tokyo. They include Air India, New India Assurance Co., Handicrafts and Handlooms Export Corporation, Bank of India, State Bank of India, Minerals and Metals Trading Corporation, Marine Products Export and Development Agency, Shipping Corporation of India, India Trade Promotion Organisation and Government of India Tourist Office.[30] Among other Indian organizations in Japan, mention may be made of Indian Social Society in Kobe, Indo-Japan Software Research Committee in Gifu Prefecture, India Club in Kobe, Indian Social Association in Okinawa, and Tokyo Marathi Mandal in Tokyo.

Indians have adopted themselves fairly well and inter-community marriages are being encouraged. Japanese rules and regulations for acquisition of citizenship are very tight but these are in no way discriminatory against Indians. The emergence of India as a power in the Information Technology sector capable of supplying quality human resource in this field has resulted in a change in the profile of the Indian community in Japan. The increase in demand of the IT professionals from India and consequent relaxation in the immigration policies of Japan for these professionals will see a greater presence and contribution of the Indian community in Japan in the years to come.

With the increase in the numbers of the Indian community, demands and expectations of the diaspora have inevitably increased. In the field of education, since education in the Japanese educational institutes is very expensive, the Indian community tries to avail of the education facilities in Indian schools and colleges. Another problem it faces is the restrictive visa regime of Japan. The Japanese authorities give only a 3-month single entry visa as against multiple-entry visa for a longer duration given by the Indian authorities, in genuine cases. This is being negotiated at top political and diplomatic channels for smooth travel of Indians to Japan. Some positive outcomes have already been achieved.

Remittances by Indian Diaspora

The millions of Indians working across the world send some of their hard-earned savings back to their home country and to support their families. India received $87 billion (Rs. 5788 billion) in 2021 with the US accounting for over 20 per cent of these funds as per the World Bank's Migration and Development Brief.[31] There is general tendency among the Indian diaspora to send remittances to support their families. This trend was more pronounced when life was disrupted during the prolonged period of the COVID-19 pandemic when most economic activities were drastically halted. This was also aided by economic recovery in Europe and the United States, and the fiscal stimulus and employment support programs. These contributed to this strong growth in remittance flows. This robust return is in line with the resilience of remittance transfers the previous year, where a decline of only 1.7 per cent was recorded despite a severe global recession brought about by COVID-19.

In 2022, remittances were projected to grow by 2.6 per cent, in line with global macroeconomic forecasts, and reach $89.6 billion for India. This reflects a decline in the overall migrant stock, as a large proportion of returnees from the Arab countries wait to return. Remittances to low- and middle-income countries are projected to have increased to 7.3 per cent and reach $589 billion in 2021. India is followed by China, Mexico, the Philippines, and Egypt in terms of overall remittance received.

The negative part of the remittances is that workers sending money back home often face hefty transaction fees. The fees vary depending on the amount transferred, methods used and countries in question. The main transfer methods are through banks, money transfer operators or post offices. But with any method, a sizable chunk of the money transferred is deducted by the transferring body. As for the latest data, Indians lost over Rs. 15,000 crore or $2.3 billion in transfer fees in 2017.[32] Recently, Christine Lagarde, the IMF chief, called for new digital currencies led by central banks to ease transactions. This could make remittance transfers cheaper.

Institutional channels of money transfer are costly as banks charge high commission and in the absence of direct bank-to-bank transfer, remittances are channelized through intra-bank arrangement, putting additional loss of money through enhanced commission costs. The differences in the buying and selling rates that banks apply further erode the value of the senders' hard-earned money. Therefore, many remittances come through hawala and informal channels. This is an issue that the Indian government needs to address to protect the interests of Indian migrants who continue to contribute indirectly to India's economic activities. Policies need to be crafted by the Indian government reforming the financial transactions from overseas. If this is done, it would result in a win-win situation for the migrants and governments of the regions alike.

This is not the only challenge. The resurgence of a new wave of COVID-19 cases with new variants emerging, there are subsequent mobility restrictions of people across globe. This poses the biggest risks to the outlook for global growth, employment, and remittance flows to developing countries.

Notwithstanding such challenges, India topped the remittance recipients with $87 billion, followed by China with $67.4 billion, the Philippines and Mexico with $34 billion each, and France with $28 billion. This constitutes 11.5 per cent, 9.8 per cent, 4.9 per cent each and 4 per cent of world total remittances of $689 billion in 2018.

It is projected that the data for the current year could be still better. Migrant workers from India are on track to send home a record amount of money in 2023, boosting the finances of Asia's third largest economy poised to retain its spot as the world's top recipient of remittances. According to World Bank's Migration and Development brief, remittance flows to India are estimated to grow 12 per cent to reach $100 billion for the first time in 2023, way ahead of Mexico, China and the Philippines, helping India to retain the top position. Several longer and short-term trends that were obscured by the pandemic were catalytic in spurring remittance flows to India. Remittances have benefitted from a gradual structural shift in Indian migrants' key destinations from largely low-skilled, informal employment in Gulf countries to a dominant share of high-skilled jobs in high-income countries such as the US, UK, Singapore, Japan, Australia and New Zealand. At $100 billion, remittances from Indians overseas will be 25 per cent higher than FDI flows, which the government estimated will reach around $80 billion in 2023.[33]

Cultural Foundation

Exchange between India and Japan is said to have begun in the 6th century AD when Buddhism was introduced to Japan via the Korean Peninsula. Subsequently, Buddhist priests from India went to Japan where they spread the Buddhist teachings. Indian culture, filtered through Buddhism, has had a great impact on Japanese culture and thought, and this is the source of the Japanese people's sense of closeness with India.

Direct exchange, however, began only in the Meiji era (1868-1912) when Japan embarked on the process of modernization. From then on, bilateral relations developed around Japanese purchases of cotton. During World War II, the Indian nationalist Subhas Chandra Bose, who advocated armed struggle to end the British colonial rule, joined forces with Japan to further Indian independence. The saga of another revolutionary, Rash Behari Bose, who escaped to Japan in 1915, mobilized public opinion in Japan against the British colonial rule is a part of Japanese folklore. After the failed Ghadar mutiny of 1912, also known as Delhi conspiracy, in which Bose was the alleged conspirator, Bose escaped to Japan after three years of a cat-and-mouse chase in 1915. The occasion was the celebratory event on December 23, 1912, where Viceroy Lord Hardinge was present to formalize the capital's transfer from Calcutta to Delhi.

After his escape, the British that had signed an alliance with Japan on January 30, 1902, used this treaty to put pressure on Japan to extradite Bose. Subsequent hostilities gave Bose a safe haven. The wealthy Soma family hid him in the basement of their Nakamuraya bakery in Shinjuku area, where he worked with the chefs to create an Indian curry that is still all the rage in Japan with six billion servings annually. Bose went on to marry Soma's daughter and had two children with her.[34]

It was in Japan that the seeds of the INA were sown and nurtured. In 1942, Rash Behari Bose established the 'Indian Independence League'—an army that would fight for India's freedom from British rule. He subsequently handed over the reins to Subhas Chandra Bose, who developed it as the Indian National Army or the Azad Hind Fauj. Rash Behari was believed to have remarked once: "Gandhi is a person whom I respect but he is an Indian saint and 'a person of yesterday' whereas Subhas Chandra Bose is the 'person of today'". Rash Behari Bose, who was eventually granted Japanese citizenship, passed away on January 21, 1945, at the age of 58 before the end of World War II.

The Japanese government honoured him with the highest title given to a foreigner—The Second Order of Merit of the Rising Sun. But the honour done by the Emperor of Japan on his demise is more touching. The Imperial coach was sent to carry the dead body of the Indian veteran revolutionary. But it is a matter of regret that an independent India failed even to get the ashes of the great patriot back to the motherland.[35] The stories of Rash Behari and Subash Chandra Bose, besides others, have already been explained in greater details in an NMML Occasional Paper available on the website.[36]

Post-War Developments

In 1949, Prime Minister Jawaharlal Nehru donated an Indian elephant to the Ueno Zoo in Tokyo. This brought a ray of hope into the lives of the Japanese, who still had not recovered from Japan's defeat in the War. The fifteen-year-old female elephant picked from the kingly state of Mysore to gift the Japanese was named after Indira, Nehru's daughter, died at the age of 49 in August 1983, ironically barely a year before her namesake was assassinated. The news was widely covered in the Japanese press and was mourned by many. Eventually, Indira's star dimmed, eclipsed by subsequent panda diplomacy with China. It is also worth noting that Nehru not only waived war reparations towards Japan but decided India not to join other non-communist countries in signing the San Francisco Peace Treaty with Japan in September 1951. Instead, India signed a separate peace treaty with Japan in June 1952, which was one of the first treaties Japan signed as an independent country after World War II. India's friendship with Japan after the War helped a great deal when Japan returned to the international arena.

In view of the economic liberalization and the increasing involvement of Japanese private sector in India's economic activities, there has been a dramatic increase in the number of people visiting each other's countries. It is beyond the scope of this Chapter to discuss such issues. What is relevant here is to mention that in the 1950s, Japan restricted overseas travel but because of the favourable political wind between the two countries, cultural interactions between the two countries centred on intellectual and officials from both countries continued.

Among non-governmental organizations, the International House of Japan (IHJ) in Tokyo played a leading role in cultural and intellectual exchange, inviting a number of prominent Indians to lecture at the IHJ, including Vice President Dr. S. Radhakrishan in October 1956 and Prime

Minister Jawaharlal Nehru in 1958. The I House, as it is popularly called, also supported the activities of the Japan-based Indian Studies Group, which was engaged in research on modern India. Scholarly exchange took place between this group and the Kolkata-based Indian Statistical Institute, headed by the distinguished statistician Chandra Mahalanobis, well known for drawing up India's first 5-year plan. Therefore, within this background of strong cultural foundation, the current position of the Indians can be studied to some extent. Interestingly, New Delhi's India International Centre is modelled on the line of the IHJ and the foundation stone was laid by the outgoing Emperor Akihito, when he visited India as Crown Prince along with the Crown Princess Michiko from November 27 to December 6, 1960.[37] The Imperial couple made another visit to India as Emperor and Empress in November 2013, further deepening bilateral ties.[38]

Mutual Expectations

The ageing population in Japan has forced Japan to reconsider its attitude towards immigration. Economic leaders are worried that shrinking workforce because of rise in longevity and declining birth rate would threaten economic growth. So much so that Sony's Chairman Iwao Nakatani has urged the government to loosen its restrictive immigration policy. But any changes may come as a shock to a nation where registered foreigners make up just over 1 per cent of the population. According to the annual report of statistics on legal migrants (2004) of the Ministry of Justice and published by Foreign Press Center Japan, the number of foreign residents in Japan totaled 1,915,030 in December 2003. In world comparison, foreign labour force in Japan constitutes 0.2 per cent of the population as compared to UK's 3.6 per cent, Germany's 9.1 per cent, Luxembourg's 55.1 per cent, to name a few.[39]

Generally, many foreigners living in Japan face discrimination. Treatment appears to be determined by a range of factors—from socio-economic status to ethnic background. Japanese avoid sitting close to a gaijin (foreigner) in a crowed train is a common complaint.[40] This observation of Japanese exercising their choice of sitting beside a gaijin in an empty seat on a train, bus or café is preposterous. The argument of empty-seat phenomena with varying frequency and intensity as constant companion that certain gaijin hold are absolutely rubbish and condemnable. Talking about foreigners as stupid is another complaint that is unacceptable. Of course, factors such as profession, income and appearance determine attitudes. The truism is Indian IT workers command respect. Japanese people think that Indians are brainy and conduct their relations with respect.[41]

Faced with calls to relax immigration restrictions, the government has shown some flexibility. According to Japanese authorities, there used to be 250,000 illegal immigrants, the majority of whom entered the country on a temporary visa and over-stayed. This number has come down to 207,299 as per the Ministry of Justice data of January 2005. Many of these people are thought to work as unskilled labourers. But the government wanted to halve that number in the next five years, and is unprepared to legalise unskilled foreign workers. However, as the population continues to age, economic arguments against bringing unskilled labour will weaken.[42] It is likely that any unskilled workers will come from countries, which are geographically close, namely China and Korea. According to Japanese government source, 2003, the numbers of registered foreigners in Japan are: Korea (613,791), China (462,396), Brazil (274,700), Philippines (185,237), (Peru (53,649), the United States (47,836), and others 277,421. Compared to this figure, the number of registered Indians is negligible, with latest count of 53,000.[43]

The Japanese have a very different image of the Indian community than they do of Koreans, Chinese, or other Southeast Asians. Indians in Japan are generally regarded as disciplined, hardworking and law-abiding. In sharp contrast, the image of the same people in their own country tells a different story. Similarly, when one wants to study the personality of the Japanese residing in India, one gets totally a different picture. Though not getting embroiled in any controversy, some believe that Japanese people generally have a split personality, often evident in how they conduct human and economic relationships.

As regards the Japanese perception of Indians in Japan, there is a large reservoir of goodwill and appreciation of their diligence, sincerity and commitment. Indians in Japan have earned the respect of the locals and while they have become an integral part of the Japanese society, they have retained their own ethnic and cultural identities. For example, when the Shinsei Bank, one of the biggest banks in Tokyo, was declared bankrupt in 2000, a small team of Indians worked hard to bring about a turnaround, and the bank regained its lost status in five years' time. The Indian team headed by Dhananjay Dwivedi, Senior Marketing Executive Officer, and assisted by a small team of young Planning Managers, all Indians, was responsible for this amazing recovery. Within three years of its being declared bankrupt, this young team turned it around into a profit-making bank. Today, books are being written on this incredible turnaround story. Shinsei Bank is not the exclusive example. The Indians are responsible for the automatic ticket dispensing system of the Japanese Bullet train, which is known around the world for its unmatched engineering and technology.[44]

Until about a decade ago, the Indian population in Japan numbered around 5,000. But in the last three years, there has been a spurt and almost 300 per cent growth every year in this figure. The basic reason behind this is the perceived image of Indians in Japan. Japanese visa regulations and citizenship conditions are very stringent as they view all foreigners with suspicious eyes. Indians are viewed differently, as trustworthy. Here again, the same story is different when one examines Japanese perception of Indians in India.

Though there is no match for Japanese engineering skills, the Indians are creating new milestones in the field of Information Technology. Not just in Tokyo, but also in the industrial towns of Nagoya, Yokohama and Kobe, there are several examples of Indian achievements. If Indians follow the same level of discipline and work culture as they do while in Japan, the developed nation status for this country will not be far off. Even though the Japanese may not chew gutka (flavoured tobacco) or paan (betel leaves) they are heavy smokers of cigarettes. However, this is changing as people grow more health-conscious. Previously, cigarette stubs and ash could only be found in the dustbin. Every smoker in Japan used to keep a personal ashtray in his or her pocket to collect cigarette ash and half-burned cigarette butts. This was not something they used to do because of any legislation, but because they felt inspired to keep cleanliness around them.

This is also changing for the worse. In Japan, the concept of cleanliness has shifted dramatically in recent years. Cigarette butts may be found on almost every street corner in Japan these days. Even though smoking is prohibited in open spaces and in public in Chiyado-ku, it is usual to observe many Japanese smoking in the street, flagrantly defying the rules. On the contrary, a foreigner who is aware of the restrictions would not dare to breach the law. There is a noticeable shift in Japanese attitude and thought that is being observed in today's culture. Violation of rules and laws has become a common cultural trait of the Japanese. So much so, that the much admired best customer-care service seems to be highly questionable these days. Japan's rich cultural legacy is gradually deteriorating, whether it be basic mannerisms in trains, classroom behaviour, road manners, driving manners, or customer service at various levels. This is not to argue that similar incidents do not occur in India. However, when comparing two societies based on economic growth, the Japanese rank worse than India, for example. Opinions may differ, however.

About a third of the registered Indian nationals in Japan live in the Kansai region. In Kobe Indian immigrants form the largest foreign community after the Chinese and Koreans. It is a successful and wealthy community, thanks to their business skills and almost effortless ability to master new languages. In the process of integrating themselves into the Japanese society, they have been careful to preserve their cultural identity. Despite this close involvement of people, there is a lot of ignorance in Japanese people about India. The persistent stereotype of India as a country of peasants and snake charmers is giving way and Japan has begun to acknowledge that the 350 million middle class consumers and the consistent high economic growth rate will take India to a major global player status.

Regrettably, Japan's awakening to the impact of India's emerging economic power at the world stage is not properly noticed. This is not to say that Japanese attitudes and knowledge of India have remained constant. The Japanese public's image of India has undoubtedly changed during the last decade and a half. The Japanese response to India's tremendous economic expansion is consistent with what the rest of the world thinks about India. When the US and other major economic powers of the world recognized the unfolding of economic potentials that the liberalization unleashed, Japan was alarmed and readily consented to the changing worldview, regardless of whether it really subscribed to such a view or not. The average Japanese even suspected if India could sustain the unprecedented growth momentum. The current phase of economic slowdown and compounded by the law and order stemming from some controversial policies of the Modi government threatened to erode for a while the confidence of Japanese on India's growth story. The cancellation of the annual Modi-Abe summit in Guwahati, scheduled for December 2019, risked delaying, if not undoing, Indian and Japanese strategies to economically develop the northeastern states, which are viewed as a gateway to further India's Act East Policy via Myanmar. Restoring confidence appeared to be a greater problem than building. As it turned out, that was a transient aberration.

The Indian Community in Edogawa (ICE) was established in 2000 at Nishi Kasai in Tokyo as a voluntary body. It was discovered that the number of Indians who were coming to live and work in Japan due to the demand for Information Technology (IT) services was increasing at a very fast pace. Further, it appeared that the new arrivals preferred to stay in the vicinity of Nishi Kasai, which is on the eastern side of Tokyo on the banks of the Nakagawa river. With the sudden rise of Indian residents, who had very little exposure to Japanese society, a few long-term residents of Edogawa, Nishi Kasai, felt that some sort of voluntary body of members of the community of Indians would be of help to all the Indian residents of Edogawa in particular, because of physical proximity, and other residents of Tokyo/Kanto region in general. Thus was born the ICE. The first objective was to get to know each other. Subsequently, cultural events such as Diwali, children's fancy dress, dance, songs and skits by adult members have since become regular activities of this association.

A 'virtual Little India' has thus emerged in this corner of Tokyo. The ethnic Indian population in Tokyo's Edogawa Ward, eastern Tokyo, totalled about 1,000 eight years ago. Earlier, there were only about 100 Indians living in the ward. Their numbers grew rapidly in recent years, with an increase of 300 per cent in 2005 alone.[45] According to the Tokyo metropolitan government, the Indian population in Tokyo rose from 1,628 in January 1,

1995, to 5,883 on January 1, 2005, with heavy concentration in the Nishi Kasai area. According to Edogawa Ward Office, there were 3,758 Indians living in the ward as of January 2018, the most of any municipality in the nation. That means about 30 per cent of the Indian people in Tokyo, as well as 10 per cent of those in the entire nation, are concentrated in Edogawa Ward.[46]

The explanation is the rapid growth of information technology. Computer engineers and their families are flocking to Japan, and young Indian engineers agree that Japan and India make great partners, with the former excelling in hardware development and the latter in software. It may be mentioned that Jagmohan S. Chandrani,[47] who settled in Edogawa in the early 1980s because of the area's proximity to both Narita International Airport and Yokohama's port became the president of the ICE and it was he who realized the need of an Indian International school for most Indian engineers who are young parents and who wanted their children to be taught in their native language and mathematics according to Indian school curriculum. The collective efforts of the Indian community in the area led to the founding of such a school in 2004 for children in the age group of 3 to 13. And yet, in both appearance and atmosphere, Edogawa's Indian neighbourhood is a far cry from New York's Little India or Indian districts around Southeast Asia. It seems Edogawa has become more like a "virtual Little India", with its residents staying connected via the Internet and cell phones.

The Indian Community Activities (ICT) in Tokyo took birth 29 years ago in Tokyo. This is an association of Indians living in the Kanto area of Japan. This is a voluntary association with no subscription or annual membership fee payable by members. The membership is open to all Indian nationals, people of Indian origin and foreign spouse of Indians living in the Kanto area.

Among the recent activities being organized by the ICT include free Yoga classes that started from January 2, 2006, at the Vivekananda Culture Centre (VCC) at the Embassy of Japan with a highly experienced Yoga teacher, Tokyo English Life Line (TELL) for the Telephone Counselors Training Program that started in mid-February 2006 and Vishnu Sahasranamam

Japan held once every month at Shimo Meguro Juku Center, Meguro. Among other cultural events being organized by the Indian community include Diwali celebration, Republic Day celebration, Rajasthan Cultural Dance Show, Independence Day celebration, Sakura Bazar, etc. Owing to the initiative of then Ambassador Manilal Tripathi, since retired and deceased, the first Oriya Community Saraswati Puja was held on February 13, 2005, at Furuishiba Bunka Centre.

Another important association in Japan is the India IT Club. India IT Club is an industry body managed by IT industry representatives in Japan. The first IT Club meeting was held on November 15, 2000, at the Indian Embassy with the participation of around 44 Indian IT professionals based in and around Tokyo. The idea behind forming the Club was to organise meeting amongst Indian IT professionals in Japan and as a platform for exchange of ideas. Subsequent meetings of India IT Club incorporate participation of members from Japanese companies interested in building network with Indian IT companies. Later on, in November 2002, the Indian Embassy handed over management of the IT Club to leaders from the IT industry.

India IT Club stands for and strongly supports the underlying value, leadership of Indian IT in IT services market in Japan. The India IT Club serves as a sales representative for India in Japan. Its primary goal involves promoting coexistence with Japanese business techniques while preserving integrity of Indian business practices. Its core purpose is to build and project Indian IT image in Japan, to promote Indian IT companies in Japan, to assist Japanese companies in learning about Indian IT and to disseminate information on Indian companies regarding visas, travel, and information exchange between India and Japan.

The India IT Club holds its meetings once in every two months in the Indian embassy. These meetings are attended by representatives of around 100 IT-related companies, both Japanese and Indian, including representations by prominent experts and business leaders in the field of IT and a business exchange party at the embassy. The bimonthly IT Club meetings were also held to coincide with high-level visits of IT-related dignitaries from India. The IT Club meetings also provide a platform for information sharing and business networking. A focus group has been formed which consists of country heads of major Indian IT companies based in Tokyo, India Club executive committee members and officials of the Embassy of India. The focus group meets at least once every month to take stock of the developments of the activities of India IT Club and also discuss various issues including building of strategies for Indian IT brand promotion, pooling of resources among Indian IT companies based in Japan, language training to Indian IT professionals, withholding tax issues, visa issues, etc.[48]

Conclusion

The aforementioned discussion demonstrates that members of the Indian diaspora are deeply conscious of their rich cultural heritage. They understand that they are the inheritors of the traditions of the world's oldest continuous civilization, and as part of such a rich inheritance, they are naturally eager to preserve their cultural identity. Deep dedication to their cultural identity has manifested itself in a variety of ways throughout the Indian diaspora. There is perhaps no other diaspora in the world with such incredible diversity.[49] It reflects the diversity of India's ethnic, linguistic, and religious communities. As a result, the initial diaspora members took with them a rich legacy of harmonising various customs, practices, values and benefits. Their unique capacity to harmonise and adapt has served Indians very well in the lands of their adoption. In almost every country of their adoption they have higher educational standards than the national averages. By and large, the divorce rates are also substantially lower.

Historical experiences have influenced and shaped the attitudes and cultures of some Indian settlers in Japan. For example, the original diaspora members remained and formed a tight community. Also, for example, the Indian population in the Kobe region prefers to isolate itself from both Japanese and other Indians. Beyond their geographical boundaries, they are little known and have little effect. The reasons can be manifold: One is the discrimination and isolation they faced in the initial years of their settlement from a community, which showed no mercy to any non-Japanese. On the contrary, the Indians emerging victorious from their initial hardship preferred to stay in a close-knit group so as not to share the benefits of their hard-won survival right with any new comers. Such exclusivist mentality is comparable to the Indian policy of non-alignment, which was pioneered by India after the close of World War II and the division of the world into two camps. India was jealous of protecting its hard-earned freedom and decided not to join either of the camps but preferred to remain non-aligned. The experience of the Indian settlers in Kobe region probably put a break to the spreading of Indian community in Japan for years to come.

Another trait of the Indian diaspora that comes out demonstrably clear is that they seldom sought conflict with their fellow citizens of the countries of their residence. This may be attributed to the deep-rooted commitment to the cultural and civilizational ethos of India. This ethos has been imbibed by the successive generations of members of the Indian diaspora, whether they are descendants of illiterate indentured labourers or of highly qualified professionals. The Indians diaspora is conscious of passing on the cultural values to their successive generations. If the Indian diaspora is to be expected to preserve and nurture its own cultural identity, Indian diplomatic missions ought to assume significantly more assertive role for its fruition.

The Indian government has in place cultural centres in many countries: Egypt, Germany, Mauritius, Suriname, Guyana, Indonesia, Russian Federation, UK, Kazakhstan, Uzbekistan, South Africa, Trinidad, Japan, South Korea, Tobago, Sri Lanka, Fiji, Caribbean and others. The High Level Committee on Indian diaspora had recommended that cultural centres in countries with a substantial Indian presence be expanded and adequate funding provided for the purpose.

As regards Japan, during the visit of Prime Minister of Japan, Junichiro Koizumi, to India in April 2005, a joint statement was issued between Prime Minister Manmohan Singh and Koizumi that stated the importance of opening an Indian Cultural Centre in Tokyo and up-gradation of the Japan Foundation New Delhi Office to a full-fledged Cultural Centre. The initial attempt by India to start such a Centre in Tokyo remained at an exploratory stage for quite some time. After a mini Cultural Centre became operational from the Indian Embassy compound in Kudanshita, the Vivekananda Cultural Centre came into being soon enough. Similarly, the Japanese attempt towards such an initiative hit a major road block as nitty-gritty issues such as reciprocity, privileges and exemptions remained to be resolved. Dialogue through diplomacy finally triumphed when the Japan Foundation New Delhi Office became Japan's cultural hub in India in 2004.

This reflects India's and Japan's determination to create a new economic/ political architecture in the region as their economic engagement increases. In this journey, the involvement of the Indian community in Japan in advancing governmental initiatives and so contributing to the complementarity between the two countries is invaluable. The Festival of India in Japan in 2007, which showcased India's rich cultural legacy, provided an opportunity to improve cultural ties between the two countries. The role of Indian immigrants in Japan in polishing and cementing cultural relationships is the most beautiful thing that has happened in the rise of Oriental civilization. The cultural diplomacy between Indians in Japan and Japanese in India strengthens the strategic and economic depth in the bilateral ties.

Notes

1. This Chapter is an expanded version of the author's lecture on the same topic delivered at the Nehru Memorial Museum and Library on February 2, 2023.
2. https://www.quora.com/Why-are-the-latest-generations-of-Japanese-Brazilians-so-mixed-more-than-60-of-them-are-children-of-inter-racial-couples-but-in-Japan-immigration-and-miscegenat
3. https://www.pewresearch.org/social-trends/rise-of-asian-americans-2012-analysis/japanese/
4. Richard Gunde, "Japanese Brazilian Return Migration and the Making of Japan's Newest Immigrant Minority", January 27, 2004, https://www.international.ucla.edu/asia/article/6996
5. Ibid.
6. "Japan House", January 8, 2023, https://www.mofa.go.jp/p_pd/pds/page25e_000145.html
7. https://www.japanhousela.com/
8. https://www.japanhouselondon.uk/about/what-is-japan-house/
9. See, Rajaram Panda, "The Brazilian Sojourn", *The Pioneer Sunday Edition*, September 3, 2017, https://www.dailypioneer.com/searchlist.php?section=&adv=Brazilian+sojourn&yr=2017
10. See, Amartya Sen, *Identity and Violence: The Illusion of Destiny*, Penguin, UK, September 2007, p. 240.
11. "Over 16L gave up citizenship since 2011, EAM tell RS", *The Times of India*, February 10, 2023.

12. "225k Indians renounced citizenship in 2022: Govt", *Hindustan Times,* February 10, 2023.
13. http://www.uohyd.ernet.in/sss/indian_diaspora/indian.html
14. Ibid.
15. Amit Bhandari, "Poor Conditions: NRIs In Saudi, Kuwait 10 Times More Likely To Die Than Those In US", August 24, 2015, http://archive.indiaspend.com/cover-story/poor-working-conditions-nris-in-saudi-kuwait-10-times-more-likely-to-die-than-those-in-us-64841
16. Shireen Aziz, "7 million Indians are Currently Living in West Asia: Report", *The Quint*, May 3, 2018, https://www.thequint.com/news/politics/indians-in-the-middle-east
17. See, Rustom Bharucha, *Another Asia: Rabindranath Tagore and Okakura Tenshin*, Oxford University Press, 2006, 236 pp. See a review of the book, David Burleigh, "A friendship's influence across Asia: Japan's Okakura Tenshin and India's Rabindranath Tagore", *The Japan Times*, October 28, 2007, https://www.japantimes.co.jp/culture/2007/10/28/books/book-reviews/a-friendships-influence-across-asia/#.XBySIlwzZPY
18. Rajaram Panda. "Bengal's Romance with Bengal: A Historical Narrative", *NMML Occasional Paper, History and Society New Series 108*, December 22, 2022, http://nehrumemorial.nic.in/downloadSeries/362
19. See, Hiroshi Shimizu, "The Indian Merchants of Kobe and Japan's trade expansion into Southeast Asia before the Asian-Pacific War", *Japan Forum*, vol. 17, no. 1, March 2005, p. 27. https://www.tandfonline.com/doi/epdf/10.1080/0955580052000337459
20. Claude Markovits, *The Global World of Indian Merchants, 1750-1947: Traders of Sind from Bukhara to Panama*, Cambridge, Cambridge University Press (2000).
21. See, G.A. Chandru Advani, "The History of Indians in Japan", in *Global Migration of Indians: Saga of Peoples Enterprises, Identity and Integration*, The Global Community of People of Indian Origin, August 27, 1989.
22. Shimizu, n. 19, p. 28.
23. Ibid.
24. For a comprehensive background of this phase of Indian settlement in Japan, see Ibid, pp. 25-48.
25. See, Markvotis, no. 20.
26. Quoted in Ibid.
27. *Report of the High Level Committee on Indian Diaspora, December 2001* (New Delhi: Indian Council of World Affairs, 2001).
28. Megha Wadhwa, "Indians in Japan – a love story beset with challenges", *The Japan Times*, June 17, 2015, https://www.japantimes.co.jp/community/2015/06/17/voices/indians-japan-love-story-beset-challenges/#.XBiiAFwzZPY.
29. See, Mimi Banerjee Dhar, "Indians in Japan: History & Dimensions of Relations", in Lipi Ghosh and Ramakrishna Chatterjee, eds., *Indian Diaspora in Asia and Pacific: Culture, People, Interactions* (New Delhi, Rawat, 2004).

30. Information in this section is heavily drawn from *Report of the High Level Committee on Indian Diaspora, December 2001*. See Chapter 21, pp. 273-288.
31. "India Receives $87 billion in Remittances in 2021" November 18, 2021, https://indbiz.gov.in/india-receives-87-billion-in-remittances-in-2021/
32. See, *Times of India*, February 6, 2019.
33. "Remittances to India set to hit record $100 bn this year, 25 per cent higher than FDI flows", *Times of India*, December 1, 2022.
34. Neera Majumdar, "The Indian freedom fighter Japan remembers as its beloved chef", *The Print*, May 25, 2018, https://theprint.in/theprint-essential/rash-behari-bose-the-indian-freedom-fighter-japan-remembers-as-its-beloved-chef/62722/
35. Rash Behari Bose, "The Greatest Indian Revolutionary", https://www.hindujagruti.org/articles/90.html
36. Rajaram Panda, "Bengal's Romance with Japan: A Historical Narrative, NMML Occasional Paper History and Society New Series No. 108, 2022, http://nehrumemorial.nic.in/downloadSeries/362
37. https://www.mea.gov.in/photo-features.htm?910/First+visit+of+Crown+Prince+and+Crown-Princess+of+Japan+to+India+1960
38. Rajaram Panda, "Significance of Royal Visit and India-Japan Relations", *C3S Paper No. 2042*, December 5, 2013, http://www.c3sindia.org/japan/3801
39. For a comprehensive overview of this issue, see Rajaram Panda, "Japan's Declining Population and Demographic Challenges", *Estudos Japoneses*, Sao Paulo, 2017, No. 38, pp. 67-80. https://www.revistas.usp.br/ej/issue/view/10766
40. Baye McNeil, "The empty seat on a crowded Japanese train: 10 years on, the 'gaijin seat' still grates", *The Japan Times*, October 17, 2017, https://www.japantimes.co.jp/community/2018/10/17/our-lives/empty-seat-crowded-japanese-train-10-years-gaijin-seat-still-grates/
41. *Japan Calling*, Embassy of Japan, New Delhi, April-June 2005.
42. Rajaram Panda, "The Greying of Japan: New Challenges", *Reitaku International Journal of Interdisciplinary Studies* (Kashiwa, Japan) vol. 6, no. 1, March 1998, pp. 67-87. Also see, Rajaram Panda "Greying in India and Japan: A Comparative Perspective", in Rajaram Panda and Yoo Fukazawa, eds., *India and Japan in Search of Global Roles* (New Delhi: Bibliophile South Asia, 2007), pp. 295-329.
43. http://news.bbc.co.uk/go/pr/fr/-/1/hi/world/asia-pacific/3708098.stm.
44. *Japan Calling*, April-September 2004.
45. *The Asahi Shimbun* (Tokyo), May 15, 2006.
46. Tsukuru Ikeda, "Tokyo's Nishikasai a second home for Indians in Japan", *The Statesman*, May 20, 2018, https://www.thestatesman.com/world/tokyos-nishikasai-second-home-indians-japan-1502638470.html
47. For information about Chandrani, see Mukesh Williams, "Jagmohan Chandrani: Father of Little India in Nishi Kasai", *Japan Spotlight*, September-October 2021, pp. 46-49, https://www.jef.or.jp/journal/pdf/239th_Special_Article_04.pdf.
48. http://www.indiaitclub.com/index.asp
49. *Report of the High Level Committee on Indian Diaspora*, n. 27, p. 403.

5

India-Japan Partnership and Northeast India

Introduction

Since the 1990s, when India adopted its Look East policy in response to liberalization, its engagement strategy has been complemented by civilizational links with the East and South eastern regions of Asia. The Narendra Modi government injected a new element of dynamism by rechristening it as Act East policy, implying thereby a departure from mere rhetoric to practical execution of projects embraced in the policy. During Modi's tenure, it is clear how far India has come in terms of political, economic, and security/strategic awareness of the area. One significant example of this engagement strategy was when India hosted all the 10 heads of states of the ASEAN member states as special guests instead of the customary one at the 69th Republic Day celebrations on January 26, 2018.

The Modi government devised a foreign policy strategy to reach out to ASEAN and aggressively integrate its economy with global markets through more forward-thinking measures. Because India shares borders with the lone ASEAN member, Myanmar, building this gateway through connection projects and upgrading the infrastructure basis in India's Northeast was prioritised. In this strategy, India joined hands with Japan to launch several developmental projects in the northeast. The focus of this Chapter is limited to this cooperation between India and Japan in order to understand the enormity of economic and strategic significance of deepening relations with Southeast Asia. Indeed, ASEAN is the fulcrum around which both India and Japan see sense to cooperate and develop the northeast region of India.

Geographical Context

India's Northeastern region has a unique standing in India because of several factors. The region has a complex ethnic composition, different experience of British control compared to the mainland, insurgency problems in the post-independent period, and sensitive location bordering five countries. Due to these factors, the government in New Delhi has been careful that involvement of foreign countries in the region is controlled. Such a line of thinking constrained the economic development of the region and fuelled the sense of alienation among the people of the region from the mainland. After Narendra Modi came to power in 2014, this policy changed. With a view to economically develop this region and remove the people's sense of alienation, India decided to join hands with Japan to develop the region by launching several connectivity projects.

During World War II, the advancement of the Japanese army into the present Manipur and Nagaland states not only brought massive destruction but also precipitated infrastructure development in the region and impacted the livelihood of the residents, although this fact has hardly caught the public's attention in both India and Japan. This Chapter intends to examine the changing narrative in the current times, investigate the conditions of connectivity in terms of economic and infrastructure development and human mobility within the region and with the neighbouring countries. India's decision to cooperate with Japan for the development of the northeast India presents a potential boost for Modi government's Act East policy.

Strategic Factor

The northeastern region of India is strategically important. The region is endowed with vast reserves of a variety of natural resources such as uranium, coal, hydrocarbons, forests, oil and gas. The biggest shortcoming, however, is poor connectivity which hinders the full exploitation of such rich resource. In a far-reaching change of the narrative of keeping foreign powers away from this region, India invited Japanese Prime Minister Abe Shinzo during his visit to New Delhi as the Chief Guest of India's 65th Republic Day Parade in 2014, and extended an invitation to Japan for partnering with India to invest and build overland infrastructure in the region.

After assuming power in May 2014, when Modi chose Japan as the country for his visit in September 2014, it signalled a new approach to deepen ties with this friendly country. Interestingly, other issues such as the nuclear deal, deepening defence ties keeping in mind the changing geopolitical dynamics in the region, and the contract to build India's first bullet (Shinkansen) train network to connect Mumbai and Ahmedabad with the construction cost of $18,148.15 million took precedence over the issue of developing India's northeastern region.[1] Subsequently, negotiations with Japan fructified to build better road connectivity and transforming the region into a manufacturing hub. It was agreed that the Japanese state-owned development agency, Japan's International Cooperation Agency (JICA) would be the donor agency through which the aid would be disbursed. The National Highways and Infrastructure Development Corporation Ltd (NHIDCL) were identified as the local Indian partner that was delegated with the responsibility of working with JICA in the region. The projects to be undertaken by JICA and NHIDCL began in April 2016 after a detailed project report got the nod from JICA and the Department of Economic Affairs via the Ministry of Roads Transport and Highways.

Defined Projects

The two main projects that were defined were the widening and improvement of Aizawl-Tuipang NH54 route (380 km) in Mizoram, which would connect India to Myanmar and the Tura-Dalu section (48 km) of NH51 in Meghalaya. The biggest strategic significance of this narrative can be deciphered from the fact that the northeast Indian states share 5,000 kilometre of international borders, with Myanmar, Bangladesh, China, Bhutan and Nepal, providing strong links to foster economic integration with both South and Southeast Asia. If the full potential is to be realized, ensuring better connectivity within and between the northeastern states is central to ensuring border security and maintaining peace and stability. Such a policy option could probably also address the issue of insurgency that has plagued the region for a long time.

As a key driver of India's Act East policy aimed to sculpt partnerships with key states in the Indo-Pacific focusing on Japan, Vietnam, Australia and other ASEAN countries, developing the region economically can serve many economic, political and strategic objectives. In order to achieve this objective, improving connectivity in the region is of utmost importance. The path to do this is not easy. In fact the challenges are huge. This includes low road density, poor quality of existing roads, inadequate intra-regional connectivity and so on. Silchar and Dimapur are the only two main rail-heads in the area and other existing rail and road infrastructure connecting to various state capitals are unable to cope with the increase in both goods and passenger traffic over the years.[2] Changing this was thought to be urgent. Indeed, if connectivity is improved by expanding road and rail links, it will benefit the local populace by providing better market access for their produce at remunerative rates, as well as facilitating imports at competitive pricing.

Japan is the only suitable country to partner with India on socio-economic development projects in the northeast region of the country. Though Japanese ODA has been made available since 1981 in key fields such as energy, water supply, forestry and urban development, there is a need to augment the loan component. JICA's known expertise in constructing durable and environmentally sustainable roads access through mountainous terrains could help. Japan's JICA has executed similar projects in several countries such as in Sri Lanka, Indonesia, Bangladesh, Ghana, Morocco and Tanzania in key areas such as building roads, railways, seaports and airports, all of which have helped quicker routes for trade and transport of critical raw materials to the resource deficient Japan, besides contributing to the host economies. Better connectivity with JICA participation also helps other Japanese companies to operate, thereby creating a win-win situation for both sides. If the connectivity projects are successfully executed, it would provide a further boost to India's Act East policy.

The other area that demands attention is cross-border connectivity and market linkages for the northeastern region with ASEAN so that a long-term vision for India-Japan partnership for economic development in the region can be generated.

India is one of the fastest growing countries in the world today, and it is catching up with the world in terms of growth rate. As a result, there is a greater need for convergence within the country, particularly between the central government and the states that are gradually growing economically. Three key areas, therefore, need extra attention—infrastructure development, institutions, and governance. It goes to the credit of the Modi government that, in this era of competitive federalism, he has focused attention on leveraging the great opportunities that exist in the northeast states, as well as other states across the country so that their productivity for rapid growth can be unleashed.

In such an endeavour, Japan appreciated the importance the central government attached to the northeastern region of the country and welcomes India's invitation to participate. In 2016, the Japanese ambassador in India Kenji Hiramatsu visited Imphal, Kohima and Assam to make on the spot study and to convey Japan's interest to engage with the region. Besides the popularity of Assam tea in Japan, Japanese people are also familiar with Imphal and Kohima due to the fierce battles which were fought there more than 70 years ago. For Japan, the expression North-East has a specific meaning because it immediately brings to mind a special link between India and Japan, as well as a worldwide and strategic cooperation. In a broader sense, Prime Minister Abe Shinzo's announcement of his foreign policy strategy as a "free and open Indo-Pacific strategy", which treated the Pacific and Indian Ocean as a wide region creates a domain for improving intra and inter-region connectivity to promote flow of people and goods.

To ensure maritime security to protect such flow of people and goods, there exists a synergy between Japanese strategy and India's Act East policy. Both India and Japan have strategic and political dialogues at various levels, including annual summit and ministerial levels and also 2+2 meetings of foreign and defence secretaries. This 2+2 dialogue is planned to be elevated to the ministerial level soon. In Tokyo in October 2018, Prime Minister Modi announced that high-level ministerial dialogue involving their respective foreign and defence ministers to work for peace and stability in the world with Japan shall commence soon. In a joint address, Modi remarked: "without the cooperation between India and Japan, the 21st century cannot be an Asian century".[3] India started similar 2+2 Ministerial Dialogue with the US in September 2018. During the visit of Japanese Foreign Minister Taro Kono to India in early January 2019, it was agreed that the 2+2 dialogue framework be upgraded to the level of ministers.[4] Kono reaffirmed the importance of cooperation in third countries and India's north eastern region, thereby realize the shared vision of a free and open Indo-Pacific. Since both India and Japan are already working closely on improving connectivity in India, and between India and its vicinity, cooperation between the two countries on the northeastern region can be placed in this wider strategic context. To boost connectivity, India and Japan agreed to work together in third countries like Bangladesh. Also, agreements were signed on cooperation in healthcare, digital and new technologies, food processing and between the naval forces of the two countries.

The perception that the state of infrastructure and connectivity are the biggest impediment to economic development in the northeastern region is now being altered, as Japan has joined to partner India in this mission. Like Japan, the northeastern region is mountainous and very vulnerable to the damage caused by heavy rain and natural disasters. It is one area where Japan's role can be crucial since it has the expertise and the required technology.

As Indian economy registers steady growth, more and more Japanese companies see business opportunities and are interested in investing in India. In the past one decade, Japanese direct investment in India has grown significantly. The Northeast region has vast economic potential—agriculture, food processing and many other industries—and by exploiting these potential, the region can benefit. Abe often observed that a strong India is in Japan's interest and vice versa, and therefore a prosperous and peaceful region is a welcome prospect. This new resurgence of Japan's partnership in the Northeast is going to be a permanent strategy of the seven sisters and Sikkim. The states need to be proactive and become stakeholders in trade and commerce.

The Assam government rightly announced a separate department for Act East Policy. The region is more than just a window for ASEAN in the context of Act East Policy, but would be the epicentre with three Cs as three pillars—Communication, Commerce and Culture. If realized, the corridor could turn into a golden corridor. Any partnership between India and Japan will find a sound foundation with Northeast as a springboard. The Modi government has a vision to make the region as an organic hub of the country. Assam is positioned to become a global business hub with Guwahati at the epicentre. The time is opportune for both India and Japan to partner to make the Northeast the new jewel of India.

While working towards developing the region economically by joining hands with Japan is laudable, there are other challenges that cannot be overlooked and must be factored in while making and executing projects. Not all the seven states are at the same level of development. Even resources are scattered. For example, while Assam is a large state, it is not wealthy. On the other hand, Sikkim is a tiny state but with a high per capita income. Therefore, in terms of economic development, the region cannot be considered as one entity. Besides, the multiplicity of social systems prevalent in the region poses challenge, especially in states which are very heterogeneous. Manipur has a very large plain area and the tension between plain and hill has been there for a long time. The three main tribes—Meitis, Kukis and Nagas—are not always on the same page. Therefore, such deep social and economic diversity must be considered while planning economic development through connection and infrastructure developments. The governments in the states ought to ensure peace so that private sector will have no worry to do business there. Besides Assam, Arunachal Pradesh are positioned to attract private sector. The region's seven states do, however, share a low population density. A regional development strategy should begin with agriculture. Farmers profit from better market access to their produce, therefore connection across states becomes more important.

Indeed, in order to attain inclusive sustainable development for the whole of India, the northeastern region ought to get primacy of focus as it is also an important gateway between India and ASEAN. Improving rural roads and forest projects could get priority. As the region is mountainous, not only the existing roads have little scope for widening but even the existing road transport network is limited. In order to secure technology for maintenance of soil and structures, JICA is implementing capacity building projects in mountainous region.

Other factors may have contributed to the region's infrastructure development being delayed. Reasons for slow pace of development could be geological issues, the soft soil, undulating terrain, law and order issue and lack of resources to include equipment and human resources. Capacity and skills of the contractors need to be developed. Involvement of the community in infrastructure development is equally important.

While there is no argument about the necessity of connectivity, it cannot be seen in isolation since other issues come into play connectedness can take numerous forms and dimensions, including physical and non-physical connectedness, financial connectivity, interpersonal connectivity, and telecommunications connectivity. Similarly, infrastructure has three effects: one direct and two indirect ones. Private firms would be enticed if developed infrastructure was accessible. Quality should not be compromised, or else maintenance expenses would soar over time. The same rationale will apply beyond the area if ASEAN's economies are to be integrated. There will also be a need to keep windows open for small enterprises along highways and railways, and this home town investment should be easily accessible.

As regards the people-to-people connectivity, private and personal education would require focused attention of the northeast expected to be an education hub with the ASEAN countries. Even here, if linkages are established with Japanese counterparts, that shall help enhance quality of delivery of technical and professional education system.

Both the governments in India and Japan face new challenges to develop the northeastern region of India as state-centric security issues could delay projects. The region remains underdeveloped because the triadic linkage between resource, production and trade could not take place in the past and changing this narrative quickly may face roadblock. Markets of the neighbouring countries have remained important so far and the main obstacle in the region remained market connectivity. This narrative can be changed in two ways: either through Bangladesh or through South East

Asia. As of now, the region has not benefitted as the whole trade takes place through the maritime route. Yet, there are potentials for trade in items like pineapples, ginger and fish from the region.

As the northeastern region is an agriculture-based economy and agricultural revolution preceded the industrial revolution, India and Japan become natural partners as envisioned by India's Act East Policy. With Myanmar as the gateway to the ASEAN, this partnership looks very promising. Prime Minister Modi's vision about the northeast is not just change but also transformation so that the aspirations of the people are fulfilled. Japan is aware that the northeastern region is strategically important for India to preserve the territorial integrity of the country, and therefore is willing to work with India to develop the region. What both sides need is result-oriented focus. Friendship with Japan is time immemorial. Memories of Japanese soldiers reaching India for the first time at Moirang in Manipur and Kohima in Nagaland during the World War II is fresh in mind. The mantra for development of the region at present should be focused on three Es—Education, Electricity and Employment.

India-Japan Forum

In September 2017, at the conclusion of the annual summit, Prime Minister Modi and Japanese Prime Minister Abe signed an MoU to establish the India-Japan Act East Forum. Subsequently, the Act East Forum aiming to provide a platform for India-Japan collaboration under the rubric of India's "Act East Policy" and Japan's "Free and Open Indo-Pacific Strategy" was set up. The aim is to identify specific projects for economic modernization of India's North-East region including those pertaining to connectivity, developmental infrastructure, industrial linkages as well as people-to-people contacts through tourism, culture and sports-related activities.

With a view to give a big infrastructure push in the northeast, both India and Japan set up the India-Japan Coordination Forum for Development of North East to aggressively develop strategic infrastructure projects such as connectivity and road network development, electricity and disaster management. The first meeting was held in September 2017. The forum is tasked to identify priority development areas of cooperation for development of northeastern region (DONER). The forum has representation from India's ministries of external affairs, road transport and highways, power and the department of economic affairs. From the Japanese side, the forum has representation from the Japanese Embassy and other government-affiliated Japanese organizations based in New Delhi.

This partnership is being viewed by some as an attempt to contain China.[5] This is because this initiative came in the backdrop of Chinese troops making repeated incursions into the Indian territory. India and China have sparred over hydropower projects in Arunachal Pradesh, a state that borders China and has the highest potential for hydropower generation in India. Several multilateral lending agencies, including the World Bank, have been unwilling to fund projects in the so-called disputed border state in India's northeast region—seen as sensitive as parts of the region are claimed by China.

While for India, development of northeast is a priority and a key to promote its Act East Policy, Japan places special emphasis on cooperation in northeast for its geographical importance connecting India to Southeast Asia and historical ties. Experts say that Japanese involvement in these projects may get expedited with the Dokalam incident acting as a trigger.

India's decision to partner with Japan in the northeastern region has, therefore, huge strategic significance as well as advantage. The region being adjacent to China, which claims Arunachal Pradesh as its territory, referring to it as "South Tibet", China is opposed to any foreign investment in the "disputed areas".[6] Chinese discomfort is to be expected, although India and Japan are less concerned but remain vigilant. Indeed, with an eye on China, India is working on a slew of road and bridge projects to improve connectivity with Bangladesh, Nepal, and Myanmar. India is also keen on expediting the South Asia Sub-Regional Economic Cooperation (SASEC) road connectivity programme in the backdrop of China's ambitious Belt and Road Initiative (BRI), aimed at connecting around 60 countries across Asia, Africa and Europe. The BRI lacks transparency and many small countries run risk of falling into debt trap. Even Malaysia abandoned certain initiatives in which it had previously promised to participate. India has been sceptical of the BRI since its inception, and it has expressed severe concerns over the development of the China-Pakistan Economic Corridor as part of the BRI, which runs through Pakistan-occupied Kashmir's Gilgit and Baltistan sectors.

Both India and Japan held the second meeting of the Japan-India Act East Forum in October 2018 in New Delhi, ahead of the annual summit between the two countries in November when Modi visited Tokyo. Both sides agreed to deepen cooperation in various sectors including building infrastructure in north eastern region, forest management projects of Tripura and Meghalaya. A new initiative to utilize bamboo, available in abundance in the region, and people-to-people exchanges were discussed.[7]

Elsewhere Japan has been helping India with some of the infrastructure projects such as the Mumbai-Ahmedabad high-speed rail corridors or bullet train, Delhi metro and others through JICA. Japan has been India's partner for a long time and there is a certain degree of comfort. This aspect is discussed in the Chapter on economic relations.

To take the development further and reinforcing Japanese commitment to engage with India in the northeast, JICA signed an agreement on 30 October 2018 to provide ODA loan of 25,483 million Japanese yen (Rs. 1,575 crore) to improve road network by constructing India's longest bridge across river Brahmaputra. Once constructed the 4-lane bridge across Brahmaputra, it would bridge the long-awaited gap between Meghalaya and Assam and the travel time will considerably be reduced. The Project is expected to contribute to "Japan-India Act East Forum" which aims to expand the cooperation between Japan and India in the north east. The Executing Agency for the Project is National Highways and Infrastructure Development Corporation Limited (NHIDCL).[8]

The Phase-III of the Project includes construction of the about 20 kilometres long four lane bridge between Dhubri in Assam and Phulbari in Meghalaya over the Brahmaputra River. The bridge will be built with emergency staircases, approach sections and necessary traffic facilities. Under Indian Road Congress (IRC) the width of each lane of the main road is 3.5 meters with the design speed at 100 kilometres/h. The bridge structure comprises the navigational portion, which has a span of 125 metres and the viaduct portion with a span of 60 metres. When completed, it will become

India's longest bridge, spanning more than 19 kilometres, surpassing the Bhupen Hazarika Setu in the state of Assam, which is 9.15 kilometres across.[9] The bridge is expected to be completed by 2026-27. The bridge will cut the distance from 250 kilometres to 19 kilometres. The bridge also would prove to be significant for international movement of traffic to other nations.

Including the amount extended for Phase–III, JICA has extended a cumulative ODA loan of 184,895 million Japanese Yen (approximately over Rs. 11,900 crore) for the North East Road Connectivity Project. Phase-I covered improvement of National Highway (NH)-51 and NH-54 in Mizoram and Meghalaya states, respectively. Phase-II helped in laying bypasses for NH-40 in Meghalaya and National Highway 54 bypasses in Mizoram. Both the Phases helped in improving connectivity in the NER through up-gradation of Transit infrastructure."[10]

Established by a specific law as an incorporated administrative institution under the Government of Japan, JICA aims to contribute to the promotion of international cooperation, as a sole Japanese governmental agency in charge of ODA implementation. JICA is the world's largest bilateral donor agency. JICA works as a bridge between Japan and emerging countries, and provides assistance in forms of loan, grant and technical cooperation so that the emerging countries can strengthen their capabilities.

India-Myanmar-Thailand Trilateral Highway Project

As a part of larger initiative and besides cooperating with Japan, India is involved in the India-Myanmar-Thailand Trilateral Highway. It was expected to be operational by the end of 2019 but is delayed because of the pandemic. Tokyo which had deep engagement with Myanmar even during the rule by military junta, now sees greater relevance to deepen ties with Myanmar as the country serves as India's land-bridge in ASEAN region. Other projects in which Japan has partnered with India are Guwahati Water supply scheme and the Nagaland Forest Management Project.

Why is this Project Important?

Under the rubric of India's Indo-Pacific strategy with Act East policy as the anchor, Prime Minister Modi's vision of SAGAR—Security and

Growth for all in the region—underpins India's vision of the Indian Ocean region and the greater Indo-Pacific region. In this strategy, ASEAN countries remain central to realizing India's vision of the Indo-Pacific. India's BIMSTEC and IORA initiatives and frameworks such as Ganga-Mekong Cooperation bring India closer to the ASEAN. India's northeast, which is being transformed by connectivity projects in cooperation with Japan, provides a land bridge with ASEAN. If understood from this larger perspective, the India-Myanmar-Thailand Trilateral Highway currently under construction is an important project in India's Act East strategy. When completed, it will connect Moreh in India with Mae Sot in Thailand via Myanmar. By linking other highways in other ASEAN states such as Vietnam and Laos, this project will boost economic growth in the region.

What is the project's history and how did it originate? The trilateral highway project was first proposed during a ministerial meeting in Yangoon in April 2002. The approximate length of the highways is 1,360 kilometres. The 160 kilometres long India-Myanmar Friendship road linking Moreh-Tamu-Kalmeya-Kalewa forms part of the trilateral highway. It was built first by the Border Roads Organisaton and was inaugurated on February 13, 2001. The BRO maintained it until 2009 when full ownership was transferred to Myanmar. India and ASEAN have plans to extend the Trilateral highway route to Laos, Cambodia and Vietnam as this connectivity will generate annually, an estimated $70 billion in incremental GDP and 20 million in incremental aggregate employment by 2025.

India initiated a preliminary survey to determine the feasibility of establishing a rail link parallel to the trilateral highway in January 2018. Japan expressed interest in collaborating with India and funding the proposed rail link. The trilateral highway project is important because it aims at opening the gate to the ASEAN through the land. The project will boost trade and commerce in the India-ASEAN Free Trade Area, as well as with the rest of Southeast Asia.

In order to deepen people-to-people contact, Japan has introduced the IRIS program, named after a mysterious link between Japan and the northeast region of India, linking one species of iris called *Kombirei* that grows mainly around Loktak Lake near Imphal and commonly used in festivals and was found to be a new species in India and identical with "Kakitsubata", which was known as "Japanese iris"[11] and considered an indigenous species of Japan for more than 1000 years. Under the IRIS program, a group of 23 young talents from Manipur and Nagaland was invited to visit Japan from October 28 to November 4 in 2017. During the visit, the group visited Tokyo, Saitama, Chiba and Hiroshima and had wide-ranging experiences such as participating in environment and disaster prevention programs, besides meeting Parliament Secretary for Foreign Affairs and learning a local government's efforts to boost eco-tourism. The programme was announced by Japanese Ambassador Hiramatsu at the commemoration of the 73rd anniversary of Battle of Imphal in May 2017. Japan hopes that the IRIS program shall bear fruit, and eventually bloom as flowers between Japan and the Northeast region of India.

Notwithstanding the thrust to boost such soft power diplomacy, the challenges are huge. Besides the lack of good quality infrastructure that requires the infusion of large amount of capital, employment opportunities are few, despite a relatively high literacy rate as compared to many parts of the country. Insurgency may have waned but stray incidents of extortions in some states in the region could pose security issue for foreigners to work there. All the seven states being stakeholders, proper coordination in executing projects shall be extremely important.

Being a sensitive region from the security point of view, the fact that India has welcomed Japan to be partner in development of the region demonstrates the level of trust, confidence and bonhomie that both share. If projects are executed as planned, one can expect dramatic turnaround in the economic prosperity in the region and its people.

Like the outgoing ambassador Kenji Hiramatsu, his successor Satoshi Suzuki is too upbeat about deepening ties with the northeast region of India by partnering with India to enhance connectivity. The ambassador is convinced that connectivity is the best area to showcase how both counties can bring about tangible benefits to the entire region.[12] Indeed, Japan's decision to become the lead country for the connectivity pillar of IPOI was a strong reaffirmation of Japan's commitment to enhancement of connectivity.

In fact, India and Japan have been advancing various connectivity projects in India as well as in third countries.

Both India and Japan are equally dedicated to developing India's northeast area in the quest for a free and open Indo-Pacific. Since none of the northeastern seven sisters have an outlet to the sea, both India and Japan are working together closely to upgrade highways all the way to the border with Bangladesh. This has emerged as an important footprint of India-Japan collaboration in the north east.

Indeed, linking northeast region with the outside world is the new narrative in Indo-Pacific construct. To take the initiative further, Prime Minister Modi inaugurated 'Maitri Setu' bridge between India and Bangladesh in March 2021. This has been built over the Feni river that flows between the Indian state of Tripura and Bangladesh. The 1.9 kilometres long bridge joins Sabroom in south Tripura with Ramgarh in Bangladesh. With this, Tripura is set to become the 'Gateway of North East' with access to Chittagong Port of Bangladesh, which is just 80 kilometress from Sabroom. From Ramgarh to Baraiyarhat, India is building a road while Japan is constructing eight bridges. Ambassador Suzuki explained that if one looks at all these joint efforts by India and Japan in a holistic way, one can notice a dynamic connectivity network in which India-Japan collaboration provides the landlocked northeast with access to the Bay of Bengal and beyond, most importantly to ASEAN countries. Indeed, the Indo-Pacific maritime domain is the source of growth and prosperity, and therefore better access to these Oceans is vital for the improvement of people' lives. Japan is also partnering India in building the 20 kilometres, four-lane bridge between Dhubri in Assam and Phulbari in Meghalaya.

Under the aegis of the Japan-India Act East Forum, both countries are also committed to boost health care in the northeast, including a 400-bed hospital in Kohima, Nagaland, and a Super Speciality Cancer and research Centre in Mizoram, besides the project on Strengthening of Health Systems and Excellence of Medical Education in Assam. In January 2021, the two countries also discussed other areas of cooperation besides reviewing the status of projects under implementation in India's sensitive northeast including roads, water supply and hydel power. The discussion took place under the framework of the Act East Forum, which is headed by India's foreign secretary on the Indian side and the Japanese ambassador in India on the Japan side. As mentioned earlier, the Act East Forum was established in 2007. It frames, evaluates and facilitates Japan-India collaboration in connectivity and developmental projects in and with the North Eastern region of India.[13]

Ongoing projects in the region are worth 231 billion yen or approximately Rs. 1,600 crore. Other potential areas cooperation include agriculture, fisheries, agro-industries, promotion of tourism, urban development forestry and connectivity.

A Japanese embassy official observed: "Japan attaches great importance to the cooperation for the development of India's North East, anchored by its historical ties, trust and friendship. The North East stands at a place strategically important to realise a free, open and inclusive Indo-Pacific; and Japan is proud to have been a partner with the people of North East in their aspirations for a better and sustainable future". Japan is one of few countries to be involved in development activity in the region—one of the others being Singapore. New Delhi views the region as a natural link with Southeast Asia. New Delhi has been looking to step up cooperation between its northeast and countries around it like Bangladesh, Bhutan and Myanmar besides the Association of Southeast Asian Nations (ASEAN) with the aim of raising the living standards of people given that the region has been as under-developed and a hotbed of militancy and separatists groups. In recent years, the Indian government has signed peace pacts with key militant and separatist groups, which has brought peace to the region.

Indeed, enhancing connectivity in the Indo-Pacific region by utilizing their expertise and complementarities is the broader vision of India-Japan partnership. This important issue was also highlighted by Modi and Suga during the Quad Leaders' Summit in March 2021. India-Japan collaborative initiative is a step in honing the synergy between India's Act East policy and Japan's Partnership for Quality Infrastructure within which both are committed to develop and strengthen reliable, sustainable and resilient infrastructures that augment connectivity within India, and between India and other countries in the Indo-Pacific region. For long, India has stressed the importance of connectivity in the Indo-Pacific region as a uniting factor rather than just enhancing trade and prosperity in the region. Indeed, robust connectivity with countries of the region, near or far, is deep rooted in Indian civilizational history. Indian culture has been enriched by ancient linkages with the rest of the world, just as the light of the Indian culture has shone in lands connected across land and seas by emissaries and merchants.[14]

The Indian diplomats stress that India has devoted more resources and assigned greater priority to building connectivity in its immediate neighbourhood. Since 2005-06, India has extended Lines of Credit worth nearly $31 billion to more than 64 countries. Its Act East Policy is at the centre of its connectivity orientation and a fulcrum of its broader approach to the Indo-Pacific. India's efforts are focused on connecting the North-East with the dynamic economies of South East Asia, and enhancing connectivity within the North East itself. Given Japan's expertise in development of quality infrastructure, India hopes that Japan's lead on the connectivity pillar of IPOI will give a boost to connectivity in the region and contribute to unlocking the potential for an equitable, positive and forward-looking change in the region contributing to security and growth of the Indo-Pacific.

Japan finds compelling reasons to collaborate in Northeast India's development. Japan believes that given its technological and infrastructural development, this is an essential component of India's Act East Policy. If both sides work together with devotion, it can boost the region's economy. Indeed, northeast India has a high level of interest in Japan's economic aid and technology. Ambassador Suzuki's travel to Assam in February 2023 is thus noteworthy.[15] Japan's interest in India's northeast region stems from historical connection with Japanese troops fighting in Nagaland and Manipur, which is consistent with India's Act East Policy.[16] JETRO is also trying to set up an industrial township in the region. Another reason for Japan's attraction to India's northeast that is often overlooked is that both India and Japan have not participated in the China-led Belt and Road Initiative (BRI), which is why collaboration between the two countries for the development of India's northeast region assumes added significance.

Because of strategic reasons and sensitivity of the region, India has avoided enlisting other countries in regional development operations.

However, Japan's situation is unique due of the relationship and trust that India and Japan enjoy. Northeast India also functions as a link between India and the ASEAN region. As a result, both parties benefit from the scenario.

However, several hurdles have to be overcome in taking the joint India-Japan development projects to fruition. Coordination at the local level between Japanese entities and different northeastern states is necessary. This is not easy given the cultural differences and exclusive mindsets of peoples of which there are many tribes with varying priorities. Moreover the level of development in the seven sisters is not uniform. The positive aspect of these projects is that the people of the region are willing to welcome the Japanese as brother and therefore coordination between different agencies at the central and regional levels and at the corporate and national levels are unlikely to face any hurdles.

As it transpires Northeast India has been an essential part of Japan's Free and Open Indo-Pacific vision, which has been the highlight of Japanese foreign policy ever since the administration of the former Japanese Prime Minister Shinzo Abe. This persisted during the Suga administration and continues throughout the Kishida administration. The collaboration between India and Japan to develop India's northeastern area exemplifies their dedication, trust, and friendship, and it will help to hone the partnership's broader security and strategic dimensions.

Notes

1. Ateetmani Brar, "Japan in Northeast India: A Potential Boost to New Delhi's 'Act East Policy'", January 18, 2016, http://www.ipcs.org/comm_select.php?articleNo=4960
2. Ibid.
3. "In Tokyo, PM Modi Announces High-Level Ministerial Dialogue With Japan", October 29, 2018, https://www.ndtv.com/india-news/in-tokyo-pm-modi-announces-2-2-ministerial-dialogue-with-japan-1939400
4. "India, Japan will upgrade 2+2 dialogue", *The Times of India,* January 9, 2019.
5. Utpal Bhaskar, "India, Japan join hands for big infrastructure push in Northeast", August 3, 2017, https://www.livemint.com/Politics/8T9Q9wBg1s4JKRwFgChMDO/India-Japan-join-hands-for-big-infra-push-in-Northeast-Indi.html
6. Debarshi Dasgupta, "Strategic location of region seen as gateway to Asean markets", *Straits Times,* November 14, 2018, https://www.straitstimes.com/asia/south-asia/japan-gives-india-aid-to-develop-north-east-states

7. Huma Siddiqui, "Japan-India Act East Forum plans major projects for northeastern region", *Financial Express*, October 10, 2018, https://www.financialexpress.com/defence/japan-india-act-east-forum-plans-major-projects-for-north-eastern-region/1344590/. See also, https://www.thestatesman.com/india/india-japan-to-step-up-cooperation-for-developing-north-eastern-states-1502695622.html
8. https://www.jica.go.jp/india/english/office/topics/press181030_02.html
9. Rupakjyoti Borah, "Japan's Infrastructure Push in Northeast India Builds on Trust Factor", July 25, 2018, https://japan-forward.com/japans-infrastructure-push-in-northeast-india-builds-on-trust-factor/
10. https://www.jica.go.jp/india/english/office/topics/press181030_02.html
11. Borah, n. 9.
12. Ateet Sharma, "India, Japan to step up work to link northeast region with Indo-Pacific", March 20, 2021, https://daijiworld.com/news/newsDisplay?newsID=814286
13. Elizabeth Roche, "India, Japan review implementation of projects in Northeastern region", January 28, 2021, https://www.livemint.com/news/india/india-japan-review-implementation-of-projects-in-northeastern-region-11611843123239.html
14. https://www.mea.gov.in/Speeches-Statements.htm?dtl/33680/Address_by_Secretary_East_at_the_Virtual_Seminar_on_Connectivity_Cooperation_for_a_Free_Open_and_Inclusive_IndoPacific
15. Rupakjyoti Borah, "Japan Shares Good Reasons to Collaborate on Northeast India's Development", *Japan Forward*, March 15, 2021, https://japan-forward.com/japan-shares-good-reasons-to-collaborate-in-northeast-indias-development/
16. Ibid.

6

India-Japan: Defence and Strategic Engagement

Introduction

Backed by the civilizational ties and nurtured by leaders in both the countries with dynamic foresight over the decades during the post-War years, bilateral ties between India and Japan have scaled to unprecedented heights. This chapter will highlight the areas in which both sides have identified mutual interests, both bilaterally, regionally, and internationally, all of which contribute to regional and global peace while also enhancing bilateral ties in a variety of domains. It will focus on and explore how defence and security cooperation has been strengthened.

To highlight the major contours in the relationship, the foremost that comes to mind is the common understanding on how the concept of Free and Open Indo-Pacific needs to be pursued. What is the main aim to pursue this policy? This concept has emerged as a response to China's belligerence and assertiveness in a host of regional issues and also at bilateral level with countries in dispute, necessitating deeper strategic cooperation with allies who share common principles. The Quad grouping of four closest partners—the United States, India, Australia, and Japan—immediately comes to mind. China has been aggressively promoting its Belt and Road Initiative (BRI) in the Indo-Pacific region, where all its projects are opaque. The smaller poorer countries are drawn into the Chinese offer of liberal funding, which they cannot resist and easily fall into debt traps. This has been China's strategy in all its BRI projects.

As a counter to China's strategy, countries sharing common values and respecting global rules are expanding their own cooperation in various fields and areas. These include non-military cooperation, primarily focusing on infrastructure-funding, supply chain resilience and technological innovations. The strategic and defence cooperation between India and Japan against this background needs to be understood when India's defence and strategic outlook has brought close ties in these domain areas with the US, Australia and other friendly countries in the Indo-Pacific region. India's deepening of ties with South Korea and Vietnam can be cited as other examples.

The geostrategic and geo-economic landscape in greater Asia has changed dramatically in recent years. The advent of China as a regional power with significant power ambitions has threatened to disrupt the present power balance. China's strategy is motivated by its recently acquired economic strength and significant military muscle. This makes the smaller countries in the region uneasy as they adjust to the great power competition between the United States and China. As a result, the term Indo-Pacific has gained popularity in describing the relevant theatre. As Japan prepares to cope with the China challenge, it is compelled to strengthen its security ties with the US and deepen cooperation with friendly countries that share common values by building strong security networks.[1] Both Japan and India have bilateral issues with China. While Japan has a long-standing territorial dispute with China over the Senkaku Islands, India's border issue continues to remain a thorn in bilateral ties. Besides, there are many regional issues on which both India and Japan share common viewpoints vis-à-vis China. These are bringing both India and Japan closer together.

Origin of the Indo-Pacific Concept

The origin of the term 'Indo-Pacific' can be traced to Indian historian Kalidas Nag who for the first time used it in his famous book *India and the Pacific World* in 1941.[2] Nag, however, used this term more in cultural and civilizational sense and not in the sense of contemporary times that has a strategic connotation. In contemporary times, the term gained currency in academic and strategic circles only in the 2000s. Former Prime Minister of Japan Shinzo Abe captured the strategic imagination of the concept during his landmark speech in the Indian Parliament in August 2007. He was the architect of Japan's Free and Open Indo-Pacific (FOIP) strategy and the Quadrilateral Security Dialogue (known later as QUAD). In his speech, Abe discussed "an arc of Freedom and Prosperity, which will be formed along the outer ring of the Eurasian continent".[3] Since then, many countries adopted the term as a geographical manifestation of Asian regionalism, replacing the existing concept of the "Asia-Pacific". Though there is no unanimity regarding the definition of Indo-Pacific, majority of analysts point to security and connectivity as twin pillars of the Indo-Pacific concept. Now the concept is viewed as "a security-oriented construct, focused on managing maritime interdependencies which span the Pacific and Indian Oceans".[4]

Main Driver of Strategic Partnership

As mentioned above, both India and Japan find China's recent assertiveness in regional issues as a new challenge to disrupt the regional order, thereby upsetting the existing power equilibrium. While Japan has territorial disputes with China over the Senkaku Islands, India has the long festering border disputes that show no sign of resolution. China's advance into the global common such as the South China Sea, and claiming almost the entire water body as its own has threatened to disrupt maritime commerce. When the Philippines, an Asian country, objected to China's intrusion into its Exclusive Economic Zone, China rejected its objection. When Philippines obtained a verdict in July 2016 from an international tribunal rejecting China's claims as illegitimate, China rejected it since the tribunal lacked enforcing authority. Since then, China has used the salami-slicing strategy to gain additional maritime space, and by constantly employing coercive tactics, smaller Asian states' security is jeopardised. In this ever-changing environment, India and Japan seek common ground to establish the status quo so that peace and security in the region is maintained. As a result, ways to create new institutional architectures and strengthen the existing institutions to manage the Asian affairs are the chosen methods.

In these complexities of power relations and balancing ties, how do India and Japan deal their ties with the US whose presence in the Indo-Pacific region can have a calming influence? After all, as the only superpower the US has enormous responsibility to help maintain global order. It has huge interests in maintaining peace and stability in the Indo-Pacific region. Both India and Japan have realised this and built close ties with the US. While Japan and the US are security partners bound by a security treaty, India too has found a great deal of commonality of interests, which converge on a host of issues, bilateral, regional and global. Again, here China seems to be the main driver.

As a throwback, it may be mentioned that after Japan's defeat in the World War II, it was the US that was instrumental in establishing democracy in Japan. That is a different story, which might not need elaboration here in detail. What is relevant here to mention that when the Peace Treaty formally ending the War was signed in San Francisco in 1951, thereby ending the occupation of Japan by the Allied forces, India that had already emerged as an independent nation from the control of the colonial power Britain, refused to join to sign the San Francisco Peace Treaty. Instead, India chose to sign a separate peace treaty with Japan in 1952. India's belief that Japan's sovereignty needed to be recognized separately dictated the Nehru government's choice and this facilitated Japan's respectable entry into the global community. This aspect has been discussed elaborately in previous Chapters.

Alongside the San Francisco Treaty, Japan signed with the US a Mutual Security Treaty. This allowed the presence of the US troops on Japan's soil. The intention was that a weak and thus a vulnerable Japan should not fall a prey to communism that has already taken birth or return to its militaristic past.

The US has also other interests. The US was keen to use this alliance with Japan to strengthen its strategic presence in East Asia because China and then the Soviet Union were on the cusp of expanding their military capabilities and drifting ideologically apart to socialistic ideology that preferred communism as the ideal driving force. The Cold War had already started because of this ideological divide with each side keen to spread influence in larger part of the world. Japan's then Prime Minister Shigeru Yoshida found the US as a key ally for Japan's security needs so that the country could devote on economic reconstruction. In 1960, the treaty was revised, allowing the US to establish bases in exchange for a commitment to defend Japan in the event of an attack by any external power. America's first strategic foothold in Asia was thus secured.[5]

Thus, two rivals during the War became close friends bound by convergence of interests. This partnership has been further strengthened in the wake of global changes and even after the Cold War ended following the disintegration of the Soviet Union. Soon a new hegemon in the form of an ambitious China is born threatening to disturb the existing global equilibrium. The US assurance to Japan for its security does not come free however. In return, Japan pays for the upkeep of the US forces in its bases. This has become problematic lately as the US has frequently been demanding that Japan enhance its security burden by paying more. This is an irritant between the two countries, though not too serious enough to derail ties as other serious issues compel both to stay engaged.

Bilateral ties passed through a turbulent phase during the presidency of Donald Trump when he chose to adopt the doctrine of "America First", which put the credibility of the alliance into test.[6] After Joe Biden came to power, his administration made attempts to mitigate the challenges caused by Trump's trade protectionism, indifference to allies and ill-conceived détente with North Korea.

However, the US continues to make repeated demands to increase the security burden, which is occasionally raised. This has put the relationship under strain at times. According to the US Department of State, the number of US military forces in various bases[7] in Japan number 55,000,[8] in addition to the thousands of civilians and family members. For the annual host-nation support called Omoiyari Yosan or sympathy budget or compassion budget, Japan pays more than 75 per cent ($4.4 billion). As of the 2011 budget, Japan no longer refers to this compensation as Omoiyari Yosan.

In view of the increasing vulnerability of Japan's security, the US has deployed its most advanced military assets to Japan, including the USS

Ronald Reagan carrier strike group and the F-35 Joint Strike Fighter. Japan procures more than 90 per cent of its defence imports from the US that has sold the F-35 Joint Strike Fighter, F-2D Airborne Early Warning Aircraft, the KC-46 Refueling Tanker, the Global Hawk Unmanned Aerial System, the MV-22 Osprey Tilt-rotor aircraft, the AIM 12-0 Advanced Medium-Range Air-to-Air (AMRAAM), UGM-84 Harpoon, and SM-3 Block IIA Ballistic Missile Defense interceptor missiles.[9]

Earlier, the US had stationed the aircraft carrier USS George Washington at Yokosuka naval base in Japan until eight years ago, when a top Japanese academic opposed to US military presence in Japan mocked the carrier as a "monster" to the author. This was replaced by the USS Ronald Reagan, which is anticipated to return to its base in 2025.[10] The aircraft carrier was commissioned in July 1992 and had to undergo mid-life nuclear refuelling and maintenance at the Newport News shipyard in Virginia. The carrier's refit-19 began in 2017 and was expected to last four years but was significantly delayed by the COVID-19 and other setbacks.

Despite the protection of US nuclear umbrella, the US has all along encouraged Japan to assume a greater security role. Though the primary focus in Japan-US security ties were premised originally for bilateral purposes, the changing security environment in the Indo-Pacific region has necessitated a rethink and reprioritizing the focus with a larger canvas. The US expects Japan to be an active responsible partner in this role of peace-keeping. As a result, Japan finds difficult navigating through volatile domestic politics where opinions are sharply divided to change the existing defence posture.

During Abe Shinzo's long reign, reform appeared to be conceivable, but as it transpired the job was half done. There wasn't much to write about during the short tenure of his successor Yoshihide Suga. The Kishida administration showed promise to align Japan's security policies to the liking of the US leadership. On its part, the US is careful not to be seen as to imposing on Japan[11] but has used diplomacy to persuade Japan to see the bigger picture, in which greater cooperation among like-minded states in the Indo-Pacific area can produce for the common good.

Thus, it transpires that during the post-Cold War era, the fundamentals underlying the Japan-US alliance have come under increased scrutiny and a bit under stress as the US has begun to put pressure on Japan to "normalize". Fears of abandonment by the US have prompted Japan to undertake essential changes to its military position in the alliance. New security challenges, such as the 1995 Taiwan Strait Crisis, North Korea's 1998 missile test, and the worldwide war on terror, enabled Japan to provide logistical support to the United States on distant beaches, modifying its role in the alliance system. Under Prime Minister Abe's "proactive pacifism" strategy, Japan's steady militarization towards a more proactive engagement in international security matters through the collective self-defence paradigm was ultimately institutionalised in 2014.[12]

Washington sees some compelling reasons for Japan to reform its security policy, with some constitutional changes playing a critical part in strengthening the alliance relationship between the two countries.[13] The common threat of China continues to drive Japan and the US closer together in pursuit of shared interests. Incidentally, Japan's efforts to implement constitutional amendments, while challenging for the time being, may benefit those who are concerned about China's assertiveness on regional problems. As previously stated, many Southeast Asian countries, as well as India, are experiencing significant uneasiness as a result of China's extraordinary growth. China has thus earned the epithet of being a threatening power. Not only has Japan resolved to make considerable increase in its defence spending and breaching its self-imposed threshold of 1 per cent of the nation's GDP, it also created a National Security Council in December 2013 to rectify a key anomaly, the lack of which was seen as a setback and symbol of Japan's apathy in strategic and security matters.[14]

After Abe's tragic assassination, when Yoshihide Suga became Prime Minister, he undertook a historic visit to Washington in April 2021. It received much attention in India.[15] During his first face-to-face meeting at the White House since taking office, President Joe Biden took advantage of the opportunity to fulfil his pledge to revitalize American alliances that were relegated to the background under his predecessor Donald Trump. Their discussions revolved around China's recent belligerence in territorial disputes in the South and East China Seas as well as in the Taiwan Strait. Underlining the importance of working with allies and partners such as India,

Australia and Japan through the Quad "to build the free, open, accessible, diverse, and thriving Indo-Pacific", Suga and Biden expressed concern about China's ambitions to dominate the development of new-age technologies such as 5G, semiconductor supply chains and quantum computing.[16] Both indicated their resolve to continue the previous policy of pressure on Beijing to address economic malpractices such as "violations of intellectual property rights, forced technology transfer, excess capacity issues, and the use of trade distorting industrial subsidies."[17]

Supported and encouraged by the US, Japan has opted to adopt a pro-active role in Asian affairs so that the US could feel less burdened to take the responsibility to manage Asia's security matters.[18] After the once-defunct Quad was resurrected and institutionalized, major stakeholders have remained engaged in discussing Asia's security issues through summit meetings and regular meetings of senior ministers of the four Quad member countries. Much of the credit for this institutional mechanism to come to fruition must go to Abe who conceptualized it and was instrumental in giving it shape. In this endeavour, India is a key factor driving the success of free and open Indo-Pacific. On the other hand, deepening engagement with Japan is one of the key pillars of India's 'Act East' policy.[19]

Japan's Indo-Pacific Strategy and new Security Posture

This shift in commitment to a "Free and Open Indo-Pacific" is quite recent. Ever since Abe spoke about confluence of two seas in his speech in Indian Parliament in August 2007, the term 'Indo Pacific' has gained currency in international diplomacy. From a Japanese perspective, this was perhaps the first articulation of evolving a cohesive strategy for the Indo-Pacific maritime space. In August 2016, during his speech at the Sixth Tokyo International Conference on African Development (TICAD) in Nairobi, Kenya, Abe delivered his vision of Free and Open Indo-Pacific. The main idea was to convey the shared importance of maritime connectivity, along with common values, to united countries in the region. He remarked that: "What will give stability and prosperity to the world is none other than the enormous liveliness brought forth through the union of two free and open oceans [the Pacific and Indian Oceans] and two continents [Asia and Africa]."[20] Clearly, Japan views the Indian Ocean and the Pacific Ocean as integral parts of the Indo-Pacific region, which should have greater military and economic connectivity, including securing large regional sea lanes. As China aggressively promotes the BRI, its global infrastructure development strategy for the Eurasian continent, and expands its military activities beyond the South China Sea, Tokyo is justified in framing a security strategy that encompasses the Pacific Ocean and the Indian Ocean.

China's coercive activities, particularly in the Senkaku islands, have unnerved Japan. This in turn has shaped Japan's policy discourse on the Indo-Pacific, allowing Tokyo to create enabling domestic environment for revisiting Japan's post-war security posture. Just before becoming Prime Minister again in December 2012, Abe had authored an article in which China stood accused of attempting to make South China Sea as "Lake Beijing", which would allow "the People's Liberation Army's navy to base their nuclear-powered attack submarines, capable of launching missiles with nuclear warheads."[21] Abe asked Japan not to "yield to the Chinese government's daily exercises in coercion around the Senkaku Islands in the East China Sea", since that would only help China "to establish its jurisdiction in the waters surrounding the islands as a fait accompli."[22] This warning sounds eerily similar to those concerning China's recent unilateral attempts to change the territorial status-quo in India's Ladakh region.

Abe's Indo-Pacific formulation has gone a long way in facilitating India to consider the Indian and Pacific Oceans in a strategic paradigm.[23] Japan's Indo-Pacific strategy seeks to ensure its strategic autonomy by shaping a favourable regional environment by expanding its options. While Japan's strategic priorities are mainly set by the US and China, its Indo-Pacific strategy is necessarily multi-layered. Balancing China and keeping the US engaged in East Asia are the key components of Tokyo's strategy. Beijing's assertive measures targeted at maritime expansion directly threaten Tokyo's security interests in the East China Sea. And frequent Chinese intrusions into Japan's territorial waters around the Senkaku Islands along with Beijing's extensive militarization of islets are perceived as dangerously undermining the freedom of navigation.[24] In order to enhance its credibility, Japan has been engaging with regional ASEAN-led multilateral organizations.

Despite several attempts by Tokyo to seek engagement with China to improve crisis prevention in the East China Sea, China has refused to scale down its coercive posturing. By deploying various military and non-military instruments of statecraft, Beijing's overall aim is to change the regional balance of power with a view to achieving greater strategic ambitions over the East China Sea.[25] Given "Beijing's three-pronged attrition strategy toward the Senkakus: normalizing Chinese presence; exercising law-enforcement rights; and taking over exclusive control",[26] Japanese push on the Quad is quite understandable.

Japan's policymakers may be averse to use the blunt language to describe the challenges China poses to Japan's territorial interests, but there seems clarity in Tokyo regarding Beijing's revisionist tendencies and its persistent attempts to gain regional pre-eminence. When the US Secretary of State Rex Wayne Tillerson in the Trump administration met with Japanese foreign minister Taro Kono in late October 2017, revival of the Quad dominated the agenda. Alice Wells, who accompanied Tillerson, had remarked on the Quad that "the Japanese foreign minister discussed would be building on a very productive trilateral we have with India and Japan", and would also include Australia to offer alternative to countries in need of infrastructure and development without "predatory financing or unsustainable debt." She termed the Quad as "a natural progression and convergence of interests between democratic countries in the Indo-Pacific region."[27]

Yoshihide Suga, who assumed office in September 2020 after Abe's sudden resignation, followed on the footsteps of his predecessor regarding Japan's foreign policy. Suga also believed that the concept of FOIP would foster peace, transparency and inclusiveness in the vast region. Within less than a month after assuming office, Suga undertook his first official visit in October to Vietnam and Indonesia as the two ASEAN countries occupy a key position in the Indo-Pacific region.[28] It needs to be noted that while Vietnam is one of the claimants in the South China Sea territorial disputes with China, Indonesia's exclusive economic zone overlaps with China's nine-dash line. Instead of visiting Washington in his first overseas visit, Suga's visit to two Asian countries was seen by some analysts as "another reminder that the traditional US "hub-and-spokes" alliance system is transforming for the better" as Tokyo started reinforcing the FOIP vision promoted by Washington.[29] Before this visit, Japan had hosted the Quad meeting of the foreign ministers of Japan, India, Australia, and the US on October 6, 2020, in which they "reaffirmed their collective vision of maintaining a free, open and inclusive Indo-Pacific."[30]

Japan's FOIP policy, aimed at countering China's rising assertiveness, has found reflection in Tokyo's official discourse on defence and threat perception. Against the backdrop of the US-China strategic competition, Japan seems to have concluded that its security environment is deteriorating at a rapid pace. China is unmistakably the elephant in the room in Japan's new Defence White Paper for 2021, which stamped Abe's proactive security policy.[31] The White Paper may be viewed in the context of Tokyo's continuing diplomatic efforts to champion a US-led rules-based international order. What was particularly noticeable in the White Paper is Japan's stance on Taiwan and the statement that "Taiwan is important for Japan's security and the stability of the international community. Noting the fast changing military balance in the Taiwan Strait, the White Paper exhorted Tokyo to "pay close attention to the situation with a sense of crisis more than ever before", signaling a significant policy shift.[32] The previous Defence White Papers avoided controversy vis-à-vis China. For instance, the 2020 White Paper did not explain the importance of military balance between China and Taiwan to Japan's security. Since Japan is approximately 70 miles away from Taiwan, China's potential attack on Taiwan with an eye to integrate it with the mainland will have serious ramifications on Japan's own security. The mention of Taiwan Strait in an official document assumed significance because Japan seems to have taken a firm public stance over the Taiwan issue realizing the Biden administration's military support to Taiwan.[33]

The mood in Japan has shifted towards increased support for Taiwan. The public statements by Japanese leaders tying Taiwan's security to Japan's own security interests indicate strong intent and resolve.[34] Also reflecting Japan's growing concerns about Chinese undesirable activities in the East

China Sea, the While Paper asserted that "China has relentlessly continued attempts to unilaterally change the status quo by coercion in the sea area around the Senkaku Islands, leading to a grave matter of concerns".[35]

China's new maritime law of February 2021 permitted Chinese Coast Guard to fire on foreign vessels for illegal entry into the waters it claims and to demolish structures built by other countries on islands claimed by Beijing. This too annoyed Japan. The Defence White Paper observed that this "included problematic provisions in terms of inconsistency with international law". The White Paper discussed many other security challenges including North Korea's nuclear belligerence, and underlined recent developments in Japan's defence technology in the new domains of space, cyberspace and the electromagnetic spectrum. Recognizing that regional security challenges "cannot be dealt with by a single country alone", the White Paper endorsed Japan's close partnership with Australia, India and European countries to uphold the regional order. Understandably, China was prompt to criticize the unusually bold language about Taiwan in the Japanese document. A Chinese Foreign Ministry spokesperson asserted that "the Taiwan question is purely China's internal affair" and that Beijing "never allows interference in the Taiwan question in any form by any country".[36]

Fumio Kishida who succeeded Suga as Japan's Prime Minister followed the security policies pursued by Abe and Suga. Kishida brought many new faces into his Cabinet and later reshuffled the key ministers of Foreign Affairs and Defence, reflecting his intention to continue Abe's push to boost security ties with Washington and the Quad partners. In particular, his creation of a new position of economy security minister received widespread attention as the choice of Takayuki Kobayashi who had been involved in protecting sensitive technology from China.[37]

Japan's relations with China remain frosty over a host of issues. Bilateral ties are dependent on a wide variety of factors, many of which seem unpredictable at this moment. The optimal scenario would be a combination of a resurgent Japan, economically and militarily, and a China that continues to be led by Xi Jinping, who has put the highest premium on a combination of economic development through increased interaction with the rest of the world via the BRI and coercive diplomacy. Even under such circumstances, the upcoming developments are likely to make the Japan-China relationship more delicate.

Despite such a troubled relationship, the economies of the two countries are intertwined in such a manner that any unilateral action by one shall hurt the other. This remains a challenge for both how to avoid such a scenario to happen. Tokyo's fear of economic coercion, manifested by China's sanctions against Australia, is an example how ties can derail quickly. Given Biden administration resetting priorities to strengthen with India and other like-minded countries, China might be deterred to calm its objective to economically punish an adversary.

It transpired, therefore, that since 2016 Japan has turned the Free and Open Indo-Pacific (FOIP) from a mere concept to a working framework of engagement with its neighbours. More countries in the region have shared this vision articulated by Japan in the changed strategic environment. Japan has injected new energy to the FOIP vision, which is endorsed by like-minded countries and a broader international community as the vision's mandate is cooperation and away from division and confrontation.[38]

In May 2023, Kishida hosted the G-7 summit at his hometown Hiroshima and invited partners including leaders of Global South countries. The event created an opportunity for those leaders to send a message towards a peaceful, stable and prosperous world. Earlier, in March, Kishida had unveiled a New Plan for a Free and Open Indo-Pacific, whose core principles were to defending "freedom", and "the rule of law", and respect for "diversity", "inclusiveness" and "openness".[39] With these principles, Japan aims to promote rule making through dialogue and equal partnership among nations. This approach focuses on "people", no matter the size of the country or the nationality of those involved. Meanwhile, it adds new areas of interest, such as climate and the environment, global health and cyberspace. Through such opportunities, Japan is attracting more countries into sharing its vision of freedom and prosperity.

Kishida's message resonated widely as there are many interconnected concepts at play. FOIP as a vision has been flexible in evolving in a way that embraces various voices, along with growing support and endorsement from the international community. Nevertheless, its fundamental concept remains unchanged. The concept of "free" indicates that, based on the rule of law, every country is equal as a sovereign state and free from unlawful interference from other countries. The concept of "open" meant to respect inclusiveness, openness and diversity. In other words, no country imposes values, and no country creates camps. FOIP is a vision which highlights cooperation rather than division or confrontation.

The Quad (Japan-Australia-India-US) has been a key platform to showcase FOIP. Japan, Australia, India, and the US share fundamental values and are committed to strengthening a free and open international order based on the rule of law. The four countries have been promoting practical cooperation in various fields, including health, infrastructure, climate change, and critical and emerging technologies, to realize a FOIP. These four countries have concurred on the importance of making a positive contribution to the region. This is in the Quad leaders' statement[40] in Hiroshima in May 2023, where all four countries renewed their "steadfast commitment to a Free and Open Indo-Pacific that is inclusive and resilient."

Over the subsequent months, Japan unveiled many new projects showcasing FOIP. Kishida travelled widely to countries in Africa, Southeast Asia and the Middle East to promote the vision of FOIP through economic security, including investment and technology from Japan. Some of the many examples include investment in practical energy transitions in Asia. In 2021, Kishida shared a preview of his sentiment in the United Kingdom at the 26th session of the Conference of the Parties to the United Nations Framework Convention on Climate Change (COP26). He had remarked, "Japan will press onward to undertake efforts toward net-zero emissions in Asia, the engine of global economic growth." Japan's commitment to this transition has encompassed $10 billion in financial support for renewable energy and energy efficiency projects.

At COP26 and elsewhere Japan committed to mobilizing up to $70 billion from both public and private sources, over five years from 2021 to 2025 to support developing countries addressing climate change, including doubling assistance for climate adaptation. Japan has steadily implemented its financial commitments.

Moreover, Japan is determined to steadily implement the commitments of the TICAD 8 as "a partner growing together with Africa", including the investment of $30 billion as the sum of public and private financial contributions over the next three years in areas such as green investment, development finance, public health and food security. Among ODA projects, promoting quality infrastructure focusing on fields such as energy and transportation were identified as priority areas. The success of some of such projects can be seen in countries such as the Philippines, Vietnam, Sri Lanka and India.

Thus in prioritising FOIP, Japan has activated diplomatic and development priorities to regional development initiatives with India, outreach to ASEAN, through TICAD, and with the Pacific Islands. Over the recent months, Kishida and his foreign ministers visited the Middle East, countries in Asia and Africa (India, Sri Lanka, Maldives, South Africa, Ethiopia and Uganda) demonstrating Japan's intent to strengthen relations with international partners, including countries of the Global South.

The rising importance of the Indo-Pacific is also visible from a security perspective. The Indo-Pacific is important for NATO, given that developments in that region can directly affect Euro-Atlantic security. This is according to the Vilnius Summit Communique[41] issued by the North Atlantic Treaty Organization heads of state and government on the occasion of the summit meeting in Vilnius on July 11, 2023. It transpires therefore that as the economic and security environment continues to shift, the concept of FOIP and the inclusion of the Global South—brought together in Hiroshima—will be international priorities well into the future.[42]

Defence White Paper 2023

As Japan enters a new era of crisis, facing its most severe and complex security environment since World War II, the Kishida government issued the Japanese version of 2023 Defence White Paper in July 2023 and the English version in September 2023.[43] This White paper was unique in the sense that it was the first since the adoption of three basic security documents. These include the National Security Strategy[44], the National Defence Strategy[45] and Defence Buildup Program[46], which provide a detailed explanation of measures to fundamentally strengthen Japan's defence capabilities.[47]

The White Paper also mentioned about Japan's need to acquire a counterstrike capability as Japan sees this as the key to deterring invasion against Japan by another country. The report called for a shift to a threat-response defence force structure. It also broke down total defence expenditures of approximately $300 billion over the five years from fiscal 2023, of which $14 billion was slated to go for ammunition and guided missiles, and $7 billion marked for an unmanned assets defence capability.

An editorial in a leading Japanese daily commended many descriptions in the White paper that helped the people understand the kind of defence capability that Japan aimed, but it was critical of overlooking some critical issues. It found that its assessment of China was inadequate, though it observed that the While Paper declared China's "military activities and other activities" are a matter of serious concern and constitute Japan's "greatest strategic challenge". The editorial observed that assessment alone was not sufficient. During the Cold War, Japan regarded the Soviet Union as a "potential threat". "Today's China does not seem any less dangerous", it observed. Indeed, the report did not refer separately to the buildup of nuclear forces by North Korea and China, though it did mention Russia's repeated threats to use nuclear weapons. The editorial therefore underlined the nuclear threat posed by North Korea, China and now Russia, and therefore urged the government to consider possessing nuclear deterrence to deal with that threat.

Positioning India-Japan Defence/Strategic Relations in Context

Against the explanation in the preceding pages, it is abundantly clear that India and Japan share plenty of common view points in the strategic domains and there exists plenty of convergence of interests. The present paradigm in bilateral ties stands in stark contrast to the Cold War era when ideological reasons kept contacts low-key. When India conducted a nuclear test in 1998, Japan became concerned. Japan's reaction was exceptionally harsh, as ODA was discontinued and ongoing agreements were put on hold. Japan failed to recognise India's compelling reasons for conducting the nuclear test. This was one of the worst points in India-Japan bilateral ties.

All this changed when then Prime Minister Yoshiro Mori paid a visit to India in August 2000 and proposed the idea of a global partnership. American President Bill Clinton's March 2000 visit to India, the first US Presidential visit to India in two decades, likely prompted Mori to do the same. Following Mori's visit, India-Japan relations dramatically improved in tandem with US-India relations. Thus, the US has been a push and pull factor in Japan's India policy.[48] Clinton had praised India's IT capabilities, and Japan most likely did not want to miss the opportunity to befriend India in this technological development process.

In December 2001, Prime Minister Atal Behari Vajpayee visited Japan. Just after he returned from a successful visit, Pakistan-based terrorists attacked Indian Parliament on December 13, 2001. While many world leaders expressed their concern, no leading Western country condemned the attack. But the visit of the leader of Japan's opposition, Yukio Hatoyama, on January 10, 2002, was a game-changer. Besides visiting the site of the Parliament attack, he went to Srinagar to lay a wreath at the Jammu and Kashmir legislative assembly building that was attacked by a suicide-bomber in October 2001. He told journalists that terrorism could not be described as freedom struggle as "terrorism is terrorism in any form".[49]

There was a sudden upswing in bilateral ties during the tenures of Shinzo Abe in Japan and Manmohan Singh in India when bilateral ties were upgraded to a "global and strategic Partnership". It was Japan which had lobbied for India's inclusion in the East Asia Summit (EAS) in 2005 despite opposition from China. The sixtieth anniversary of the two countries' diplomatic relations saw Prime Minister Noda visit India in 2011, during which he signed a 'Comprehensive Economic Partnership Agreement'.[50] In 2014, Modi and Abe elevated bilateral relationship further to a 'special strategic and global partnership.' This unique bilateral relationship is driven as much by economic complementarity as by their shared concerns over China's rise and other global issues.

Soon maritime security issue took the centre stage as securing sea lanes of communication emerged as important in the wake of certain power threatening to either control or disrupt maritime commerce. The world's attention aimed at India as India enjoys a distinctive geography that gives it a major commercial and geostrategic space astride the sea lanes of communication between West Asia and East Asia.[51] The emergence of China as a regional hegemon in Asia is perceived by New Delhi, Tokyo and many others as adversely affecting their security interests, making them adopt a broadly convergent outlook of Asia's security architecture. China's military modernization has also aroused concerns in New Delhi.

Shivshankar Menon, India's former National Security Advisor, observed that China's People's Liberation Army (PLA) is now the transformed product of two decades of double-digit budgetary growth. This entails the building of hard infrastructure to support the military, and military reform under Xi Jinping to convert it into an expeditionary force. China has modernized its nuclear and intercontinental ballistic missile forces into a more capable second-strike force and developed medium range ballistic missile and cruise missile capabilities and systems that are altering the regional military balance. The PLA is now an instrument for power projection, tasked to fight short, intense, high-technology wars in "informationized" conditions, outside China's own territory, dominating its periphery.[52] This has huge ramifications for security of not only India and Japan, but the whole Indo-Pacific region.

As a result, India's relationship with Japan has become the cornerstone of a larger coalition of like-minded countries to resist China's growing might.[53] Japan has used its FOIP strategy as a linchpin to develop deeper trilateral cooperation among the four countries. When the second India-US-Japan trilateral foreign ministers' meeting took place in New York in September 2017, it was "agreed to strengthen their cooperation in the fields of maritime security and regional connectivity in order to realize a free and open Indo-Pacific."[54] The Malabar naval exercise may also be seen as a part of collaboration under the Indo-Pacific vision.[55]

Despite Tokyo's attempts to pursue stable diplomatic relations with China during 2016-18 when the Japanese strategy demonstrated a shift "from pure balancing to hedging comprised of multiple policy options including soft balancing, engagement, and economic-pragmatism", Japan did not hesitate in offering subtle support for India's stance over the Doklam border stand-off with China in June-August 2017. Kenji Hiramatsu, former Ambassador of Japan to India, said that all parties concerned should not seek to "resort to unilateral attempts to change the status quo by force, and resolve the dispute in a peaceful manner."[56] This statement may appear diplomatically innocuous, but "could be interpreted as giving support to India because the Indian government had accused China of changing the status quo by force."[57]

Strengthening the American alliance system through the Indo-Japanese partnership is an important element of Japan's balancing efforts for encouraging China to play a more responsible regional role. In October 2018, Japan and India agreed to establish a 2+2 dialogue mechanism of regular consultations between foreign and defence ministers.[58] During a meeting between Abe and Modi, in October 2018 in Tokyo, both the countries agreed to strengthen maritime domain awareness, and also began to negotiate the Acquisition and Cross-Servicing Agreement (ACSA) that is aimed at facilitating joint manoeuvres, including three-way exercises involving the US Navy in the Indian Ocean and the Pacific. Japan hopes to project its rising naval power in the Indian Ocean that would also allow Japanese vessels to secure access to Indian naval facilities in the Andaman and Nicobar islands near the Malacca Straits.[59] Clearly, Japan has been developing strategic cooperation with India as a form of mini-laterals in the Indo-Pacific. The Japan-American-India (JAI) along with the India-Japan-Australia trilateral partnership seems functioning as an alternative form of Quadrilateral cooperation.[60] To a certain extent, the Quad in its current form is an expanded mini lateral of the existing various security bilaterals and trilaterals among its member states.[61]

India has given its unconditional commitment to work closely with Japan in its vision known as 'Partnership for Quality Infrastructure' (PQI). India and Japan are keen to explore synergies between Act East Policy and PQI.[62] Set up in December 2017, the India-Japan Act East Forum has become a driving force in advancing bilateral cooperation to boost connectivity within India's northeast region and its neighbouring countries.[63] Japan has signed the Acquisition and Cross-Servicing Agreement (ACSA) with India in September 2020, which is seen as a sign of growing convergence of interests between the two sides.[64] Several recent developments have indisputably underscored the growing convergence of interests between them. Japan joined hands with India to launch a development project, the Asia-Africa Growth Corridor (AAGC) in 2017 in order to increase connectivity and cooperation between Asian and African continents. The AAGC seeks to provide a mechanism for India and Japan to invest in infrastructure projects in the Indo-Pacific region from East Asia to Africa, and this is seen as a response to China's BRI.[65] Although the AAGC is way behind the BRI in many respects because of India's own infrastructural needs, lack of financing capacity, and the exclusive investment focus of AAGC in only maritime regions, yet it is a significant step toward providing infrastructure finance to a region critical to the Indo-Pacific.[66]

The infrastructure cooperation by Quad's member states in the context of economic competition between the US and China has not escaped Beijing's attention. China has come to recognize that the Quad, which understands the urgency of limiting China's dominance in infrastructure investment in the region, have been making efforts to constrain China's economic development inside and outside of its territory. In order to counter potentially negative impact of these efforts on China's overall trade strategy, its decision-makers are responding by partially fixing the debt trap of the BRI.[67] What makes investments from Japan particularly attractive is that, unlike their Chinese counterparts, they not only comply with international standards of good governance and environmental sustainability, but also create more job opportunities for the local populations. While most of China's BRI projects and the terms and conditions are opaque; that of Japan's are transparent genuinely aimed at the economic development of the hosting countries of the project.

Post-pandemic Scenario

Viewed from the perspective of global peace and prosperity, the Indo-Pacific has now emerged as the most important strategic space. The region is geographically extensive and politically diverse and contains geopolitical hotspots, competing interests among emerging powers, overlapping economic partnerships. All of these contain potential risks of conflicts.

Besides, the growing rivalry between the U.S. and China has introduced new geopolitical and geo-economic tensions. This trend was accelerated in the COVID-19 pandemic era. Such changes in the geopolitics and geo-economics of the post-COVID-19 world draw Japan closer to India.

During their phone conversation on September 10, 2020, both prime ministers, Modi and Abe, agreed that strong partnership between their countries would play a "critical role in charting the course for the global community in the post-COVID world", while reaffirming that the leadership change in Japan would not affect the upward trajectory in bilateral ties.[68] The 'Acquisition and Cross-Servicing Agreement' (ACSA) was signed just two days before the Abe-Modi virtual meeting.

With an eye on China's expansionist behaviour in the Indo-Pacific and beyond, Modi and Abe signed the much anticipated Mutual Logistic Support Arrangement during the virtual meeting. At a press conference on 28 August, Abe had already announced his decision to demit office on health grounds. However, this did not deter him to go ahead with the leadership level dialogue which was already scheduled for September 10. With the signing of the pact, the Quad grouping of India, Japan, Australia and the US is set to gain more heft now.[69]

Bottom of Form

The pact was signed by Defence Secretary Ajay Kumar and Japanese Ambassador Suzuki Satoshi in New Delhi on September 10, 2020. India has signed similar agreements with the US, France, South Korea, Singapore and Australia. The Logistics Exchange Memorandum of Agreement (LEMOA) inked with the U.S. in 2016 gives India refuelling facilities and access to American bases in Djibouti, Diego Garcia, Guam and Subic Bay. With the six countries with which India has such agreements, India can now support each other's warships and aircraft as well as boost defence ties. Such a move shall enhance India's strategic reach in the Indian Ocean and can counter China's expanding footprint across the Indo-Pacific.

The India-Japan relationship has assumed a multi-dimensional perspective in recent times in the wake of geopolitical changes in the region, demanding a unified response to the threats perceptions stemming from such changes. During Abe's long tenure at the helm, India-Japan ties scaled new heights as convergence of interests on a host of issues provided a stronger spine to bilateral ties. Apart from defence and security cooperation, cultural and economic ties also deepened.

The deepening of defence ties in recent years is in response to China's growing weight across the region. The India-Japan MLSA agreement will enhance the inter-operability between the armed forces of both countries. The agreement will provide their militaries access to each other's bases for supplies and services. The significance of the pact could not be missed as it came amid tensions with China along the Line of Actual Control and Beijing's aggressive behaviour across the Indo-Pacific region.

The agreement will facilitate the smooth provision of supplies and services between the forces on the ground, thereby contributing further to global peace and security. During their telephone conversation, Modi and Abe concurred on a wide range of topics such as security, the economy and economic cooperation including the high-speed rail project where both countries can work together closely. Indeed, Abe has been a pillar of strength for India's Look East and Act East Policy, someone who developed a close bonhomie with Modi and his predecessor Dr. Manmohan Singh.

Abe's speech in Parliament in August 2007 during his first term wherein he proposed the Indo-Pacific construct and partnership across the region based on the confluence of two seas and ushered in the Asia-Africa Growth Corridor with India as a key partner amid Beijing's BRI and Maritime Silk Route initiatives still reverberate in Indian minds. The subsequent quadrilateral concept including India, Japan, Australia and the US originally floated by Abe in 2007 and again reactivated gained currency soon bearing Abe's footprint. The Malabar exercise between the navies of India, Japan, Australia and the U.S. confirms to this assertion.

In recent times, bilateral, trilateral and quadrilateral naval exercises between the countries in the Indo-Pacific have been taking place with regularity. The main objective is to send a message to China as it tries to unilaterally change the established regional order by trying to impose its will to the detriment of the interests of other nations in the region. China's rise coincides with the relative decline in American power. It was further aggravated by then U.S. President Trump's inward-looking and 'America First' policies sought to correct the trade deficit with China. That has further complicated global politics. Such a stance has given rise to a trade war between the two largest economies in the world with ripple effect across the globe.

This has not deterred China from pursuing its assertiveness on a host of regional issues, even though many countries in Asia like India, Japan, South Korea and also in Europe such as France and Germany started looking to shift their production bases from China either back to their home countries or other countries. The suspicion over information on the Coronavirus released to the world by China is another trigger, leading to mistrust. This does not suggest that the US has abdicated its responsibility as a security provider to its allies in Asia. On the contrary, it has deepened security ties with a view to reassure allies and friends in the wake of perceived threat from China. The Biden administration has proved this assertion.

India and the US signed the bilateral Logistics Exchange Memorandum of Association (LEMOA), the first of three foundational agreements proposed by Washington to deepen bilateral military cooperation between the two countries in August 2016. This logistics support pact with the US helps naval ties between the two countries. Following the signing of the LEMOA, a significant number of at sea replenishments have taken place between the Indian and US navies. Indian and US warships are being refuelled regularly by each other's tankers at sea, easing logistical constraints under the LEMOA legal framework. For example, an Indian warship deployed in the Gulf of Aden for anti-piracy patrols was refuelled by a US tanker. All issues relating to cash payment or the reciprocal provision of logistics support were straightened out.

Similarly, the amphibious transport dock, the *USS Anchorage*, with the Marine Expeditionary Unit that arrived in Visakhapatnam on December 22, 2018 for a four-day port visit was provided supplies and services under the LEMOA framework. At a time when China-US ties nosedived, those between India and the US grew to new heights. The full scope of the LEMOA enables the navies of the two countries in terms of reciprocal provision of logistics support, supplies and services.

The pact served as a template for similar arrangements with other countries, with which India subsequently entered into such pacts. After tough negotiations, India and the U.S. also signed the Communication Compatibility and Security Agreement (Comcasa), valid for 10 years. Comcasa aims to provide a legal framework for the transfer of highly sensitive communication security equipment from the U.S. to India that will streamline and facilitate interoperability between their armed forces. This effectively means opening up India's military communications network to the U.S. military.

Both nations are also exploring to sign the third foundational agreement, the Basic Exchange and Cooperation Agreement (BECA), to share geospatial intelligence.

Negotiations on the military pact between India and Japan, on the 'reciprocal provision of supplies and services' between the armed forces of the two countries signed on September 10, 2020 had commenced in October 2018. With the signing of the pact, it is hoped that the 10-year agreement, to be extended automatically every decade unless one side decides to terminate it, will contribute to peace and security in the Indo-Pacific.

With this, the Quad grouping of four countries is set to gain more heft now, complimenting then Chief of Defence staff General Bipin Rawat's remarks about the Quad as a 'good mechanism' to ensure freedom of navigation in the Indo-Pacific. An optimistic view on the churning of the geopolitics in the Indo-Pacific in the wake of the perceived Chinese threat would be that these pacts with six countries shall have a stabilising effect and dispel any alarmist perspective of a potential conflict.

Thus, it transpires that bilateral defence ties between Japan and India have been further strengthened. It needs to be noted that ACSA was one of the key items on the 2019 Abe–Modi summit agenda which was scheduled for December 2019 in Guwahati, capital of India's northeastern state of Assam. But the summit had to be postponed due to political protests against the anti-Citizenship Amendment Act (CAA).[70]

Since Abe was the Quad's major proponent, there were considerable concerns about whether it would survive after his departure in September 2020. However, these concerns were unfounded, since Abe's successors in Japan, first Suga and now Kishida, and other leaders of other Quad countries have been supportive of the framework.[71] Japan and India can potentially play a greater role in concretizing the Quad, should some of the domestic challenges be sorted out and their respective diplomatic strengths be exercised to the fullest.

Due to economic upheavals caused by the COVID-19 pandemic, many countries have become sensitive to the risks of over-dependence on China in their supply chains, particularly in the areas of medical care and 5G communications. Tokyo has now taken the lead in launching the India-Japan-Australia trilateral initiative to ensure the resilience of supply chains in the Indo-Pacific, and this is likely to accelerate economic and diplomatic de-coupling from China by the Quad governments.[72] During their first virtual meeting on the issue in early September 2020, ministers from the three countries expressed their determination to "take a lead in delivering a free, fair, inclusive, non-discriminatory, transparent, predictable and stable trade and investment environment." They also invited other countries in the region with similar views to join the resilient supply chain initiative, which has been viewed as adding economic pillar to the existing political and strategic pillars of the Quad.[73] In April 2021, India, Japan and Australia formally launched the Supply Chain Resilience Initiative (SCRI) to build resilient supply chains in the Indo-Pacific region. The three countries "acknowledged that the COVID-19 pandemic was having an unprecedented impact in terms of lives lost, livelihoods and economics affected, and that the pandemic had revealed supply chain vulnerabilities globally."[74] The primary objective of SCRI is to reduce dependence on China's vast supply chains in the Indo-Pacific.

The first summit of Quad leaders, held virtually on March 12, 2021, was also received positively in Japan. The summit was held about a year-and-half after the Quad was upgraded to the level of foreign ministers in September 2019 and clearly reflected the desire of the Quad members to present a united front to key challenges in the Indo-Pacific region, including China's assertiveness. An editorial published after the summit in *Japan Times*, captured the enthusiasm when it wrote that the holding of summit must "quiet fears that the forum would be just a talk shop, unable to provide concrete deliverables that would improve Indo-Pacific security. The establishment of three working groups—on vaccines, climate change and emerging technologies—shows that those governments have a sophisticated understanding of regional security and recognize the need for a realistic and appropriate division of labor to get the most from each member."[75]

As the second wave of COVID-19 became uncontrollable, wreaking unimaginable havoc across India, Tokyo came forward to provide vital assistance to New Delhi for fight against the pandemic. In April 2021, Modi had a telephonic conversation with his Japanese counterpart, Suga Yoshihide, and thanked him for Japan's help to deal with the ongoing second wave of COVID-19. Both the leaders "highlighted the importance of close India-Japan co-operation to overcome these challenges, such as by working together to create resilient, diversified and trustworthy supply chains, ensuring reliable supply of critical materials and technologies, and developing new partnerships in manufacturing and skill development."[76] It needs to be recalled that in January 2021, Japan agreed to provide a loan of 50 billion Yen (Rs. 3,468 crore) to help India ease the socio-economic impact of the COVID-19.

Hurdles before Japan

While Japan's intentions to relook its security doctrine that stems from the prevailing challenges are undisputed, the path to realize those objectives is not easy. The constitutional constraints limiting Japan's capacity to expand its security posture and amending Article 9 to overcome this constraint is not easy. Japan can only use force in response to existential threat and it must use minimal force to achieve its goals.[77] Although attempts are being made to overcome these defence limitations, these have proved to be half-measures. During his tenure, Abe with his realist and incremental approach tried to change but was unsuccessful. Instead, he interpreted the peace clause, thereby diluting the spirit of the Article 9 to some extent. This he did by introducing the measures of collective self-defence.

The Japanese public is opposed to their country to return to the pre-War nationalist postures. The threats from North Korea and China on continuous basis are not enough to influence the people to change their opinion. Abe's attempt to tinker with Article 9 evoked sharp reactions from Korea and

China. As argued by an observer, "if Abe wants to bring Japan's defense cooperation with the "quad" countries beyond what it is already doing, he may be met with considerable domestic resistance."[78] It seems fair to contend that it would take a while for the Japanese citizens, who have become pacifist after 1945, to internalise the Quad's rationale.

There is a view gaining currency in Japan to revisit its nuclear option in the wake of North Korea's growing nuclear capabilities and repeated missile firings, many of which have over the northern island of Hokkaido. China's intensified maritime presence near Japan and military assertiveness in the Indo-Pacific as well as Tokyo's diminishing confidence in Washington's ability to protect make Japan's argument convincing.[79] Also, notwithstanding America's extended nuclear deterrence or its security, South Korea has also witnessed a similar nuclear debate.[80] However, if both Japan and South Korea choose to take the nuclear path, it would have serious consequences for the region, and thus the US would not be inclined to help its two key East Asian allies having their own nuclear weapons. Beijing's efforts to protect North Korea's political stability have resulted in strengthening of the trilateral relationship among Washington, Tokyo and Seoul. Therefore, if the security situation deteriorates due to failure of North Korea's denuclearization, it would be difficult for the governments in Tokyo and Seoul to skirt public demands for a serious rethink on the issue. Japan, which is often described as a "de facto" nuclear state, is technologically so advanced that building a weapon within a year is not difficult.[81] Moreover, the public support for Japan's nuclear armament is likely to grow with rising threat from China and North Korea.

However, given the deep economic interdependence between Japan and China, it is not easy for Japan to pursue an overtly anti-Chinese policy. Despite misgivings about China's intensions, Japan does not seem to force a complete break with China. Some observers draw attention to the fact that "Tokyo has always avoided aggressively presenting its FOIP vision as a containment strategy towards China. Tokyo has so far refrained from securitising its relations with its big neighbour, despite its concerns about China's foreign policy ambitions and the domestic political changes in the country."[82] This is, however, understandable as Japan has deep economic linkages with China. It underlines the huge challenge of managing a relationship which is characterized by security concerns and economic interdependence. However, Japan is not alone in facing this dilemma; India and Australia have to balance this imperative as well.

On the other hand, pessimists held the view about India's ability to pursue a more ambitious role in the Indo-Pacific as they suspected that Indian economy might not overcome and recover fast following multiple setbacks induced by the COVID-19 pandemic. Such a view proved wrong as the Indian economy bounced back in quick time to be back on its growth path. Therefore, its ambitions to become a regional and global player remain as strong as during the pre-COVID days.

A new trilateral security partnership between Australia, UK and the US, named AUKUS, understandably generated a lot of curiosity and attention. Despite the initial reservations, this new security construct was soon viewed as strengthening other mini-laterals in the Indo-Pacific besides enhancing Australia's naval deterrent capabilities. Though both India and Japan are not part of the AUKUS, it is an acknowledgment among leading Anglosphere democracies that China is now the main strategic competitor to the democratic world.[83]

Coming against the backdrop of an unusually hasty and unilateral withdrawal of the US troops from Afghanistan, AUKUS hoped to assuage the widespread concerns across the Indo-Pacific about America's regional commitments and convey Washington's willingness to invest heavily in enhancing the defence potential of its allies through the sharing of highly-sensitive technology.[84] This opens new opportunities for both India and Japan to strengthen their security cooperation with the US.

AUKUS is particularly a positive development for India, which had shown discomfort in militarizing the Quad. Though India is a crucial player in the geopolitics of the Quad, without India, Quad would lose credibility in Asia. India remains extremely wary about formally joining a military pact despite abandoning its non-alignment rhetoric.[85] If India's strategic leadership seems satisfied with India being left out, Tokyo might be feeling let down by Washington's unwillingness to expand AUKUS to include Japan. But Japan's defence industry seems unprepared for the depth and breadth of security cooperation that is required for an AUKUS-like partnership.[86] If Japan decides to create a similar security framework with the US, its defence establishment must make necessary reforms.

India-Japan and the Role of the Middle Powers

India-Japan strategic cooperation needs to be examined against the background of some emerging powers, whose roles interplay in achieving strategic objectives. In international relations parlance, these emerging powers are called "middle powers". Though this term has been in use for quite some time, there is no broad consensus on what constitutes a middle power in global politics. Andrew Cooper has identified four different types of middle powers: geographic—a state located between two great powers; normative—a state which acts as honest broker or trusted mediator in crises; positional—a state whose power is relative to both great and small states; and behavioural—a state that can engage in 'niche diplomacy'.[87]

Therefore, one may define a middle power as a country that is neither great nor small in terms of its power and influence. The concept of middle power has been further refined to enhance its explanatory power. In contrast to traditional middle powers, which are seen as wealthy, stable and egalitarian, the emerging middle powers are defined as "semi-peripheral, materially inegalitarian and recently democratized states that demonstrate much regional influence and self-association. Behaviourally, they opt for reformist and not radical global change, exhibit a strong regional orientation favouring regional integration but seek also to construct identities distinct from those of the weak states in their region".[88]

As the world enters a new Cold War, a new geopolitical contest between the Indo-Pacific and Eurasia has started. The final outcome of this emerging divide is likely to be decided by four middle powers—India, Japan, Iran and Turkey—which have the capacity to project power regionally, build alliances, and support or disrupt the strategies of international powers pursuing their interests in the region.[89] There is another country in Asia, South Korea, which too possesses the credentials and claims to aspire to be a middle power and play a role in regional and global affairs accordingly.

The US-allied middle powers such as Japan and South Korea, and now India considered to be added to this group, have become increasingly vulnerable to China's coercive diplomacy as Beijing attempts to weaken their support for US-led regional security order. Recent examples include China's economic coercion against Australia, South Korea, Canada and India. China's threat and the US-China strategic rivalry require a new form of middle power diplomacy in the Indo-Pacific. The Indo-Pacific states which are considered as middle powers—India, Japan, South Korea and Australia—need to strengthen effective regional cooperation and thereby shape future regional order in the Indo-Pacific.[90] In fact, these middle powers are already cooperating to manage changing regional dynamics. The Biden administration seems interested in pushing these middle powers further to bolster their ties with one another. It transpires from the discussion in this Chapter that India and Japan are on the cusp of a stronger partnership in the defence, strategic, including maritime domains. A strong partnership between the two leading Asian economies shall contribute to regional peace and stability.

Notes

1. Purnendra Jain and Takenori Horimoto, "Japan and the Indo-Pacific", in Priya Chacko (ed.) *New Regional Geopolitics in the Indo-Pacific Drivers, Dynamics and Consequences*, Oxon: Routledge, 2016, pp. 38-39.
2. Kalidas Nag, *India and the Pacific World*, Calcutta Book Company Ltd, 1941.
3. Ministry of Foreign Affairs of Japan, "Confluence of the Two Seas" Speech by H.E. Mr. Shinzo Abe, Prime Minister of Japan at the Parliament of the Republic of India", August 22, 2007, https://www.mofa.go.jp/region/asia-paci/pmv0708/speech-2.html
4. J.D. Wilson, "Investing in the economic architecture of the Indo-Pacific", Perth US-Asia Centre, Indo-Pacific Insight Series, August 2017, https://perthusasia.edu.au/getattachment/be3d8ec4-50f2-4e4d-8c4b-46943500f726/PU-27-IPIS-8-WEB-170817.pdf.aspx?lang=en-AU
5. Lindsay Maizland and Beina Xu, "The US-Japan Security Alliance", Council on Foreign Relations, November 4, 2011, https://www.cfr.org/backgrounder/us-japan-security-alliance
6. James L. Schoff, "Political Change in America and Implications for the US-Japan Alliance", *Asia Pacific Review,* vol. 25, no. 2, 2018, pp. 45-63.
7. "US Military Bases in Japan", https://militarybases.com/overseas/japan/

8. US Department of State, "U.S. Security Cooperation With Japan", Bureau of Political-Military Affairs, January 20, 2021, https://www.state.gov/u-s-security-cooperation-with-japan
9. Ibid.
10. Alex Wilson, "USS George Washington destined for Japan to replace USS Ronald Reagan, report says", March 3, 2023, https://www.stripes.com/branches/navy/2023-03-03/george-washington-carrier-yokosuka-japan-9330654.html
11. Takashi Inoguchi, G. John Ikenberry, and Yoichiro Sato, "Alliance Constrained: Japan, the United States, and Regional Security", in Takashi Inoguchi, G. John Ikenberry and Yoichiro Sato, *The U.S.-Japan Security Alliance: Regional Multilateralism*, New York: Palgrave Macmillan, 2011, p. 4.
12. Adam P Liff, "Japan's Security Policy in the 'Abe Era': Radical Transformation or Evolutionary Shift?", Texas National Security Review, vol. 1, no. 3, 2018, https://tnsr.org/2018/05/japans-security-policy-in-the-abe-era-radical-transformation-or-evolutionary-shift/. Also see, Rajaram Panda, "Debate on Collective Self-Defence and Constitutional Revision in Japan", *Reitaku Journal of Interdisciplinary Studies*, vol. 26, 2018, pp. 1-19, https://reitaku.repo.nii.ac.jp/index.php?action=pages_view_main&active_action=repository_view_main_item_snippet&index_id=476&pn=1&count=20&order=17&lang=japanese&page_id=13&block_id=29
13. David Vergun, "U.S.-Japan Alliance Increasingly Strengthened Since End of WWII", US Department of Defence, August 14, 2020, https://www.defense.gov/News/Feature-Stories/Story/Article/2306658/us-japan-alliance-increasingly-strengthened-since-end-of-wwii/
14. Lionel P. Fatton, "'Japan is back': Autonomy and balancing amidst an unstable China–U.S.–Japan triangle", *Asia and the Pacific Policy Studies*, vol. 5, no. 2, May 2018.
15. Gurjit Singh, "Why Japan-US summit holds promise for India", *Indian Express*, April 21, 2021.
16. The White House, "U.S.-Japan Joint Leaders' Statement: 'U.S. – JAPAN GLOBAL PARTNERSHIP FOR A NEW ERA'", April 16, 2021, https://www.whitehouse.gov/briefing-room/statements-releases/2021/04/16/u-s-japan-joint-leaders-statement-u-s-japan-global-partnership-for-a-new-era/
17. Ibid.
18. Tomohiko Satake and Ryo Sahashi, "The Rise of China and Japan's 'Vision' for Free and Open Indo-Pacific", *Journal of Contemporary China*, 2020. DOI: 10.1080/10670564.2020.1766907
19. Ministry of External Affairs, Government of India, "Launch of India-Japan Act East Forum", December 5, 2017, https://www.mea.gov.in/press-releases.htm?dtl/29154/Launch_of_IndiaJapan_Act_East_Forum
20. Ministry of Foreign Affairs of Japan, "Address by Prime Minister Shinzo Abe at the Opening Session of the Sixth Tokyo International Conference on African Development (TICAD VI)", August 27, 2016, Kenyatta International Convention Centre, Nairobi, Kenya, https://www.mofa.go.jp/afr/af2/page4e_000496.html

21. Shinzo Abe, "Asia's Democratic Security Diamond", Project Syndicate, December 27, 2012, https://www.project-syndicate.org/onpoint/a-strategic-alliance-for-japan-and-india-by-shinzo-abe?barrier=accesspaylog
22. Ibid.
23. Hidetaka Yoshimatsu, "The Indo-Pacific in Japan's strategy towards India", *Contemporary Politics*, vol. 25, no. 4, 2019.
24. Céline Pajon, "Japan's Indo-Pacific Strategy: Shaping a Hybrid Regional Order", *War on the Rocks*, December 18, 2019, https://warontherocks.com/2019/12/japans-indo-pacific-strategy-shaping-a-hybrid-regional-order/
25. Toshi Yoshihara, "China's Coercive Posturing in the Senkakus: A Quest for Dominance", *Japan Forward*, August 23, 2019, https://japan-forward.com/chinas-coercive-posturing-in-the-senkakus-a-quest-for-dominance/
26. Alessio Patalano, "What is China's Strategy in the Senkaku Islands?", *War on the Rocks*, September 10, 2020. https://warontherocks.com/2020/09/what-is-chinas-strategy-in-the-senkaku-islands/
27. David Brunnstrom, "U.S. seeks meeting soon to revive Asia-Pacific 'Quad' security forum", *Reuters*, October 28, 2017, https://www.reuters.com/article/us-usa-asia-quad-idUSKBN1CW2O1
28. Kyodo "Suga leaves for Vietnam and Indonesia on first overseas trip as PM", *Japan Times*, October 18, 2020, https://www.japantimes.co.jp/news/2020/10/18/national/politics-diplomacy/yoshihide-suga-vietnam-indonesia-2/. Also see, Rajaram Panda, "Japan-Vietnam Security Matrix in the Indo-Pacific Region", October 19, 2020, https://www.vifindia.org/article/2020/october/19/japan-vietnam-security-matrix-in-the-indo-pacific-region,
29. Michael J. Green and Gregory B. Poling, "Suga in Southeast Asia: Japan's Emergence as a Regional Security Hub", Center for Strategic and International Studies (CSIS), October 27, 2020, https://www.csis.org/analysis/suga-southeast-asia-japans-emergence-regional-security-hub
30. Ministry of External Affairs, "2nd India-Australia-Japan- USA Ministerial Meeting", Government of India, October 6, 2020, https://www.mea.gov.in/press-releases.htm?dtl/33098/2nd_IndiaAustraliaJapan_USA_Ministerial_Meeting
31. Thomas Wilkins and Daisuke Akimoto, "Japan signals more robust security posture in new defence white paper", The Strategist, Australia Security Policy Institute, July 29, 2021, https://www.aspistrategist.org.au/japan-signals-more-robust-security-posture-in-new-defence-white-paper/
32. Ministry of Defense, "Defense of Japan 2021", https://www.mod.go.jp/en/publ/w_paper/wp2021/DOJ2021_Digest_EN.pdf
33. Rajaram Panda, "Japan's Defence White paper 2021: China Riled by Mention of Taiwan Strait", July 22, 2021, https://www.vifindia.org/article/2021/july/22/japans-defence-white-paper-2021-china-riled-by-mention-of-taiwan-strait
34. Brian Waidelich and Elizabeth Barrett, "Japan's New Defense White Paper Elevates Security Concerns Over Taiwan Strait", CAN, July 23, 2021, https://in.search.yahoo.com/search?fr=mcafee&type=E210IN1274G91769&p=%2C+

https%3A%2F%2Fwww.cna.org%2Fnews%2FInDepth%2F2021%2F07%2Fjapans-defense-white-paper-security-concerns-taiwan-strait

35. Ministry of Defense, "Defense of Japan 2021", https://www.mod.go.jp/en/publ/w_paper/wp2021/DOJ2021_Digest_EN.pdf
36. Ministry of Foreign Affairs, the People's Republic of China, "Foreign Ministry Spokesperson Zhao Lijian's Regular Press Conference on July 13, 2021", https://www.fmprc.gov.cn/mfa_eng/xwfw_665399/s2510_665401/t1891749.shtml
37. Andrew Oros, "Kishida a status quo prime minister facing escalating foreign policy challenges", *East Asia Forum*, October 10, 2021; Greg Earl, "Economic diplomacy: Japan's new PM joins the (supply) chain gang", Lowy Institute, 76, October 2021, https://www.lowyinstitute.org/the-interpreter/economic-diplomacy-japan.
38. Arielle Busetto, "Japan Sets World Agenda with Expanding Vision of Prosperity in a Free and Open Indo-Pacific", *Japan Forward*, September 5, 2023, https://japan-forward.com/sets-international-agenda-with-expanding-free-open-indo-pacific-vision/
39. "New Plan for a "Free and Open Indo-Pacific (FOIP)", March 2023, https://www.mofa.go.jp/files/100477660.pdf
40. "Quad Joint Leaders' Statement", May 24, 2023, https://www.mofa.go.jp/fp/nsp/page1e_000401.html
41. "Vilnius Summit Communique", July 11, 2023, https://www.nato.int/cps/en/natohq/official_texts_217320.htm
42. Arielle Busetto, "Japan Sets World Agenda with Expanding Vision of Prosperity in a Free and Open Indo-Pacific", *Japan Forward*, September 5, 2023, https://japan-forward.com/sets-international-agenda-with-expanding-free-open-indo-pacific-vision/
43. Defense of Japan 2023, https://www.mod.go.jp/en/publ/w_paper/wp2023/DOJ2023_EN_Full.pdf
44. National Security Strategy, April 5, 2023, https://www.mofa.go.jp/fp/nsp/page1we_000081.html
45. National Defense Strategy, December 16, 2022, https://www.mod.go.jp/j/policy/agenda/guideline/strategy/pdf/strategy_en.pdf
46. "Defense Buildup Program", December 16, 2022, https://www.mod.go.jp/j/approach/agenda/guideline/plan/pdf/program_en.pdf
47. "The New Defense White Paper is Out; Now get the Public On Board", *Japan Forward,* August 3, 2023, editorial, https://japan-forward.com/editorial-the-new-defense-white-paper-is-out-now-get-the-public-on-board/
48. Tomoko Kiyota, "Forward Together we go with Japan: 'Dazalling' US-Japan Rapprochement for Tokyo", PacNet 74, Pacific Forum CSIS Honolulu, Hawaii, October 6, 2014.
49. Indirani Bagchi, "New Japanese PM is an old friend of India", *The Times of India*, September 23, 2009.
50. Guibourg Delamotte, "Japan's Foreign Policy beyond Short-term Politics", *Asia-Pacific Review,* vol. 19, no. 2, 2012, p. 54.

51. Ramesh Thakur, "The Quad isn't a knight in shining armor to slay the dragon", *The Japan Times*, July 9, 2018, https://www.japantimes.co.jp/opinion/2018/07/09/commentary/japan-commentary/quad-isnt-knight-shining-armor-slay-dragon/
52. Shivshankar Menon, *India and Asian Geopolitics: The Past, Present*, New Delhi: Penguin Random House India, 2021, pp. 51-52.
53. Christophe Jaffrelot, "The picture after Doklam stand-off", *Indian Express*, September 12, 2017.
54. Ministry of Foreign Affairs of Japan, "Japan-U.S.-India Trilateral Foreign Ministers' Meeting", September 19, 2017, http://www.mofa.go.jp/s_sa/sw/in/page3e_000752.html
55. Rajaram Panda, "Malabar 2023: Reinforcing Maritime Security in the Indo-Pacific", September 11, 2023, https://www.vifindia.org/article/2023/september/11/malabar-2023-reinforcing-maritime-security-in-the-indo-pacific
56. TNN, "Doklam stand-off: Japan backs India, says no one should try to change status quo by force", *Times of India*, August 18, 2017.
57. Hidetaka Yoshimatsu, "Partnership against the rising dragon? Japan's foreign policy towards India", *The Pacific Review,* 2019, DOI: 10.1080/09512748.2018.1563210
58. Rezaul H Laskar, "Narendra Modi, Shinzo Abe pledge to work for Indo-Pacific peace, 2+2 dialogue on cards", *Hindustan Times*, October 29, 2018.
59. Axel Berkofsky, "Japan and the Indo-Pacific: Alive and Kicking", in Axel Berkofsky and Sergio Miracola (eds), *Geopolitics by Other Means: The Indo-Pacific Reality,* Ledizioni Ledi Publishing, February 2019, pp. 110-12.
60. Yasuyuki Ishida, "China's OBOR Initiative and Japan's Response: The Abe Doctrine, Free and Open Indo-Pacific Strategy and Japan-India Strategic Partnership", in Jagannath P. Panda and Titli Basu, *China-India-Japan in the Indo-Pacific Ideas, Interests and Infrastructure*, New Delhi: Institute for Defence Studies and Analyses and Pentagon Press, 2018, p. 174.
61. Wooyeal Paik & Jae Jeok Park, "The Quad's Search for Non-Military Roles and China's Strategic Response: Minilateralism, Infrastructure Investment, and Regional Balancing", *Journal of Contemporary China*, vol. 30, no. 127, 2021.
62. Darshana M. Baruah, "Toward Strategic Economic Cooperation between India and Japan", Carnegie Endowment for International Peace, December 1, 2016, https://carnegieendowment.org/files/Darshana_Baruah_India_and_Japan.pdf
63. Ministry of External Affairs, Government of India, "Launch of India-Japan Act East Forum", December 5, 2017, https://www.mea.gov.in/press-releases.htm?dtl/29154/Launch_of_IndiaJapan_Act_East_Forum
64. Abjijnan Rej, "India and Japan Sign Military Logistics Agreement for All to See", *The Diplomat*, September 12, 2020, https://thediplomat.com/2020/09/india-and-japan-sign-military-logistics-agreement-for-all-to-see/
65. Shahana Thankachan "Japan's 'Free and Open Indo-Pacific Strategy': Reality before the Rhetoric?", *Maritime Affairs: Journal of the National Maritime Foundation of India*, 2018.

66. Emre Demir, "Competing regional visions China's Belt and Road Initiative versus the Indo-Pacific Partnership", in Ash Rossiter and Brendon J. Cannon (eds), *Conflict and Cooperation in the Indo-Pacific New Geopolitical Realities*, New York: Routledge, 2020.
67. Wooyeal Paik and Jae Jeok Park, "The Quad's Search for Non-Military Roles and China's Strategic Response: Minilateralism, Infrastructure Investment, and Regional Balancing", *Journal of Contemporary China*, 2020, DOI: 10.1080/10670564.2020.1766908
68. Rezaul H Laskar, "India, Japan ink pact to bolster defence forces", *Hindustan Times*, September 10, 2020.
69. Rajaram Panda, "With China in mind, Abe departs with military pact with India", September 12, 2020, https://www.rediff.com/news/column/eyeing-china-japan-signs-military-pact-with-india/20200912.htm
70. Shishir Gupta, "At India-Japan Summit next month, Modi and Abe to sign off on key military pact", *Hindustan Times*, August 17, 2020.
71. Rajaram Panda, "Rethinking the 'Quad' Security Concept in the Face of a Rising China", Jamestown Foundation, *China Brief* 20 (19), October 30, 2020.
72. Rajeswari Pillai Rajagopalan, "Australia-Japan-India Trilateral Sets Sights on Supply Chain Resilience", *The Diplomat*, October 2, 2020, https://thediplomat.com/2020/10/australia-japan-india-trilateral-sets-sights-on-supply-chain-resilience/
73. "India, Australia and Japan to launch resilient supply chains for Indo-Pacific", *Hindustan Times*, September 1, 2020, https://www.hindustantimes.com/india-news/india-australia-and-japan-to-launch-resilient-supply-chains-for-indo-pacific/story-0e4j7CfG9kz0AmH0tK1ndL.html
74. Kirtika Suneja, "India, Japan, Australia launch supply chain resilience initiative, may be expanded based on consensus", *Economic Times*, April 28, 2021.
75. "A demonstration of strength by the Japan-U.S. alliance", *Japan Times*, editorial March 18, 2021, https://www.japantimes.co.jp/opinion/2021/03/18/editorials/quad-china-north-korea-u-s-military-senkakus-disputed-islands-south-korea-u-s-japan-relations/
76. Prime Minister's Office, "Phone call between Prime Minister Shri Narendra Modi and H.E. Mr. Suga Yoshihide, Prime Minister of Japan", Press Information Bureau, April 26, 2021, https://pib.gov.in/PressReleaseIframePage.aspx
77. Robert Farley, "The Key to Securing the Indo-Pacific: Japanese Constitutional Reform?", *The Diplomat*, September 11, 2018, https://thediplomat.com/2018/09/the-key-to-securing-the-indo-pacific-japanese-constitutional-reform/
78. Yuki Tatsumi, "Is Japan Ready for the Quad? Opportunities and Challenges for Tokyo in a Changing Indo-Pacific", *War on the Rocks*, January 9, 2018, https://warontherocks.com/2018/01/japan-ready-quad-opportunities-challenges-tokyo-changing-indo-pacific/
79. Rajaram Panda, "Should Japan go Nuclear?", *The Korean Journal of Defense Analyses (Seoul)*, vol. 26, no. 4, December 2014, pp. 407-425.

80. Rajaram Panda, "Should South Korea go Nuclear?", *Asia Pacific Review (Tokyo)*, vol. 21, no. 1, 2015, pp. 148-176.
81. David E. Sanger, Choe Sang-Hun and Motoko Rich, "North Korea Rouses Neighbors to Reconsider Nuclear Weapons", *New York Times*, October 28, 2017, https://newyorktime2017.wordpress.com/2017/10/28/north-korea-rouses-neighbors-to-reconsider-nuclear-weapons-by-david-e-sanger-choe-sang-hun-and-motoko-rich/
82. Felix Heiduk, Gudrun Wacker, "From Asia-Pacific to Indo-Pacific Significance: Implementation and Challenges", SWP Research Paper 2020/RP 09, German Institute for International and Security Affairs, July 2020.
83. Vinay Kaura, "AUKUS is no counter to Quad, both have common vision of Indo-Pacific region", *Economic Times,* September 25, 2021.
84. Harsh V Pant, "A signal to China from America and two of its oldest major allies", *Livemint*, September 20, 2021.
85. Manjari Chatterjee Miller, "The Quad, AUKUS and India's Dilemma", Council on Foreign Relations, October 13, 2021, https://www.cfr.org/article/quad-aukus-and-indias-dilemmas
86. Yuki Tatsumi, "AUKUS: Lessons for Japan's Defense Industry", *The Diplomat*, September 28, 2021, https://thediplomat.com/2021/09/aukus-lessons-for-japans-defense-industry/
87. Andrew F. Cooper, Richard A. Higgott, and Kim Nossal, *Relocating Middle Powers: Australia and Canada in a Changing World Order*, Vancouver: University of British Columbia Press, 1994.
88. Eduard Jordaan "The Concept of a Middle Power in International Relations: Distinguishing Between Emerging and Traditional Middle Power", Politikon: South African Journal of Political Studies, vol. 30, no. 1, 2003.
89. Talmiz Ahmad, "A multipolarity, scripted by the middle powers", *The Hindu*, April 16, 2021.
90. Yoshihide Soeya, "Middle powers can shape a new security framework", *East Asia Forum,* September 23, 2020, https://www.eastasiaforum.org/2020/09/23/middle-powers-can-shape-a-new-security-framework/

7

Conclusion and Policy Recommendations

The discussion and analyses in all the Chapters in this manuscript makes it abundantly clear that India-Japan relationship is the most cherished partnership between both the countries. It is the most defining collaboration in contemporary times. The relationship dates back to centuries, and there is a strong cultural and religious connect bound by Buddhism and common Asian values that resonated in the past and continue to resonate today. This is further honed and complemented by strong economic and security/strategic considerations.

This is not to suggest that the journey throughout history has always been smooth. There have been occasional hiccups with particular concerns, but they have proven to be fleeting, like passing clouds. When differences arose, dialogue and discussion were used to successfully resolve them. Both have supported each other through terrible times. Some of these are covered in the introductory chapter. Such experiences have taught both parties to increase their mutual understanding, ultimately strengthening the partnership.

The small number of the Indian diaspora in Japan has also contributed to foster the relationship. Though language has often been cited as a main barrier, the strength of the cultural and religious connections is so powerful that such barriers have never stood in the way of dealing with each other.

Some recent developments in the Asian region have further drawn both closer to seek a common solution. Aberrations of history are never permanent, though the nuisance value of some past happenings keep the political leaders alert and engaged.

The post-War environment in the world has witnessed many tumultuous events. Ties between countries are affected and also repaired. The world is never static, but humanity continues in the journey of life. Some countries that were once economically and military powerful have lost their shine, while others that were weak have gained strength. In such a journey, the values of the past are never diminished. Within four decades of the end of World War II, the Soviet Union crumbled when perestroika and glasnost were unleashed, dividing the globe into two camps based on ideological principles, each led by the US and subsequently the USSR. The world structure abruptly shifted, leaving the world unipolar. With the emergence of China in economic and military strength, this structure has again come under threat of crumbling. The focus of the world has thus begun to shift from the Orient to the Occident.

Thus the world finds itself at the crossroads of a predicament. The outbreak of the COVID-19 virus demanded calls from all countries for collective approach to address this menace. The immediate need in the Indo-Pacific region was to seek ways that makes the region safe and prosperous.

As the word starts perceiving the US as a declining power and starts seeing China as a rising power, strategic competition between intensifies. This has put the world at the edge. In this new strategic matrix, a growing expectation has emerged from the middle powers such as Japan, India and South Korea to play decisive roles to ensure peace and stability in the Indo-Pacific region.

While ties between India and South Korea, India and Japan and Japan and South Korea have expanded in all dimensions and become complex, the cultural aspect has always offered value addition to the strengthening process in security/defence and economic areas. India and Japan have emerged as active partners in this remarkable transformation process and reshaping the world.

In this journey of building ties, the obvious complementaries between the economies of India and Japan cannot be missed. When it comes to improving economic fundamentals, both parties' benefit, and bilateral relations are seldom viewed as a zero-sum game. Japan's technology and investment has the potential to help India upgrade its infrastructure and manufacturing sector, and India's growing consumer market and investment requirements offer immense opportunities for Japan's economy.

However, as the article has shown, it is the strategic dimension of the relationship that is most significant. Given Japan's prominent role in the FOIP plan, collaborating with countries such as India makes sense for Tokyo. The changing nature of maritime security and commercial connections in the Indo-Pacific, as well as China's growing aggressiveness in the South China Sea and along the Ladakh border, have pushed Japan closer to India. Since both Japan and India depend hugely on sea trade for sustaining their economies, while strongly committed to respecting freedom of navigation and uninterrupted commercial interactions, they remain united in their stand that outstanding disputes in the Indo-Pacific region should be resolved without resorting to threats or use of force by any third country. However, the test of this evolving partnership will be the extent to which Japan commits to assisting India in the event of a crisis.

As Tokyo and New Delhi recognize the huge significance of an enhanced strategic role that Japan-America-India trilateral alliance can play in the Indo-Pacific for ensuring regional and global peace, Japan is likely to press the Biden administration for a robust American presence while also accelerating the momentum of joint military exercises in all the three branches. This would make it even more difficult for Japan and India to play a larger role in guaranteeing peace and stability in the evolving global geopolitical architecture alongside the United States.

India and Japan are partners in the Quad along with the US and Australia. Both the US and Japan are India's 2+2 dialogue partners. Malabar exercise is another important initiative that addressed the issue of maritime security. Other regional forums have allowed India, Japan, and the United States to discuss their perspectives on regional and global concerns, ensuring that the region and the world remain peaceful.

At the bilateral level, the post-Cold War years have been very enriching for both India and Japan. Both have high expectations of each other and deep mutual trust. The past decade has seen sudden spurt in understanding of all aspects of the relationship. While Japan has begun to reconsider its security policy and debates to shed some of its previous inhibitions, like-minded democratic and friendly countries have stood by each other during this realignment process.

Though bilateral ties have expanded and deepened in all dimensions of the relationship, two areas—economic and security—have assumed added attention from both. This does not mean that the cultural aspect is given less importance and does not get much visibility. For example, while Indian cuisine is very popular in Japan, Japanese food is yet to receive such acceptability. However as the number of Japanese companies grow and presence of Japanese increase, more Japanese restaurants shall come up, thereby spreading the popularity of Japanese food in India. In fact, that process had already started. The soft power component shall provide additional heft to other dimensions of the relationship.

Thus, based on recent changes in Japan's security actions, the Indo-Japanese alliance has evolved into a longer-term plan. That approach has concentrated on strengthening Japan's connections with other middle powers in favour of the 'rules-based international order'. There is a growing recognition that Japan should cooperate to build connectivity infrastructure inside and outside of India. It is also an opportune moment for Japan and India to look beyond the post-pandemic situation. The bilateral ties have become too important and to make this more relevant, current institutional mechanisms ought to be strengthened and new ones created if changed in the region demand for such a need.

How does India-Japan bilateral tie move from here? Here certain recommendations are in order, which might be relevant to policy makers. First: Given the existing robust strategic partnership, the defence component needs to be deepened. For this to happen, Japan needs to loosen some of the existing restrictions and bring in exports of defence technologies in the reform process. As both India and Japan face the same challenge from China, expanding their relationship in the defence sector is a logical step. The Malabar exercise, 2+2 dialogue, maritime security, securing the critical lanes of sea route for safe maritime commerce would be the propelling factors to expand the defence ambit of the relationship.

Second: in terms of economics, Japan has already established a visible presence in India by establishing manufacturing bases to meet domestic needs in the electrical and automotive sectors. Efforts may be made to establish more collaborative projects in India to meet India's domestic needs as well as exports to Africa and Middle East.

Third: India and Japan might consider setting up a joint India-Japan Friendship University by co-funding and designing courses and departments by honing each other's strength and make the India-Japan friendship more visible. Faculties can be drawn both from India and Japan and students from both countries may be encouraged to join the courses for study. Like the South Asia University, the proposed University must be restricted only between the two countries in terms of students and faculty. To begin with, two or three main schools may be started in the field of Japanese language for the benefit of Indian students, and two or three India's regional language, besides Hindi, for the benefit of Japanese students. Since Japan is strong in engineering, the other school could focus on this area of study. Depending on progress, other schools may be added in the future. Like the South Asia University that comes directly under the administration of the Ministry of External Affairs, the proposed University should be directly administered by the Union Education University, with full autonomy given to the University head in terms of setting up admission criteria, faculty recruitment and other policy-related matters with minimum government interference. A special budget for this project may be created in the forthcoming budget, putting the project on fast-track mode. A steering committee by experts drawn from both sides can be tasked to design and make the blueprint that would be doable and can deliver results soon. The Japan Foundation can also offer special grants to the University for more fellowships and exchange of scholars between the two countries. By this, the people-to-people contact and cultural component of the relationships could be further strengthened.

These are some of the proposals for policymakers to consider, as they are all easily implementable. What is necessary is political will, which exists in abundance.

Select Bibliography

Primary Sources

Masood, Sayyid Ross, *Japan and Its Educational System: Being a Report Compiled for the Government of His Exalted Highness the Nizam* (Hyderabad, Andhra Pradesh, India: Government Central Press, 1923).

Toshiya Kaneko, "Cultural light, political shadow: Okakura Tenshin (1862–1913) and the Japanese crisis of national identity, 1880–1941", https://repository.upenn.edu/dissertations/AAI3054959/

Abe's address on "Confluence of the two Seas", August 22, 2007, https://www.mofa.go.jp/region/asia-paci/pmv0708/speech-2.html

https://www.mea.gov.in/bilateraldocuments.htm?dtl/7012/Treaty_of_Peace

https://www.mofa.go.jp/region/asia-paci/india/data.html

https://www.mofa.go.jp/region/asia-paci/india/data.html https://www.mofa.go.jp/region/asia-paci/pmv0708/speech-2.html

https://www.mofa.go.jp/policy/oda/region/sw_asia/india_o.pdf

Ministry of Foreign Affairs, Government of Japan, http://www.mofa.go.jp/policy,oda/white/2008/parts3-2-3.pdf

http://www.meti.go.jp/english/report/downloadfiles/2009WhitePaper/sumary.pdf

https://www.in.emb-japan.go.jp/files/100365125.pdf

https://dipp.gov.in/programmes-and-schemes/delhi-mumbai-industrial-corridordmic

https://dipp.gov.in/japan-plus/delhi-mumbai-industrial-corridor-dmic

"Report of the India-Japan Joint Study Group, June 2006", http://www.mofa.go.jp/region/asia-paci/india/report0606.pdf

https://www.mofa.go.jp/press/release/press23e_000032.html.

https://www.in.emb-japan.go.jp/files/100187212.pdf

https://www.in.emb-japan.go.jp/PDF/2020_co_list_en.pdf

"India-Japan Economic Relations", Embassy of India, Tokyo, https://www.indembassy-tokyo.gov.in/coityo_pages/NjA

"India-China Trade and Economic Relations", Embassy of India, Beijing, https://www.eoibeijing.gov.in/economic-and-trade-relation.php

https://www.jica.go.jp/india/english/office/topics/press181030_02.html

https://www.mea.gov.in/Speeches-Statements.htm?dtl/33680/Address_by_Secretary_East_at_the_Virtual_Seminar_on_Connectivity_Cooperation_for_a_Free_Open_and_Inclusive_IndoPacific

https://www.quora.com/Why-are-the-latest-generations-of-Japanese-Brazilians-so-mixed-more-than-60-of-them-are-children-of-inter-racial-couples-but-in-Japan-immigration-and-miscegenat

https://www.pewresearch.org/social-trends/rise-of-asian-americans-2012-analysis/japanese/

"Japan House", January 8, 2023, https://www.mofa.go.jp/p_pd/pds/page25e_000145.html https://www.japanhouselondon.uk/about/what-is-japan-house/

Report of the High Level Committee on Indian Diaspora, December 2001 (New Delhi: Indian Council of World Affairs, 2001).

https://www.jica.go.jp/india/english/office/topics/press181030_02.html

Secondary Sources

Books

Chitoshi Yanaga, *Japan Since Perry* (New York: 1949) p. 692.

Rajaram Panda, ed., *India-Vietnam Relations: Retrospect and Prospect* (New Delhi: ICCR and Northern Book Centre, 2016), p. 240.

Rajaram Panda, *Pacific Partnership: Japan-Australia Resource Diplomacy* (Rohtak: Manthan Publications, 1982).

Rajaram Panda, "Changing Dynamics of India-Japan Relations: Future Trends", in Akihiro Iwashita, ed., *India-Japan Dialogue: Challenge and Potential* (Slavic Research Center, Hokkaido University, Sapporo.

Rajaram Panda and Yoo Fukazawa, eds., *India and Japan in Search of Global Roles* (New Delhi: Bibliophile South Asia, 2007).

Chaturvedi Badrinath, *Swami Vivekananda: Living Vedanta* (Penguin Books, 2006), p. 452.

Sir M. Visvesvaraya, *Reconstructing India* (London: P.S. Kings and Sons Ltd, 1920), p. 352.

Rustom Bharucha, *Another Asia: Rabindranath Tagore & Okakura Tenshin*, (New Delhi: Oxford University Press, 2006), p. 236.

A.M. Nair, *An Indian Freedom Fighter in Japan* (Vikas Publishing House, 1986), p. 364.

An Indian Freedom Fighter in Japan: Memoirs of A.M. Nair (New Delhi: Orient Longman, 1982), p. 346.

Takeshi Nakajima, *Bose of Nakamuraya: An Indian Revolutionary in Japan* (New Delhi: Bibliophile South Asia, 2009), p. 324.

Harin Shah, *Verdict from Formosa: Gallant End of Netaji* (Atam Ram & Sons, 1956), p. 158.

Anju Dhar and Chandrachur, *Conundrum: Subhas Bose's Life After Death*, (New Delhi: Vitasta Publishing Pvt Ltd, 2019), p. 834.

William Sebald, "With MacArthur in Japan: A Personal History of the Occupation", (Tokyo: Asahi Shimbun Co, 1965), p. 318.

J.D.B. Miller, ed., *India, Japan, Australia: Partners in Asia* (Canberra: Australian National University Press, 1968).

Hiroshi Yoshikawa, *Japan's Lost Decade* (Tokyo: I-House Press, 2002).

Sir John Crawford and Saburo Okita, eds., *Australia and Japan: Issues in the Economic Relationship* (Canberra, 1979).

Krishna Bose (Edited and Translated by Sumantra Bose), *Netaji Subhas Chandra Bose's Life, Politics & Struggle,* (Picador India, 2022), p. 332.

Maj Gen (Dr) G D Bakshi, *Bose, The Military Dimension: A Military History of INA and Netaji*, (Delhi: KW Publishers Pvt Ltd, 2022), p. 374.

Sujan R Choinoy and Jagannath P Panda, eds., *Asia Between Multipolarism and Multipolarity*, (Delhi: KW Publishers Pvt Ltd, 2020,) p. 587.

K V Kesavan and Lalima Varma, eds, *Japan-South Asia: Security and Economic Perspectives*, (Lancer Books, 2000), p. 555.

Herbert P Bix, *Hirohito and the Making of Making Japan* (Harper Perennial, 2000) p. 818.

Pallavi Aiyar, *Orienting: An Indian in Japan* (Harper-Collins, 2021) p. 290.

Arka Biswas. "Framework for Indo-Japanese Strategic Partnership and Cooperation", (New Delhi: Vivekanand International Foundation, 2013), p. 80.

"India and Japan: Growing Partnership and Opportunities for Cooperation" (Kochi: Centre for Strategic Studies, 2019), p. 73.

Adarsha Verma, *The Heavenly Land and the Land of the Rising Sun: Historical Linkages, Security Cooperation and Strategic Partnership*, (Delhi: KW Publishers Pvt Ltd, 2020), p. 271.

Shamshad Ahmad Khan, Changing Dynamics of India-Japan Relations: Buddhism to Special Strategic Partnership (Delhi: Pentagon Press, 2017), p. 196.

Sanjay Baru, ed., The Importance of Shinzo Abe: India, Japan and the Indo-Pacific (Harper Collins, 2023), p. 256.

Takenori Horimoto and Lalima Varma, eds., *India-Japan Relations in Emerging Asia* (Manohar Publisher, 2013), p. 299.

Asok Kumar Ray, *Party of Firebrand Revolutionaries: The Dacca Anushilan Samiti 1906-1918*, (Kolkata: Minerva Associates Publications Pvt Ltd, 1999), p. 200.

Buddhadeva Bhattacharyya, ed., *Freedom Struggle and Anushilan Samiti, Vol. 1*, Kolkata: Anushilan Samity, 1978), p. 335.

Research/Website/Newspaper Articles and links

"Japan's Longest-Serving Prime Ministers", 20 November 2019, https://www.nippon.com/en/features/h00296/japan%E2%80%99s-longest-serving-prime-ministers.html

Savitri Vishwanathan, "India and Japan: Changing Perceptions", https://www.jpf.go.jp/e/about/award/archive/2010/dl/Savitri_Vishwanathan.pdf

J.A.A. Stockwin, "New Directions in Japan under the Abe government: Constitution, Defence and Nationalism", July 18, 2018, https://think.iafor.org/new-directions-in-japan-under-the-abe-government-constitution-defence-and-nationalism/

https://www.japanpitt.pitt.edu/timeline/tokugawa-period-1603-1868

"Tokugawa Shogunate Closed Country Policy", http://world-history-education-resources.com/tokugawa-shogunate/country-closed-tokugawa-shogunate.html

https://www.britannica.com/biography/Shomu-emperor-of-Japan

John Carroll, "Bodhisena: The Indian Monk Who Opened Eyes in Nara", *Japan Forward*, September 26, 2020, https://japan-forward.com/bookmark-bodhisena-the-indian-monk-who-opened-eyes-in-nara/

Gopi Karelia, "The Bond that moved Swami Vivekananda to say 'You Are (my) only Friend in This Life", August 23, 2021, https://www.thebetterindia.com/261033/swami-vivekananda-letters-read-online-maharaja-khetri-friendship/

Rajaram Panda, Bengal and Japan-I, and "Bengal and Japan-II, *The Statesman*, July 9 and 10, 2021, https://www.thestatesman.com/opinion/bengal-and-japan-i-1502979918.html, and https://www.thestatesman.com/opinion/bengal-and-japanii-1502980307.html

David Burleigh, "A friendship's influence across Asia: Japan's Okakura Tenshin and India's Rabindranath Tagore", *The Japan Times*, October 28, 2007, https://www.japantimes.co.jp/culture/2007/10/28/books/book-reviews/a-friendships-influence-across-asia/

https://everything.explained.today/Yone_Noguchi/

"Rabindranath Tagore and Japan", *The Japan Times*, editorial, September 7, 2003.

https://www.japantimes.co.jp/opinion/2003/09/07/editorials/rabindranath-tagore-and-japan/

"Uemon and Hariprabha Takeda: Travelling into Lives", https://refugeewatchonline.wordpress.com/2017/10/04/uemon-and-hariprabha-takeda-travelling-into-lives/.

Mukesh Williams, "Hariprabha Takeda's Diary – an Indian Woman's Observations of Taisho & Meiji Japan", *Japan Spotlight*, September-October 2021, pp. 50-53. https://www.jef.or.jp/journal/pdf/239th_HRAC.pdf

Subrat Kumar Das, "Manmathanath Ghosh's Japan Probas: The initial Bangla-language book on Japan".

https://www.academia.edu/12143810/Manmathanath_Ghosh_s_Japan_Probash_The_initial Bangla_language_book_on_Japan

"Freedom Fighter Rash Behari Bose's Favourite Indian Curry: A Taste of Romance and Revolution in Japan", https://www.indianeagle.com/travelbeats/

"Rash Behari Bose: The founder of Indian National Army", November 29, 2009, https://haindavakeralam.com/rash-behari-bose-founder-of-hk10962

Sanchari Pal, "The Other Bose: How an Indian Freedom Fighter's Curry Became a Sensation in Japan", July 21, 2017, https://www.thebetterindia.com/109063/rash-behari-bose-ina-nakamuraya-curry-japan/

Peter Tasker, "What Have Love, Curry, and the Quad Got to Do with Japan's Security?", *Japan Forward,* June 6, 2021, https://japan-forward.com/bookmark-what-have-love-curry-and-the-quad-got-to-do-with-japans-security/

Pallavi Aiyar, "Bose of Nakamuraya", *The Hindu*, February 6, 2018, https://www.thehindu.com/opinion/op-ed/bose-of-nakamuraya/article22661567.ece

Yukihiko Yamada, "The tale of two Boses, their Japanese connect and authentic Indian curry", November 10, 2019, https://www.asiancommunitynews.com/the-tale-of-two-boses-their-japanese-connect-and-authentic-indian-curry/#:~:text=He%20married%20Toshiko%20in%201918%2C%20and%20he%20acquired,the%

Peter Tasker, "Curried Narratives: Indian Alternative History of Modern Japan", *Japan Forward*, July 29, 2021, https://japan-forward.com/curried-narratives-indias-alternative-history-of-modern-japan/

Peter Tasker, "Love, Curry, and the Quad: A Curious Story of Japan's Indian Connection", *Japan Forward*, June 5, 2021, https://japan-forward.com/bookmark-love-curry-and-the-quad-a-curious-story-of-japans-indian-connection/

Peter Tasker, "What have Love, Curry, and the Quad Got to Do with Japan's Security?", *Japan Forward*, June 6, 2021, https://japan-forward.com/bookmark-what-have-love-curry-and-the-quad-got-to-do-with-japans-security/

Priyanka Basu, "Netaji and Gumnami Baba - An Uncanny Resemblance", January 21, 2021, https://monomousumi.com/netaji-and-gumnami-baba-an-uncanny-resemblance-one-mystery/

Latha Varadarajan, "The trials of imperialism: Radhabinod Pal's dissent at the Tokyo tribunal", *European Journal of International Relations,* December 10, 2014, https://journals.sagepub.com/doi/10.1177/1354066114555775

Norimitsu Onishi, "Decades After War Trials, Japan Still Honors a Dissenting Judge", *The New York Times,* August 31, 2007, https://www.nytimes.com/2007/08/31/world/asia/31memo.html

Naotaka Fujita, "Tojo's ashes scattered over ocean with those of 6 others", *The Asahi Shimbun*, June 8, 2021, http://www.asahi.com/ajw/articles/14368165

"The Dissenting Indian", *Deccan Herald,* August 14, 2021, https://www.deccanherald.com/content/88645/dissenting-indian.html

Ryuichi Kitano, "Diary: Hirohito prepared for U.S. war before Pearl Harbor attack", *The Asahi Shimbun*, December 6, 2021, https://www.asahi.com/ajw/articles/14496398

John F. Burns, "India sets 3 nuclear blasts, defying a worldwide ban; tests brings a sharp outcry", *The New York Times,* May 12, 1998, https://www.nytimes.com/1998/05/12/world/india-sets-3-nuclear-blasts-defying-a-worldwide-ban-tests-bring-a-sharp-outcry.html

Sanjna Sudan, "Indo-Japan Civil Nuclear Agreement: A Win-Win?", November 16, 2016, https://www.diplomaticourier.com/posts/indo-japan-civil-nuclear-agreement-win-win

Peter Symonds, "Clinton visit to the Indian subcontinent sets a new strategic orientation", 23 March 2000, https://www.wsws.org/en/articles/2000/03/ind-m23.html

Abhijnan Rej, "India and Japan Sign Military Logistics Agreement for All to See", *The Diplomat,* September 12, 2020, https://thediplomat.com/2020/09/india-and-japan-sign-military-logistics-agreement-for-all-to-see/#:~:text=On%20September%209%2C%20India%20and%20Japan%20signed%20an

Rajaram Panda, "A Revolution in store for Indian Railways", February 10, 2016, https://www.indiaglobalbusiness.com/igb-archive/revolution-store-indian-railways

Rajaram Panda, "Japan and South Korea: Prisoners of History", *IIC Quarterly*, Summer 2021, vol. 48, no. 1, pp. 111-121.

Rajaram Panda, "India and Japan" Strengthening Defence Cooperation", December 22, 2009, https://idsa.in/idsacomments/IndiaandJapanStrengtheningDefenceCooperation_rpanda_221209

Rajaram Panda, "Significance of Royal Visit and India-Japan Relations", *C3S Paper No. 2042*, December 5, 2013, http://www.c3sindia.org/japan/3801

Rajaram Panda, "Abe Shinzo: A giant departs Japanese politics", August 29, 2020, https://www.rediff.com/news/column/abe-shinzo-a-giant-departs-japanese-politics/20200829.htm

Rajaram Panda, "How is Suga Crafting Japan's Policies towards Russia?", December 15, 2020, https://www.vifindia.org/article/2020/december/15/how-is-suga-crafting-japan-s-policies-towards-russia

Rajaram Panda, "Japan and South Korea talk but Old Issues Continue to Figure", May 14, 2021, https://www.vifindia.org/article/2021/may/14/japan-and-south-korea-talk-but-old-issues-continue-to-figure

Rajaram Panda, "Can Article 9 of the Japanese Constitution be ever Amended", May 25, 2021, https://www.vifindia.org/article/2021/may/25/can-article-9-of-the-japanese-constitution-be-ever-amended

Rajaram Panda, "Fallout from Covid-19: Japanese, S. Korean & US Companies likely to Relocate Production Bases from China to India", *Japan SPOTLIGHT* (Tokyo), July-August 2020, pp. 68-69. https://www.jef.or.jp/journal/pdf/232nd_Readers_Response.pdf

Rajaram Panda, "India Opts Out of RCEP: Cost-Benefit Analysis", *Mainstream,* 30 November 2019, vol. lvii, no. 50, pp. 11-15.

Rajaram Panda, "Is the RCEP China's gain and India's loss?", *China Brief: A Journal of Analysis and Information,* vol. 20, no. 22, December 23, 2020, pp. 26-31, https://jamestown.org/wp-content/uploads/2020/12/Read-the-12-23-2020-CB-Issue-in-PDF.pdf?x30227

Rajaram Panda, "A Step Too Far: Why India Opted Out of RCEP", *Global Asia*, vol. 14, no. 4, December 2019, pp. 82-88, http://globalasia.org/v14no4/feature/a-step-too-far-why-india-opted-out-of-rcep_rajaram-panda

Rajaram Panda. "Bengal's Romance with Bengal: A Historical Narrative", *NMML Occasional Paper, History and Society New Series 108*, December 22, 2022, http://nehrumemorial.nic.in/downloadSeries/362

Rajaram Panda, "Japan's Declining Population and Demographic Challenges", *Estudos Japoneses*, Sao Paulo, 2017, no. 38, pp. 67-80.

https://www.revistas.usp.br/ej/issue/view/10766

Rajaram Panda, "The Greying of Japan: New Challenges", *Reitaku International Journal of Interdisciplinary Studies* (Kashiwa, Japan) vol. 6, no. 1, March 1998.

Arielle Busetto, "Shinzo Abe on His 8 Years as Prime Minister: 'Many Challenges, But Also Successes'", August 29, 2020, https://japan-forward.com/shinzo-abe-on-his-8-years-as-prime-minister-many-challenges-but-also-successes/

Bill Emmott, "The Japan that Shinzo Abe has left behind", *The Japan Times*, August 29, 2010, https://www.japantimes.co.jp/opinion/2020/08/29/commentary/japan-commentary/japan-shinzo-abe-resignation/

Reiji Yoshida, "Suicide note reignites Moritomo scandal that rocked Abe administration", *The Japan Times,* March 18, 2020, https://www.japantimes.co.jp/news/2020/03/18/national/suicide-note-reignites-moritomo-gakuen-cronyism-scandal-abe/

Eric Johnston, "With suicide note and lawsuit, Moritomo scandal back to haunt Abe", *The Japan Times,* April 2, 2020, https://www.japantimes.co.jp/news/2020/04/02/reference/moritomo-gakuen-back-to-haunt-abe/

"Ex-Japan justice minister, lawmaker wife charged over vote buying", July 8, 2020, https://english.kyodonews.net/news/2020/07/01547c4c74d5-update1-ex-justice-minister-wife-indicted-over-election-voting-scandal.html

W.R. Purcell, "The Nature and Extent of Japanese Commercial and Economic Interests in Australia, 1932-41, *Australia-Japan Economic Relations Research Project Research Paper no. 53,* Canberra, October 1978.

Lalima Varma, "Japan's Official Development Assistance to India: A Critical Appraisal", *India Quarterly* (New Delhi), vol. 65, no. 3, July-September 2009, pp. 237-244.

Japan's Official Development Assistance (ODA) to India", February 28, 2023, https://www.newsmania.co.in/2023/02/28/japans-official-development-assistance-oda-to-india/

Srabani Roy Choudhury, "Japan's Foreign Direct Investment Experiences in India: Lessons Learnt from Firm Level Surveys", *ICRIER Working Paper No. 243,* December 2009, New Delhi.

Rupakjyoti Borah, "Japan's Infrastructure Push in Northeast India Builds on Trust Factor", July 25, 2018, https://japan-forward.com/japans-infrastructure-push-in-northeast-india-builds-on-trust-factor/

Amartya Sen, *Identity and Violence: The Illusion of Destiny,* Penguin, UK, September 2007, p. 240.

Rustom Bharucha, *Another Asia: Rabindranath Tagore and Okakura Tenshin*, Oxford University Press, 2006, p. 236.

Hiroshi Shimizu, "The Indian Merchants of Kobe and Japan's trade expansion into Southeast Asia before the Asian-Pacific War", *Japan Forum*, vol. 17, no. 1, March 2005, p. 27, https://www.tandfonline.com/doi/epdf/10.1080/0955580052000337459

Claude Markovits, *The Global World of Indian Merchants, 1750-1947: Traders of Sind from Bukhara to Panama*, Cambridge, Cambridge University Press (2000).

G.A. Chandru Advani, "The History of Indians in Japan", in *Global Migration of Indians: Saga of Peoples Enterprises, Identity and Integration*, The Global Community of People of Indian Origin, August 27, 1989.

Mimi Banerjee Dhar, "Indians in Japan: History & Dimensions of Relations", in Lipi Ghosh and Ramakrishna Chatterjee, eds, *Indian Diaspora in Asia and Pacific: Culture, People, Interactions* (New Delhi, Rawat, 2004).

Mukesh Williams, "Jagmohan Chandrani: Father of Little India in Nishi Kasai", *Japan Spotlight*, September-October 2021, pp. 46-49, https://www.jef.or.jp/journal/pdf/239th_Special_Article_04.pdf

Debarshi Dasgupta, "Strategic location of region seen as gateway to Asean markets", *Straits Times*, November 14, 2018, https://www.straitstimes.com/asia/south-asia/japan-gives-india-aid-to-develop-north-east-states

Rupakjyoti Borah, "Japan's Infrastructure Push in Northeast India Builds on Trust Factor", *Japan Forward*, July 25, 2018, https://japan-forward.com/japans-infrastructure-push-in-northeast-india-builds-on-trust-factor/

Rupakjyoti Borah, "Japan Shares Good Reasons to Collaborate on Northeast India's Development", *Japan Forward*, March 15, 2021, https://japan-forward.com/japan-shares-good-reasons-to-collaborate-in-northeast-indias-development/

Index